Family Tree of the American Silverware Industry: 1815-1965

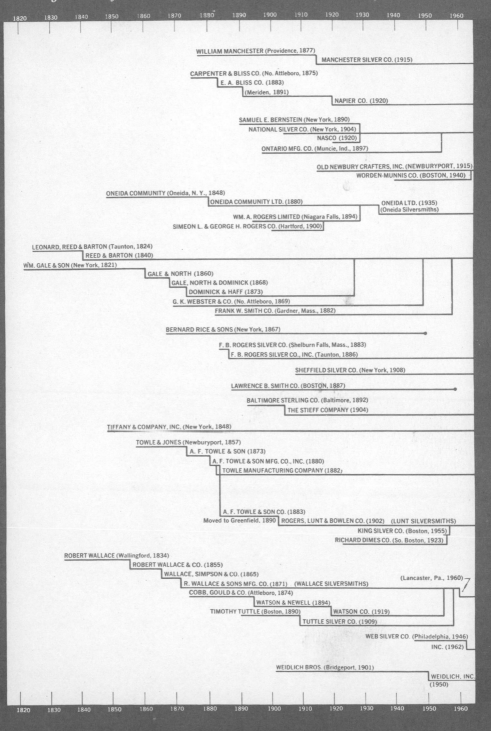

WILLIAM MANCHESTER (Providence, 1877)
MANCHESTER SILVER CO. (1915)

CARPENTER & BLISS CO. (No. Attleboro, 1875)
E. A. BLISS CO. (1883)
(Meriden, 1891)
NAPIER CO. (1920)

SAMUEL E. BERNSTEIN (New York, 1890)
NATIONAL SILVER CO. (New York, 1904)
NASCO (1920)
ONTARIO MFG. CO. (Muncie, Ind., 1897)

OLD NEWBURY CRAFTERS, INC. (NEWBURYPORT, 1915)
WORDEN-MUNNIS CO. (BOSTON, 1940)

ONEIDA COMMUNITY (Oneida, N. Y., 1848)
ONEIDA COMMUNITY LTD. (1880)
ONEIDA LTD. (1935)
(Oneida Silversmiths)
WM. A. ROGERS LIMITED (Niagara Falls, 1894)
SIMEON L. & GEORGE H. ROGERS CO. (Hartford, 1900)

LEONARD, REED & BARTON (Taunton, 1824)
REED & BARTON (1840)
WM. GALE & SON (New York, 1821)
GALE & NORTH (1860)
GALE, NORTH & DOMINICK (1868)
DOMINICK & HAFF (1873)
G. K. WEBSTER & CO. (No. Attleboro, 1869)
FRANK W. SMITH CO. (Gardner, Mass., 1882)

BERNARD RICE & SONS (New York, 1867)

F. B. ROGERS SILVER CO. (Shelburn Falls, Mass., 1883)
F. B. ROGERS SILVER CO., INC. (Taunton, 1886)

SHEFFIELD SILVER CO. (New York, 1908)
LAWRENCE B. SMITH CO. (BOSTON, 1887)

BALTIMORE STERLING CO. (Baltimore, 1892)
THE STIEFF COMPANY (1904)

TIFFANY & COMPANY, INC. (New York, 1848)

TOWLE & JONES (Newburyport, 1857)
A. F. TOWLE & SON (1873)
A. F. TOWLE & SON MFG. CO., INC. (1880)
TOWLE MANUFACTURING COMPANY (1882)

A. F. TOWLE & SON CO. (1883)
Moved to Greenfield, 1890   ROGERS, LUNT & BOWLEN CO. (1902)   (LUNT SILVERSMITHS)
KING SILVER CO. (Boston, 1955)
RICHARD DIMES CO. (So. Boston, 1923)

ROBERT WALLACE (Wallingford, 1834)
ROBERT WALLACE & CO. (1855)
WALLACE, SIMPSON & CO. (1865)
R. WALLACE & SONS MFG. CO. (1871)   (WALLACE SILVERSMITHS)
(Lancaster, Pa., 1960)
COBB, GOULD & CO. (Attleboro, 1874)
WATSON & NEWELL (1894)
TIMOTHY TUTTLE (Boston, 1890)   WATSON CO. (1919)
TUTTLE SILVER CO. (1909)

WEB SILVER CO. (Philadelphia, 1946)
INC. (1962)

WEIDLICH BROS. (Bridgeport, 1901)
WEIDLICH, INC.
(1950)

AMERICAN SILVER MANUFACTURERS, THEIR MARKS, TRADEMARKS AND HISTORY

American
Silver
Manufacturers

DOROTHY T. RAINWATER

EVERYBODYS PRESS · HANOVER, PENNSYLVANIA

DEDICATION

To THE MEMORY OF Carl W. Dreppard and W. G. Snow, both persistent researchers in the history of American silver manufacturers, and whose tireless endeavors inspired this volume, it is most humbly dedicated.

INTRODUCTION

THIS BOOK is the natural outgrowth of an insatiable curiosity about who made it and where. While many excellent books have been published on early American silversmiths and their marks, almost nothing was to be found on those who were *manufacturers*.

As more and more early American silver finds its way into museums and less and less is available to collectors, 19th century silver has become the major pool from which collectors can draw.

Colonial silversmiths marked their wares with a stamp containing the first initial of the given name and surname in a shaped device such as a square, a heart, a star, a rectangle or shaped cartouche. After the first quarter of the 18th century the maker's name was often stamped in full, or the initials of the first name and full surname was used. "Pseudo hallmarks," in imitation of English hallmarks were often used about the middle and latter part of the century.

The name of the city, or location, of the silversmith was often used in the beginning of the 19th century as were other marks such as COIN, STANDARD, PURE COIN, DOLLAR, D or C (to indicate the standard of coin from which the piece was made). Shortly before 1860, the word STERLING came into use.

Dating a piece of American silver is difficult because, unlike England, no official stamps or date letters were used. Nor, was there ever established a guild hall for keeping records of silversmiths.

A few companies adopted their own system: Samuel Kirk & Son silver can be dated through the changes in the maker's mark—especially early pieces which also bear the Baltimore Assay Office stamps (1814–1830); William Gale & Sons of New York always dated their work; the Gorham Company adopted a system of dating flatware in 1868; the Tiffany Company uses the surname initial of the incumbent president of the firm and Tuttle Silversmiths, during the administration of President Calvin Coolidge, adopted a crescent enclosing the initials of the current President of the United States as a dating device.

Other silver can be dated only through records of the years the maker worked, or, in the case of a manufacturer, the years the company operated under the same name. Even this is not precise as records are scarce and often a mark was carried over and used after the company had changed hands.

United States Patent Office records cannot always establish the date a trademark was used as many companies used trademarks for years before they were registered—and, many were never registered at all.

The serious collector will study not only the marks, but, the styles as well. Silver has followed changing tastes just as faithfully as have clothing, hair styles, furniture and architecture.

The *manufacture* of silverware in the United States began about 1842. Prior to that time there were no real factories in this country. Almost all the silver was custom made with the buyer dealing directly with the silversmith. With the rise of manufactured goods, a new relationship of manufacturer-wholesaler-retailer-consumer developed. Many of these wholesalers and retailers had their own marks put on articles made for them or to be sold by them exclusively. In addition, there were numerous manufacturing companies who made nickel silver wares that were sold "in the metal" for plating by jobbing firms who then stamped them with their own or with retailers' marks.

Very few records are available on the silver manufacturers who worked between the 1840's and the present. Only a thorough study of old city directories, county histories, newspapers and legal documents *in each locality* would make possible a complete history of all the companies listed—and reveal those who are omitted.

The function of trademarks is a social one—historically essential in placing the responsibility for quality. One of the oldest of human institutions, maker's marks are found on excavated materials from the early civilizations of Crete, Egypt, Greece and Rome. The guild system of the Middle Ages was characterized by their use.

In some silversmith's shops the stamp of the owner or Master was accompanied by the personal stamp of the individual craftsman, but, trademarks, as we think of them, were not used on American silver until the establishment of factories.

The first major effort to collect American silver manufacturers' trademarks was the publication in 1896, by the JEWELERS' CIRCULAR (now the JEWELERS' CIRCULAR-KEYSTONE) of *Trade-Marks of the Jewelry and Kindred Trades.* This was followed by editions in 1898, 1904, 1909, 1915, 1922, 1943, 1950 and, most recently, in 1965.

Every effort has been made to determine whether the marks are those of the manufacturer or retailer. In the late 1890's almost every manufacturing jeweler also made various types of silver products. Many of the jewelry marks included appear on silver articles and may, or may not, also be stamped "STERLING."

The trademarks of some manufacturers, wholesalers, retailers and jobbers are included for the purpose of identification.

When the records show different marks for sterling and for plated silver, this has been indicated. Trademarks known to have been used only on jewelry are not included.

The names and marks of a few pewterers and britannia ware makers have been included, in tracing company histories, because some silver manufacturers started as pewterers and later made britannia ware. It replaced pewter in the American home, just as pewter had earlier replaced woodenware.

Only a few companies known to have started in business after 1920 have been included. These are companies that have become part of larger, already established firms. The stopping point of 1920 was not an arbitrary one. It was selected because many companies went out of business following World War I, when, in 1921, American business went through a post-war depression.

Even before the enactment of laws regarding the quality of silver products, most manufacturers had adopted the standard of not less than 900/1000, raised to 925/1000 fine after 1868 when the Gorham Company switched to the English standard and others followed their lead.

When plated silver production first began, some manufacturers either ignored indicating the quality or marked their products "Triple" or "Quadruple" plate. About this, the JEWELERS' CIRCULAR had this to say:

SILVER PLATED WARE

NOTE:—Manufacturers of silver plated flatware, in addition to their trade-mark, stamp the quality upon their goods, almost all of them adopting the same signs and figures. These quality signs and figures are as follows:

A.I . . . . represents standard plate.
XII . . . . represents sectional plate.
4 . . . . represents double plate, tea spoons.
6 . . . . represents double plate, dessert spoons and forks.
8 . . . . represents double plate, table spoons.
6 . . . . represents triple plate, tea spoons.
9 . . . . represents triple plate, dessert spoons and forks.
12 . . . . represents triple plate, table spoons.

There is an amount of cheap plated ware on the market stamped with names of fictitious companies, such as "Quadruple Silver Plate Co.," "Royal Sterling Plate Co.," etc. These goods are furnished, bearing no stamp, to department storekeepers, conductors of gift enterprises and jobbers of cheap merchandise, who stamp the goods themselves with such names as suit their fancy. It is, therefore, practically impossible to trace these stamps.

The 1896–1915 editions of the JEWELERS' CIRCULAR publications, *Trade-Marks of the Jewelry and Kindred Trades* are the principal source of the trademarks illustrated. These volumes are referred to by the abbreviation "J C-K." The dates given in referring to J C-K listings are those of publication of the various editions and are not to be construed as actual dates a particular company was in business unless specifically stated.

ACKNOWLEDGMENTS

ACCORDING TO John Donne, the English poet, "No man is an island," and in no field of endeavor is this more clearly demonstrated than in research. Without the help of many friends, librarians and officials of silver and jewelry manufacturing companies, wholesalers and retailers, this book would not have been possible. The list is long and the indebtedness is great.

Most of the trademarks illustrated are from the 1896, 1898, 1904, 1909 and 1915 editions of *Trade-Marks of the Jewelry and Kindred Trades*, published by the JEWELERS' CIRCULAR (now the JEWELERS' CIRCULAR-KEYSTONE, a Chilton publication) and are reproduced through the kindness and gracious permission of the Editor, Donald S. McNeil. Other trademarks were obtained from United States Patent Office records; from silver and jewelry manufacturers, wholesalers and retailers still in business; from numerous old company catalogs; from pieces in the writer's collection and from hundreds of pieces examined in antique shops all over the country.

The writer also wishes to thank Mr. McNeil for permission to use material from numerous articles on the progress of the silverware industry in the United States, published in the JEWELERS' CIRCULAR-KEYSTONE and for permission to reproduce the *Family Tree of the American Silverware Industry: 1815–1965*, from the 1965 JEWELERS' DIRECTORY ISSUE.

E. P. Hogan, Historical Research Librarian, for the International Silver Company, not only supplied much of the information regarding the complicated history of the company and its predecessors, but also very graciously consented to read that part of the manuscript to insure its accuracy. His encouragement also merits particular appreciation.

A special note of gratitude is due S. Kirk Millspaugh, Vice-President, Samuel Kirk & Son and to Joseph S. Student and Jeannette Christopher, also of Kirk's for the company history and for the photographs from which the writer made drawings of assayer's and maker's marks.

Ann Holbrook, of the Gorham Company, was more than generous in supplying information and copies of Gorham trademarks as well as the date marks used on Gorham flatware.

To Arthur L. Roy, Manager—Advertising, Towle Silversmiths, goes credit for much information concerning that company and also permission to reproduce the marks of the Moulton family who were its predecessors.

Arlene Hershey, of Public Relations of Tuttle and Wallace Silversmiths, now both Divisions of the Hamilton Watch Company, supplied histories of the two companies as well as the many Presidential crescent marks by which Tuttle sterling can be dated.

In the United States Patent Office, Wayne R. Campbell, Chief Librarian; C. A. Calk and R. L. Birch, also of the Scientific Library; W. G. Lanham, Jr., Document Services; John Merchant, H. T. Pitta, Alex Revis and Kenneth Russell, of the Trademark Division were all most gracious in giving assistance.

To the following librarians, for their painstaking research—sometimes supplying publications from their private collections—the deepest gratitude is expressed: Catherine M. Bagdon, Welles-Turner Memorial Library, Glastonbury, Connecticut; Gloria Carter, Victor Public Library, Victor, Colorado; Chicago Historical Society; Chicago Public Library; Julia L. Crawford, The Free Library of Philadelphia; June K. Csoltko, Henry A. Bishop Historical Room, Bridgeport Public Library, Bridgeport, Connecticut; Julia M. Cunningham, Carnegie Library of Pittsburgh; Isabel Erlich, Atlanta Public Library; Kay Fox, Keene Public Library, Keene, New Hampshire; Alys Freeze, Denver Public Library; Marvin Fryatt, Portland Public Library, Portland, Maine; Deborah Gans, Public Library of New Rochelle, New Rochelle, New York; Frances Gilchrist, Public Library, Taunton, Massachusetts; Elfriede Gudelius, Tacoma Public Library; Mary A. Henegan, Providence Public Library; Ann B. Honea, Santa Fe Public Library, Santa Fe, New Mexico; Thelma Jackman, Los Angeles Public Library; Mary V. Jennings, New York State Library, Albany, New York; Myrtle M. Jillson, Silas Bronson Library, Waterbury, Connecticut; Astrid P. Johnson, Wallingford Public Library, Wallingford, Connecticut; Elizabeth Anne Johnson, Library Association of Portland, Portland, Oregon; Katherine M. Kuechle, Newburyport Public Library, Newburyport, Massachusetts; Rita B. Kusek, Chicopee Public Library, Chicopee, Massachusetts; Library of Congress, Washington, D. C.; Vera L. Lindsley, Haverhill Public Library, Haverhill, Massachusetts; Kathrine C. Little, Lynn Public Library, Lynn, Massachusetts; C. Frances Manwaring, Public Library, Washington, D. C.; Elizabeth C. Martin, The Danbury Library, Danbury, Connecticut; Metropolitan Museum of Art; New Milford Public Library, New Milford, Connecticut; Helen E. Monson, Newburgh Free Library, Newburgh, New York; Setsuko Nakata, Bernice P. Bishop Museum, Honolulu, Hawaii; B. Joseph O'Neil, Boston Public Library; Thelma Paine, Free Public Library, New Bedford, Massachusetts; Gerald J. Parsons, Syracuse Public Library; Eleanor Plain, Aurora Public Library, Aurora, Illinois; Enoch Pratt Free Library, Baltimore, Maryland; William L. Ramirez, San Francisco Public Library; Eleanor B. Rench, St. Louis Public Library; Josephine W. Sale, Hartford Public Library, Hartford, Connecticut; Edwin G. Sanford, Boston Public Library; Janet Schroeder, Duluth Public Library; Mabel R. Schell, Public Library of Cincinnati and Hamilton County; Stacia N. Simmons, Amesbury Public Library, Amesbury, Massachusetts; Alice E. Station, Omaha Public Library; Emma Swift, Rochester Public Library; Mrs. Milford J. Taylor, Yalesville, Connecticut; Dorothy M. Vaughn, Portsmouth Public Library, Portsmouth, New Hampshire; Florence A. Wales, Niagara Falls

Public Library, Niagara Falls, New York; Rowell L. Waller, Attleboro Public Library, Attleboro, Massachusetts; Patricia Weiherer, Reading Public Library, Reading, Pennsylvania; Elizabeth P. Whitten, Public Library of New London, New London, Connecticut; Marjorie F. Williams, City Historian, Niagara Falls, New York and Anna Holmes Wise, Beardsley and Memorial Library, Winsted, Connecticut.

To these silver and jewelry manufacturers, wholesalers and retailers, whose responses to inquiries reflected their pride in this important industry, the writer feels especially grateful: Milton Baker, President, Majestic Silver Company; Swift C. Barnes, President, Old Newbury Crafters; John R. Blackinton, R. Blackinton & Company; O. L. Binder, Binder Bros., Inc.; Alfred H. Dickinson, House of Dickinson; D. L. Bromwell, Inc.; Barbara Edgerton, Tiffany & Company; Paul A. Frey, Black, Starr & Frost, Ltd.; Galt & Bro., Inc.; George L. Graff, Redlich & Company; Austin F. Grant, Webster Company; Joseph C. Hickingbotham, Chairman of the Board, Shreve & Company; William T. Hurley, Jr., Vice-President, Reed & Barton; E. Nelson Jenkins, J. Jenkins Sons Co., Inc.; Harold F. Johnston, Oneida Silversmiths; G. Keiver, Shreve, Crump & Low, Co.; C. F. Klinke, Bates & Klinke, Inc.; George J. LeMire, Executive Vice-President, Whiting & Davis Company; Gladys Loesing, Manning-Bowman; Denham C. Lunt, President, Lunt Silversmiths; E. B. McAlpine, Manchester Silver Company; R. J. Nolan, President, Saart Bros. Company; William P. Pike, R. Harris & Company; Herbert J. Pollack, President, Crown Silver Inc.; Irene Redmond, C. F. Rumpp & Sons; Elmer N. Riley, Vice President & Treasurer, H. F. Barrows Company; Charles R. Rodgers, Poole Silver Company; Nathaniel D. Rogers, Rogers Silver Plate Company; Frank J. Ryder, President, Walter E. Hayward Company; Berthe M. Schofield, Schofield Company; Wolfgang Schroth, President, Hickok Matthews Company— Silversmiths; The Sheffield Silver Company; Gideon N. Stieff, Sr., Chairman of the Board, The Stieff Company; Herbert L. Thomae, Charles Thomae & Sons, Inc.; W. H. Thurber, President, Tilden-Thurber Company; E. J. Towle, President, E. J. Towle Manufacturing Company and F. D. Young, Russell Harrington Cutlery Company.

The wise editorial counsel of Marcia Ray and Richard B. Alleman, of THE SPINNING WHEEL, has been especially helpful.

Donna H. Felger, College Park, Maryland, gave freely of her time and talent in typing the bibliography, glossary and final manuscript.

Acknowledgment is made to the following collectors who supplied information about companies and trademarks not previously known to the writer: Helen Hoegsberg, Coronado, California; Floy Mitchell, Boca Raton, Florida; Dorothy Seefurth, Chicago, Illinois; and Gertrude Schmidt, Long Beach, California who generously loaned her 1915 edition of the JEWELERS' CIRCULAR.

Finally, the writer acknowledges the understanding of her husband, Ivan, who for many years has patiently endured late dinners while she contemplated the mark on the back of a piece of silver, neglecting the preparation of food with which to fill it.

A

ALBERT ABRECHT
Newark, New Jersey

ABRECHT & COMPANY
(See Albert Abrecht)

ABRECHT & SULSBERGER
(See Albert Abrecht)

A & S

Listed in the Jewelers' Weekly in 1896 as Abrecht & Sulsberger. Listed in J C-K as Abrecht & Co., 1896-1904; succeeded by Albert Abrecht before 1915. Manufacturers of sterling and plated silver, gold chains, pendants, scarf pins and brooches. Last listing found was 1936-37.

ACME SILVER PLATE CO.
Boston, Massachusetts

Reported to have made plated silverware c. 1885. Not listed in U. S. Patent Office records.

GEORGE C. ADAMS
Baltimore, Maryland

Listed in the 1864 Baltimore City Directory as a silversmith.

THE ADAMS & SHAW CO.
New York, New York

First record found was for March 6, 1877. Out of business by 1896. Silversmiths and makers of hard metal electroplate.

ADELPHI SILVER PLATE CO.
New York, New York

(Quadruple Plate.)
(Hollowware.)

STERLING $\frac{925}{1000}$

(Quadruple Ware.)

(Special Goods in Hollowware.)

First record, 1890. Listed in the Jewelers' Weekly in 1896. Out of business between 1904-1915. John Schimpf & Sons, proprietors. They designed and made gold, sterling and plated silver holloware. Advertised "sterling silver mountings for cut glass a specialty."

AHRENDT & KAUTZMAN
(See Ahrendt & Taylor Co., Inc.)

AHRENDT & TAYLOR CO., INC.
Newark, New Jersey

First listed as Ahrendt & Kautzman; succeeded by Wm. G. Ahrendt and became Ahrendt & Taylor Co., Inc. between 1922–36. Not listed after 1943. Manufacturers and distributors of sterling silver novelties.

WM. G. AHRENDT
(See Ahrendt & Taylor Co., Inc.)

ALBANY SILVER PLATE CO.
. (See Barbour Silver Co.)
(See International Silver Co.)
(See I. J. Steane Co.)

ALBANY SILVER PLATE CO.
TRIPLE PLATE.

C. A. ALLEN
Chicago, Illinois

Specialized in plating pieces "in the metal" manufactured by others. Said to have been in the wholesale business from 1887 to c. 1900.

ALVIN CORPORATION
Providence, Rhode Island
(See Gorham Corporation)

ALVIN

SILVERPLATE

Founded in 1886 as Alvin Mfg. Co. Known as Alvin Silver Co. c. 1915–1920. Incorporated between 1943 and 1950. Makers of sterling silver flatware, holloware, dresserware, silver deposit ware and plated silver flatware. Purchased by the Gorham Corporation in 1928 and the title changed to the Alvin Corp.

ALVIN STERLING

AMERICAN RING CO.
Waterbury, Connecticut

KLEVER KRAFT

Manufacturers of plated silverware c. 1920.

AMERICAN SILVER CO.
Bristol, Connecticut
(See Bristol Brass & Clock Co.)
(See Holmes & Tuttle Mfg. Co.)
(See International Silver Co.)

Established in 1901 as successor
to Holmes & Tuttle Mfg. Co. and
Bristol Brass & Clock Company.
Bought by International Silver Co.
in 1935.

INDEPENDENCE
BRAND

"WORLD BRAND"

Windsor
Table Spoons.

ASC°

(Stamped on Nickel Silver Wares.)

AMERICAN SILVER CO.
12 DWT.

A. S. CO.

BRISTOL CUTLERY CO.

NEW ENGLAND CUTLERY CO.

OLD ENGLISH BRAND, B.

BEACON SILVER CO.

CROWN SILVER CO.

1857 WELCH-ATKINS

EASTERN SILVER CO.

H. & T. MFG. CO.

NEW ENGLAND SILVER PLATE CO.

PEQUABUCK MFG. CO.

ROYAL PLATE CO.

WELCH SILVER

CROWN SILVER PLATE CO.
STERLING PLATE ◁ B ▷

(Flatware.)

AMERICAN SILVER PLATE CO.
(See Simpson, Hall, Miller & Co.)

AMERICAN STERLING CO.
Naubuc, Connecticut
(See F. Curtis & Co.)
(See Thomas J. Vail)
(See Williams Bros. Mfg. Co.)

Successors to the Curtisville Mfg.
Co. in 1871 when they took over
the property of Thomas J. Vail,
manufacturer of German silver
and plated ware. In business till
1880 when it was bought by
James B. and William Williams
and the name changed to Williams
Bros. Mfg. Co.

TRIPLE PLATE

AMES MFG. COMPANY
Chicopee, Massachusetts

Nathan Peabody Ames and James Tyler Ames, founders of the Ames Mfg. Co., in 1829, began with the production of swords and sabers, many of which were presentation pieces for such eminent figures as Ulysses S. Grant and Zachary Taylor.

It was at the Ames company that the process of electroplating was introduced into the United States, according to Chicopee historian, Ted M. Szetela. His account says that Charles R. Woodworth, an artist employed by Ames, was the pioneer plater of the country. They made silver services for the leading hotels of the country. Among the elaborate plated silverware they exhibited at the New York World's Fair, 1853–54, were a wine cooler, a sword and standing salt cellar.

James T. Ames became head of the company after the death of his elder brother in 1847.

In 1853, the company added the manufacture of bronze statuary becoming the first company in the United States to cast bronze statues. The bronze doors of the United States Capitol in Washington, D. C., were cast at Ames from designs by Thomas Crawford, American sculptor. These were commissioned in 1853. The East doors were installed in 1868 and the West doors in 1905. Both doors are made up of panels which depict scenes of important events in American history.

During the Civil War, Ames became the largest producers of light artillery and third largest supplier of heavy ordinance.

James T. Ames retired in 1874 and was succeeded by his son-in-law, Albert C. Woodworth. The company was later owned by Emerson Gaylord and James C. Buckley and went out of business in 1920.

ANCO SILVER CO.
New York, New York

Manufacturers of sterling silverware c. 1920–1925.

ANCHOR SILVER PLATE CO.
Muncie, Indiana and St. Paul,
Minnesota

Listed in 1898 and 1904 J C-K.
Listed in 1909 J C-K as out of
business.

ANCHOR SILVER PLATE CO.
(On Quadruple Plate.)

INDIANA BRAND
(On Triple Plate.)

ANCHOR BRAND
(On High Grade Novelties.)

L. D. ANDERSON JLY. CO.
Reading, Pennsylvania

L. D. A.

Louis D. Anderson was listed in
the Reading City Directories from
1914-1939 as a manufacturer of
jewelry and souvenir spoons.
Listed again 1941-44. No further
listing and no record of store.

ANDOVER SILVER PLATE CO.
(See R. Wallace & Sons Mfg. Co.)

APOLLO SILVER CO.
New York, New York
(See Bernard Rice's Sons)

Succeeded by Bernard Rice's Sons
before 1899.

ARCHIBOLD-KLEMENT CO., INC.
Newark, New Jersey

Successor to C. F. Kees & Co. c. 1909. No record after 1922. Trademark used on sterling and gold lorgnettes.

JAMES R. ARMIGER
Baltimore, Maryland

Successor in 1893 to Justis & Armiger who were first listed in the Baltimore City Directory in 1891. Advertised plated silver-ware. Succeeded by James R. Armiger Co. in 1900 which was listed in business to 1936.

ART MFG. CO.
Meriden, Connecticut
(See International Silver Co.)

ART MFG. CO.
(Match Boxes.)

Name used on sterling silver match boxes.

THE ART SILVER SHOP
Chicago, Illinois

Listed in 1922 J C-K as The Art Silver Shop. Makers of hand-wrought sterling silverware, bar pins, rings and novelties. Still in business as Art Metal Studios.

ART STAMPING & MFG. CO.
Philadelphia, Pennsylvania

A. S. & M. CO.

Listed in 1909 J C-K as manufac-turers of sterling and plated silverware. No record after 1915.

ASSOCIATED SILVER CO.
Chicago, Illinois

YOUREX

Listed in 1915 and 1922 J C-K. Last record 1931. Probably jobbers of plated silver flatware.

H. F. ATKINSON & CO.
Baltimore, Maryland

Listed in Baltimore City Direc-tories 1887–1889 under plated silverware.

ATTLEBORO CHAIN CO.
Attleboro, Massachusetts

Listed in J C-K 1909–1915. Trade-mark used on sterling dresser-wares.

ATTLEBORO MFG. CO.
Attleboro, Massachusetts

(*Novelties.*)

Listed in J C-K 1898–1915, as manufacturers of sterling silver novelties. Out of business before 1922.

AURORA SILVER PLATE CO.
Aurora, Illinois
(See Mulholland Bros., Inc.)

(*On Best Grade.*)

1869
AURORA SILVER PLATE M'F'G. CO.
12 Dwt.
(*Flatware.*)

(*Hollowware.*)

Organized under charter from Illinois Legislature in 1869 when the city's industries were few in number and the population of the city was only 10,000. It employed 65 people at the start. The company was an important factor in the development of the city. Its rolling mill was "the only one west of Cincinnati" at that time. They made plated silver flatware and holloware. Succeeded by Mulholland Bros., Inc. between 1915–1922.

Built on Stolph's Island, the business was founded by J. G. Stolph (president for several years), Charles L. Burphee, Daniel Volintine, George W. Quereau, A. N. Shedd, D. W. Young, Charles Wheaton, Samuel McCarty, M. L. Baxter, William Lawrence, William J. Strong and James G. Barr.

AZTEC COIN METAL
(See Holmes & Edwards)

B

BACHRACH & FREEDMAN
New York, New York

Listed in 1896 J C-K under sterling silver. Out of business before 1904.

BAILEY, BANKS & BIDDLE CO.
Philadelphia, Pennsylvania

Jewelers and silversmiths since 1833. Founded by Joseph T. Bailey, jeweler. Known as Bailey & Kitchen from 1839-1846 when Andrew B. Kitchen joined the firm. Became Bailey & Company when Kitchen retired. Other early members of the firm were Eli W. Bailey, Jeremiah Robbins, J. T. Gallagher, A. N. Raymond and James R. Balding.

Joseph T. Bailey died in 1854 and the business was conducted by his brothers. In 1878 the older Baileys retired. George Banks and Samuel Biddle joined with Joseph T. Bailey, Jr., and the firm became Bailey, Banks & Biddle before 1904. They are still in business under that name.

ROSWELL & B. M. BAILEY
Woodstock, Ludlow & Rutland,
Vermont

In 1837-72, with partners, Parmenter & Parker, made silverware. The Bailey's apprentices made doll-size spoons as evidence of their craftsmanship and were allowed to sell them for their own profit for 25¢ each.

Roswell Bailey established his own large shop in 1839 and kept a dozen journeymen and apprentices busy. He was in business until 1875.

BRADBURY M. BAILEY
Ludlow and Woodstock, Vermont

A brother-in-law of Roswell Bailey of Woodstock, he worked as a silversmith in Ludlow before moving to Rutland in 1852. Closed his business in 1885. Born 1824–died 1913.

BAKER-MANCHESTER MFG. CO.
Providence, Rhode Island
(See Manchester Silver Co.)

A short-lived concern in operation from c. 1914-1915 to the early 1920's. Manufacturers of sterling silver fancy flatware, souvenir spoons, holloware and novelties.

BALDWIN, FORD & CO.
New York, New York
(See Cohen & Rosenberger)
(See Ford & Carpenter)

Listed in the 1896 J C-K as Baldwin, Ford and Co. Succeeded by Ford & Carpenter before 1904. They, in turn, were succeeded by Cohen & Rosenberger before 1915. Baldwin, Ford & Co., whose factory was in Providence, Rhode Island, advertised that they made "the only one piece stud in the market," patented May 6, 1884.

BALDWIN & JONES
(See Shreve, Crump & Low Co., Inc.)

BALDWIN, MILLER CO., INC.
Indianapolis, Indiana

B. & M.
Present trademark

B. M. CO.
Not used after 1915

First established in 1883. Manufacturers, wholesalers and jobbers of silverware, jewelry, clocks, and appliances. Their early trademarks have been found on souvenir spoons. Still in business.

BALL, BLACK & COMPANY
New York, New York
(See Black, Starr & Frost, Ltd.)

BALLBLACK&CO

Successors to Ball, Tompkins & Black in 1851. Partners were Henry Ball and William Black. In the 1860's they bought Reed & Barton wares "in the metal" and operated their own plating establishment. Succeeded by Black, Starr & Frost in 1876.

EDWARD BALL CO.
New York, New York

Manufacturers of sterling silverware. The only record found was in the early 1920's.

BALL, TOMPKINS & BLACK
New York, New York
(See Black, Starr & Frost, Ltd.)

Successors to Marquand & Co. in 1839. Partners were Henry Ball, Erastus O. Tompkins and William Black. Succeeded by Ball, Black & Co. in 1851.

THE BALLOU MFG. CO.
Attleboro, Massachusetts

Manufacturers of gold, gold-filled and sterling silver jewelry, materials and findings. Listed in J C-K 1915 and 1922.

BALTES-CHANCE CO., INC.
Irvington, New Jersey

BALTCO

Manufacturers of sterling silver novelties. First record found in early 1920's. Succeeded by Baltes Mfg. Co. before 1931.

BALTIMORE NICKEL PLATING
WORKS
Baltimore, Maryland

Listed in Baltimore City Directories 1874–1886 as silverplaters.

BALTIMORE SILVER CO.
Baltimore, Maryland

Listed in Baltimore City Directories 1906–1908 as silverplaters. Successors to Baltimore Silver Plating Co. (?)

BALTIMORE SILVER PLATE CO.
Baltimore, Maryland
(See Balt. Silver Plating Co.)

Listed in Baltimore City Directories as silverplaters 1894–1907. Succeeded by Baltimore Silver Plating Company.

BALTIMORE SILVER PLATING CO.
Baltimore, Maryland

In business from 1905–1907 as successors to the Baltimore Silver Plate Company which was first listed in 1894. Succeeded by the Baltimore Silver Co. (?)

BALTIMORE SILVERSMITHS
MFG. CO.
Baltimore, Maryland
(See Heer-Schofield Co.)
(See Schofield Co., Inc.)

BALTIMORE STERLING SILVER
BUCKLE CO.
Baltimore, Maryland

Listed c. 1900–1904 at the same address as the Baltimore Sterling Silver Co.

BALTIMORE STERLING
SILVER CO.
Baltimore, Maryland
(See Stieff Co.)

C. A. BAMEN
Boston, Massachusetts

Listed as specialist in plating
c. 1860.

BANCROFT, REDFIELD & RICE
New York, New York

In the 1860's they purchased Reed
& Barton wares "in the metal"
and operated their own plating
establishment. Possibly related to
Redfield & Rice, Shepard & Rice
and Bernard Rice's Sons.

BARBOUR BROS. CO.
Hartford, Connecticut
(See Barbour Silver Co.)
(See I. J. Steane & Co.)

Samuel L. Barbour, of Chicago,
moved to New Haven, Conn. about
1881-82, to join his brother
Charles who was in business
there. They marketed the plated
silverware produced by I. J. Steane
& Co. Succeeded by Barbour
Silver Co. in 1892.

BARBOUR HOBSON CO.
Hartford, Connecticut
(See Barbour Silver Co.)

The Barbour Hobson Company
was organized in 1890 for manufacturing sterling silver. The interests of I. J. Steane, the Barbour
Bros. Co. and the Barbour Hobson
Co. were so nearly identical that it
was thought best to unite them
and the Barbour Silver Co. was the
result.

BARBOUR SILVER CO.
Hartford, Connecticut
(See International Silver Co.)

B. S. C.

BARBOUR SILVER Co.
QUADRUPLE PLATE

When the Barbour Silver Co. was
organized in 1892 by Samuel L.
Barbour, Isaac J. Steane and J. L.
Dalgleish, they succeeded I. J.
Steane & Co., Barbour Hobson Co.
and Barbour Bros. Co. In August of
1893, they took over at least some
of the machinery and stock of the
Hartford Silver Plate Co., organized in 1882 and believed to have

been carried on for a short time under the name of Hartford Silver Co.

When the International Silver Co. was formed in 1898, Samuel L. Barbour, who had been active head of the Barbour Silver Co. for several years, continued as manager of that branch (known as Factory "A") and was made a director of the new company and remained in that capacity for several years after the plant was moved to Meriden to the buildings formerly occupied by the Meriden Silver Plate Co.

Samuel L. Barbour was born in Norwalk, Conn., about 1865 and died in San Francisco, Nov. 11, 1925. He was identified with A. I. Hall & Son.

One of the original companies to become part of International Silver Co. in 1898.

BARDEN, BLAKE & CO.
Plainville, Massachusetts
(See Chapman & Barden)

B. B. & CO.
STERLING.

C. B. BARKER MFG. CO.
New York, New York

(Quadruple Plate.)

Manufacturers of sterling (?) and plated silverware. First listed in J C-K in 1896. Out of business before 1915.

GEORGE BARRETT
Baltimore, Maryland

Listed in the Baltimore City Directories 1873-1898 as silverplaters (electroplate). Successors to Barrett & Rosendorn who were first listed in 1871 as silversmiths.

BARRETT & ROSENDORN
Baltimore, Maryland

Listed 1871-1872 as silversmiths and silverplaters (electroplaters). Succeeded by George Barrett in 1873.

H. F. BARROWS & CO.
North Attleboro, Massachusetts

In business since 1851. Listed in 1896 J C-K under sterling silver and under jewelry in all subsequent listings. Still in business as manufacturers of jewelry in sterling silver and gold filled, 10k and 14k gold. A new line of religious medals and symbols has recently been added.

N. BARSTOW
Providence, Rhode Island

Successors between 1904–1915 to Barstow & Williams.

BARSTOW & WILLIAMS
Providence, Rhode Island
(See N. Barstow Co.)

Listed in 1896 Jewelers' Weekly as makers of sterling silver. Trademark found on souvenir spoons. Listed in J C-K 1896–1904.

E. BARTON & COMPANY
New York, New York
(See Black, Starr & Frost, Ltd.)

In business 1815–1823. Partners were Erastus Barton and Isaac Marquand.

BASCH BROS. & CO.
New York, New York

Listed in 1904 J C-K under sterling silverware. Out of business before 1915.

E. & J. BASS
New York, New York

Manufacturers of sterling silver wares, sterling silver deposit wares and plated silver and jewelry. In business from 1890– c. 1920.

THE BASSETT JEWELRY CO.
Newark, New Jersey

Manufacturers of sterling silver and gold jewelry. Listed in J C-K 1896–1943.

J. C. BATES
Northfield, Vermont

Advertised in 1859 and 1860 that he sold watches, jewelry, silver, clocks, toys and fancy goods.

BATES & KLINKE, INC.
Attleboro, Massachusetts

Established in 1919 as a die cutting and jobbing firm by Harold Bates and Oscar F. Klinke. Both are accomplished die cutters who served their apprenticeship before World War I. After serving in the army, they started business in November, 1919. The company was incorporated in 1929. The company gradually moved into the jewelry business. They now manufacture convention and special jewelry and souvenir spoons, mostly of sterling silver.

BATTIN & CO.
Newark, New Jersey

STERLING **B.**

STERLING

Listed in J C-K 1896–1922. Manufacturers of 14k and sterling silver match boxes, cigarette cases, eyeglass cases, belt buckles and pocket knives.

BAY STATE JEWELRY & SILVERSMITHS CO.
Attleboro, Massachusetts

Patent No. 104,012. Registered April 27, 1915. Application filed October 20, 1914. Serial No. 82,010. Trademark used continuously since August 1, 1914. For jewelry and precious metal ware; silver novelties, match boxes, purses, dresserware, cigarette cases, vanity cases and coin holders. Filed by Carrie L. Saart, Treasurer.

BAY STATE SILVER CO.
North Attleboro, Massachusetts

(Novelties.)

BEACON SILVER CO.
(See American Silver Co.)
(See F. B. Rogers Silver Co., Inc.)

ERNST GIDEON BEK, INC.
Pforzheim, Germany
(See Binder Bros., Inc.)

Manufacturers of sterling silver, gold and platinum mesh bags. Prior to World War I, Bek's was represented in the United States by Binder Bros., Inc. Following the war, Binders purchased the Bek stock from the alien custodian. The German company is thought to be still in operation. Pforzheim is the center of the German silver industry.

GEORGE BELL CO.
Denver, Colorado

Retail jewelry company. Listed in J C-K 1904-1922. Their trademark was found on souvenir spoons.

O. E. BELL COMPANY
Cincinnati, Ohio
(See Cincinnati Silver Co.)

Founded in 1892 as the Cincinnati Silver Company. O. E. Bell was general manager in 1898 and took over the company in 1899. They were manufacturers of plated silver holloware and novelties. Out of business c. 1900.

BENEDICT MFG. CO.
East Syracuse, New York

BENEDICT
INDESTRUCTO
SHEFFIELD PLATE
E.P.N.S.
MADE IN U.S.A.
PATENTED

BENEDICT
INDESTRUCTO
SHEFFIELD PLATE
E.P.N.S.
MADE IN U.S.A.

BENEDICT
TABARD SILVER

ESC
QUADRUPLE PLATE
24 KT GOLD LINED

BENEDICT

Sheffield Reproduction

EMPIRE SILVER CO
E.S. CO.
QUADRUPLE PLATE

T. N. Benedict & Co., founded in 1894; the Benjamin Clark Silver Co., founded c. 1890 and Benedict Dunn Co., founding date unknown, merged to form the M. S. Benedict Mfg. Co. of East Syracuse, N. Y. which became the Benedict Mfg. Co. before 1909 and went out of business in 1953.

Manufactured plated silverware.

EMPIRE SILVER CO
ESC
NICKEL SILVER
SHEFFIELD PLATE

BENEDICT-PROCTOR MFG. CO.
Trenton, Ontario, Canada

Listed c. 1920 to 1935 as manufacturers of plated silverware.

T. N. BENEDICT
East Syracuse, New York
(See Benedict Mfg. Co.)

BENNETT-MERWIN SILVER CO.
New Milford, Connecticut
(See Merwin-Wilson Co., Inc.)

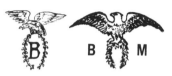

U. S. Patent No. 91,548, May 13,
1913, registered for use on plated
silver flat, hollow and tableware.

WM. BENS CO., INC.
Providence, Rhode Island

Listed 1915–c. 1920 as manufacturers of sterling silver dresserware.

FREDERICK BERENBROICK
Weehawken, New Jersey

Established c. 1850 at 15 John
Street (New York?) by Frederick
Berenbroick, the pioneer maker of
filigree in the United States. In
1858 the business was taken over
by his nephew, Gottlieb Berenbroick, who made filigree and
silver jewelry and novelties at
78 Duane St. In 1889, at death of
Gottlieb, the business was taken
over by Berenbroick & Martin,
Frederick Berenbroick and Max
Martin. Max Martin retired in 1919
and Frederick Berenbroick continued. The last listing found was
1935. He manufactured reproductions of old Dutch, English and
French silverware.

ODO BERGMANN
Baltimore, Maryland

Listed in Baltimore City Directories 1897–1900 under silverware, solid and plated.

BERNDORF METAL WORKS
Berndorf, Austria
(Arthur Krupp)

    OR

  OR

Manufacturers of plated silverware c. 1910. No record after 1915.

SAMUEL E. BERNSTEIN
New York, New York
(See National Silver Co.)

Founded in 1890 and succeeded by the National Silver Company in 1904.

BEVAN & CO.
Baltimore, Maryland

Listed in 1872 Baltimore City Directory as silverplaters.

B. H. CO. STERLING

Known only from name found on novelty flatware c. 1910.

BIGGINS-RODGERS CO.
Wallingford, Connecticut

D

Manufacturers of plated silverware c. 1870-c. 1920.

BINDER BROS. INC.
New York, New York

Prior to 1919, Binder Brothers Incorporated were the exclusive American agents for Ernst Gideon Bek, Inc., Pforzheim, Germany. To their knowledge the Bek Company is still doing business in Germany today.

Since 1919, when Binder Brothers Incorporated purchased the Ernst Gideon Bek stock from the alien custodian who had taken it over during World War I, Binder has manufactured, imported and had made up exclusively under its own trademark, jewelry, watchbands, sterling novelties, etc.

JAMES BINGHAM
Philadelphia, Pennsylvania

Listed from 1896 to c. 1910 as manufacturer of sterling silverware and jewelry.

BIXBY SILVER CO.
Providence, Rhode Island

Listed in J C-K as manufacturers of sterling silverware 1896–c. 1909.

BLACK, STARR & FROST
New York, New York
(See Black, Starr & Frost, Ltd.)

BLACK, STARR & FROST, LTD.
New York, New York

Black, Starr & Frost traces its early history to Marquand & Paulding who began their partnership in Savannah, Georgia c. 1801. Other firm names which succeeded in direct line, or were related, are as follows: H. Lord & Co., c. 1805; Marquand, Harriman & Co.; Marquand, Paulding & Penfield; Marquand & Brother; E(rastus) Barton & Company; J. Penfield & Company; Marquand & Company; Ball, Tompkins & Black; Ball, Black & Company; Black, Starr & Frost in 1876; Black, Starr, Frost-Gorham, Inc. in 1929, when The Gorham Corporation retail store merged with them. In 1940, the firm name was shortened to Black, Starr & Gorham, Inc. In 1962 The Gorham Company sold its interests and the name became Black, Starr & Frost, Ltd.

BLACK, STARR, FROST-GORHAM,
INC.
New York, New York
(See Black, Starr & Frost, Ltd.)

BLACK, STARR & GORHAM, INC.
New York, New York
(See Black, Starr & Frost, Ltd.)

R. BLACKINTON & CO.
North Attleboro, Massachusetts

(Nethersole Bracelets.)

Founded in 1862 in North Attleboro, Massachusetts and has been owned and operated by members of the same two families to the present day. The original trademark was used till c. 1900. Their products have consisted mostly of sterling silver and 14 karat gold novelties, flatware, holloware and dresserware, with a small amount of costume jewelry.

W. & S. BLACKINTON CO.
Meriden, Connecticut

W. & S. BLACKINTON

Founded in 1865 by the Blackinton brothers who specialized in gold jewelry. Acquired by the Ellmore Silver Co. in 1938. While owned by Ellmore, operations expanded to include plated silver holloware. Production was curtailed during World War II and resumed with new lines in 1945. Independently owned since 1961. Incorporated between 1961-65.

CHARLES BLAKE
Baltimore, Maryland

Silverplaters listed in Baltimore City Directories as Charles Blake 1868-1876, and as Charles W. Blake 1877-1886.

JAMES E. BLAKE CO.
Attleboro, Massachusetts

Manufacturing jewelers. Also registered U. S. Patent No. 44,102, January 31, 1905, for use on sterling silver and silver inlaid with 14k gold cigarette and vanity cases, match boxes, men's belt buckles and pocket knives. Listed in J C-K as makers of plated silverware. In business from 1897-1936. Their factory building is now occupied by Bates & Klinke.

E. A. BLISS CO.
Meriden, Connecticut
(See Napier Company)

(Stamped on Nickel Silver Wares.)

Successor to Carpenter & Bliss in
1883.
    Succeeded by Napier-Bliss Co.
c. 1915.

Used on World's Fair souvenirs,
Chicago, 1893 (U. S. Patent
18,479, September 30, 1890.)

L. D. BLOCH & CO.
New York, New York

BONTON
B
SILVERPLATE

Manufactured plated silver novelties c. 1920.

LUTHER BOARDMAN & SON
East Haddam, Connecticut

L. BOARDMAN & SON

The company was founded by
Luther Boardman in the 1820's;
became L. Boardman & Son between 1840–44 and went out of
business about 1905.
    Luther Boardman was born at
Rocky Hill, Connecticut, December
26, 1812. He was apprenticed to
Ashbil Griswold at Meriden, Connecticut, where he learned the
britannia trade. In 1833 he worked
for Burrage Yale at South Reading,
Massachusetts and became owner
of the shop in 1836. In 1837 he
returned to Meriden and married
Lydia Ann Frary. In 1838 he
worked for Russell & Beach at
Chester, Connecticut and later
made britannia spoons in his own
shop there. In 1842 he moved to
East Haddam, Connecticut. Most
of his work after this time was
silver plated britannia.

F. L. BOSWORTH CO.
Minneapolis, Minnesota

GOPHERBRAND

Founding date not known. Jobbers who bought wares "in the metal" from manufacturers and plated them in their own shop. Succeeded by P. M. Vermaas before 1921.

D. C. BOURQUIN
Port Richmond, N. Y.

Founding date not known. Listed in J C-K 1904, under sterling and jewelry. Out of business before 1909.

BOWLER & BURDICK CO.
Cleveland, Ohio

Listed in J C-K 1904-1922. Wholesaler whose trademark was found on souvenir spoons. In business before 1890.

WM. N. BOYNTON
Manchester, Iowa

Registered trademark June 27, 1882 for manufacture of gold, silver and platedware. This is essentially the same trademark used by the United States Jewelers' Guild until c. 1904. This latter mark was also used by J. H. Purdy & Co., wholesale and retail jeweler in Chicago, listed c. 1896-1924.

BRAINARD & WILSON
Danbury, Connecticut

B. & W.

(On Silver Plated Art Ware.)

Listed 1909-1922 in J C-K under plated silver art wares.

W. J. BRAITSCH & CO.
Providence, Rhode Island

W J B & Cọ
TRADE MARK

STERLING

Listed in J C-K 1896 as silversmiths. They were manufacturers of sterling dresserwares. Out of business before 1922.

BRAZIL SILVER
(See Weinman Co.)

BRIDE & TINCKLER
New York, New York

Wholesalers of sterling silverware and jewelry. Listed J C-K 1896-1922.

BRINSMAID & HILDRETH
Burlington, Vermont

A. Brindsmaid   B & H

Brinsmaid's,   B (us) D   Brinsmaid

Brinsmaid & Hildreth

Abram Brinsmaid, father of James Edgar and William, first advertised as a silversmith and clockmaker 1809–1841.

Brinsmaid & Hildreth were silversmiths c. 1830–? The name has been spelled Brindsmaid and Brinsmaid. Family pieces belonging to the writer have only the latter spelling.

BRISTOL BRASS & CLOCK CO.
Bristol, Connecticut
(See American Silver Co.)
(See International Silver Co.)

1857 WELCH-ATKINS
NEW ENGLAND SILVER PLATE CO.
H. & T. MFG. CO.
WELCH SILVER.
ROYAL PLATE CO.

Successor to Holmes & Tuttle Mfg. Co. in 1857. In 1901 became The American Silver Co. which was bought by International Silver Co. in 1935. Bristol Brass & Clock Co. owned the entire stock of American Silver Co. until 1913 when a distribution of stock was made.

Makers of silver tableware, solid and plated.

Patent 26,297, March 26, 1895.

BRISTOL CUTLERY CO.
(See American Silver Co.)

BRISTOL MFG. CO.
Attleboro, Massachusetts

SILVEROIN
Novelties

GERMAN SILVER
(On Mesh Bags.)

Founding date not known. They were manufacturers of plated silverware, cut and plain glass. Succeeded by Bristol Silver Co. c. 1910.

BRISTOL PLATE CO.
New Bedford, Massachusetts
(See Pairpoint Corporation)

BRISTOL SILVER COMPANY
Attleboro, Massachusetts

(Sterling Finish.)

Successors to Bristol Mfg. Co. Out of business before 1915.

BRISTOL SILVER CORP.
Taunton, Massachusetts
(See Poole Silver Company, Inc.)

BRITANNIA ARTISTIC SILVER
(See M. T. Goldsmith)

BRITANNIA ARTISTIC SILVER

BRITANNIA METAL CO.
(See Van Bergh Silver Plate Co.

BRODGERS SILVER CO.
Taunton, Massachusetts

The trademark shown here has previously been attributed to a "Brodgers" Silver Company. It is actually the trademark of F. B. Rogers Silver Company of Taunton, Massachusetts, successor to the West Silver Company.

THOMAS S. BROGAN
New York, New York

Listed J C-K 1896–1922 under sterling silverware and jewelry.

D. L. BROMWELL, INC.
Washington, D. C.

Founded in 1873 by James Bromwell as a small silver and nickel-plating plant. Wet cells were used for the electroplating process, but the buffing wheels that were used to develop the gleaming finish employed a huge mastiff dog, named Cleo, as the motive power. So well did Cleo love the work that it was a problem getting the dog out of the wheel when his efforts were no longer needed. An old-style gas engine was installed later to replace Cleo's power potential, but it broke down periodically and Cleo was allowed to return to the beloved wheel.

James Bromwell's shop, which was capable of making or repairing almost anything, soon became the popular refuge of inventors, who would bring their problems there to be solved. One inventor was trying to develop a gramaphone at about the time Edison was perfecting his. While working with the inventor on the basis of a coated cylinder to retain the sound impressions, James discovered how to plate babyshoes with precious metals, a branch of the business which is still active.

Requests for repair and replacement of antique door knockers, fireplace andirons, fenders and fire tools led to new fields and the development of a bewildering array of metal products spread the fame of the establishment all over the country.

In 1907 James Bromwell died, and his son, Dwight, took over the business. His own son, Berton also began to learn the business, but his interests were in its administration. In 1924 the firm was incorporated under its present name. It is presently operated by the fourth generation of Bromwells. The country's oldest silver platers, they are still active in this field and in custom work.

J. T. BROMWELL
Baltimore, Maryland

Listed in the Baltimore City Directories 1881–1888 under the name J. T. Bromwell, silver plater; listed 1889 as Bromwell Plating Works; 1898–1901 as John T. Bromwell and 1902–04 as Bromwell Plating Works.

BROOKLYN PLATE CO.
(See Schade & Co.)

BROOKLYN SILVER CO.
(See Schade & Co.)

"Satin finish" on plated silver patented in 1870 by James H. Reilly.

BROWER & RUSHER
New York, New York
(See Walter S. Brower)

Listed in New York City Directories 1837–1842 as retailers for S. D. Brower; Hall, Hewson & Co.; Hall, Hewson & Brower.

WALTER S. BROWER
Albany, New York

CHRONOLOGY

Carson & Hall	1810–1818
Hall & Hewson	1818–1829
	1842–1847
Hall, Hewson & Co.	1839–1842
	1847–1850
Hall, Hewson & Merrifield	1845
Hall, Hewson & Brower	1849–1850
Hall & Brower	1852–1854
Hall, Brower & Co.	1854
S. D. Brower & Son	1850
Walter S. Bower	1850

The history of the Walter S. Brower company of Albany, New York can be traced to Carson & Hall (Thomas Carson & Green Hall, 1810–1818); Hall & Hewson (Green Hall & John D. Hewson, listed in City Directories 1818–1829; 1842–1847); Hall, Hewson & Co. (Green Hall, John D. Hewson and S. Douglas Brower, listed in the City Directories 1839–1842; 1847–1850); Hall, Hewson & Merrifield (Green Hall, John D. Hewson & Thomas V. Z. Merrifield, in business c. 1845); Hall, Hewson & Brower (Green Hall, John D. Hewson & S. D. Brower, listed in the City Directory 1849–1850); Hall & Brower (Green Hall & S. Douglas Brower, listed in the City Directories 1852–1854); Hall, Brower & Co. (Green Hall and S. D. Brower, listed in City Directories after 1854): S. D. Brower & Son (S. D. Brower & Walter S. Brower, in business around 1850) and finally Walter S. Brower, who began around 1850 in Albany. Walter S. Brower was the son of S. Douglas Brower, who had been apprenticed to Hall & Hewson before setting up his own shop in Troy, New York in 1834. S. Douglas retired to a farm temporarily and then returned to silversmithing with the firm of Hall, Hewson & Brower c. 1849–50. Father and son were in business together soon afterwards. Walter S. Brower retired in 1898.

BROWN & BROS.
Waterbury, Connecticut

U. S. Patent registered September 21, 1875 for brass, German silver and plated silver goods. Out of business before 1904.

THOMAS G. BROWN & SONS
New York, New York

(Goods made for Gorham Mfg. Co.)

Listed 1896-1915 J C-K as manufacturers of sterling silver goods for Gorham Mfg. Co. Out of business before 1922. The Gorham Co. has no record.

THOMAS J. BROWN
Baltimore, Maryland

Listed in Baltimore City Directories 1867-1874 as a gold and silversmith. The company name was changed to Thomas J. Brown & Son in 1875 and continued under this listing through 1883.

BROWN & WARD
New York, New York

Listed J C-K 1896 under sterling silver. Out of business before 1904.

BROWNE, JENNINGS & LAUTER
New York, New York
(See Jennings & Lauter)

BRUN-MILL CO.
Pittsfield, Illinois

BRUN-MILL CO.
MADE IN U. S. A.

Manufacturers of plated silverware c. 1920.

B. S. CO.
(See Holmes & Edwards
Silver Co.)

FRED BUCHER
Baltimore, Maryland

Listed in Baltimore City Directories 1877-79 as a gold and silversmith.

BUCK SILVER COMPANY
Salamanca, New York

Listed as Buck Silver Company c. 1900-1914 when it became Buck Plating Co. Out of business before 1922.

BUCKER & ROHLEDER
Baltimore, Maryland

Listed in Baltimore City Directories 1901-04 as silverplaters.

SILAS E. BUCKER
Baltimore, Maryland

Listed in Baltimore City Directories 1907-13 as a silverplater.

CALEB H. BURGESS
Baltimore, Maryland

Listed in 1864 Baltimore City Directory as a silverplater. Listed as Caleb H. & John Burgess 1865-1883—Caleb H. Burgess 1884-89.

JOHN BURGESS
Baltimore, Maryland

Listed in 1864 Baltimore City Directory as a silverplater.

OWEN D. BURGESS
Baltimore, Maryland

Listed in Baltimore City Directories 1894-1899 as a silverplater.

CHAS. B. BYRON CO.
New York, New York

Successors to Byron & Vail Co. before 1909.

BYRON & VAIL CO.
New York, New York
(See Chas. B. Byron Co.)

Succeeded by Chas. B. Byron Co.
Founding date not known.
Manufacturers of sterling silver-

ware, gold and platinum cigarette and vanity cases, match boxes and powder boxes.

C

J. E. CALDWELL & CO.
Philadelphia, Pennsylvania

J. E. C. & CO.

Jewelers, silversmiths and antiquarians since 1839.

J. D. CAMIRAND & CO.
Montreal, Canada

Manufacturers of plated silver c. 1920.

A. CAMPBELL
Chicago, Illinois

Listed in Chicago City Directories 1853-1855 as a silverplater.

ARCHIBOLD CAMPBELL
Baltimore, Maryland

Listed in 1864 Baltimore City Directory as a silverplater.

JAMES J. CAMPBELL
Baltimore, Maryland

Listed in Baltimore City Directories 1874-1877 as silverplaters.

SAMUEL K. CAMPBELL
Baltimore, Maryland

Listed in 1864 Baltimore City Directory as a silverplater.

CAMPBELL-METCALF SILVER CO.
Providence, Rhode Island

Manufacturers of sterling silverware. Founding date not known. Out of business before 1904.

CANADIAN JEWELERS, LTD.
Montreal, Quebec

DEPOS-ART

Manufacturers of silver deposit ware c. 1915-1920.

CANADIAN WM. A. ROGERS CO., LTD.
Toronto, Canada
(See Oneida Silversmiths)
(See Wm. A. Rogers Co.)

"HEIRLOOM"
"WM. A. ROGERS"

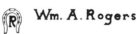

CANFIELD & BROTHER
Baltimore, Maryland

Ira B. Canfield and William B. Canfield, silversmiths in Baltimore c. 1830.

CANFIELD BRO. & CO.
Baltimore, Maryland

Ira B. Canfield, Wm. B. Canfield and J. H. Meredith. Importers and manufacturers of watches, jewelry and silverware, "Albata & Plated ware." Listed in Baltimore City Directories 1850-81.

CARLBERT MFG. CO.
New York, New York

GONDOLA SILVER

Listed J C-K 1915 as manufacturers of plated silver. Out of business before 1922.

CARON BROS.
Montreal, Canada

Listed in J C-K as manufacturers of metal products and jewelry. Their trademark has been found on souvenir spoons.

CARPENTER & BLISS
North Attleboro, Massachusetts
(See Napier Company)

Began business as Carpenter & Bliss in 1875 in North Attleboro, Massachusetts. Succeeded by E. A. Bliss Co. in 1883.

SANDERS W. CARR
Baltimore, Maryland

Listed in 1876 Baltimore City Directory as a silverplater. Succeeded by W. S. Carr & Co. in 1877.

W. S. CARR & CO.
Baltimore, Maryland

Successors to Sanders W. Carr, silverplater, first listed in 1876 Baltimore City Directory. In business through 1886.

CARTER-CRUME CO.
Niagara Falls, New York

EXTRA {COIN SILVER N°12} PLATE

U. S. Patent 30,185, June 15, 1897 to be used on spoons, forks, knives and plated flatware.

RSMC

U. S. Patent 30,962, December 14, 1897, to be used on blades of knives, shanks of spoons and forks.

Listed in the Niagara Falls City Directory as the earliest manufacturers of salesbooks in this country. Succeeded by American Salesbook Co., now Moore Business Forms, Inc.

They were also listed in the 1898 J C-K as manufacturers of plated flatware.

These two trademarks were registered at the U. S. Patent Office for use on plated flatware.

LEWIS CARY
Boston, Massachusetts

Silversmith c. 1820. One of his apprentices was Newell Harding.

CATTARAUGUS CUTLERY CO.
Little Valley, New York

YUKON SILVER
98-100 FINE.

Manufacturers of fine cutlery since 1876.

CENTRAL STERLING CO.
Brooklyn, New York
(See J. Wagner & Son, Inc.)

Discontinued between 1909-14

CHAPIN & HOLLISTER CO.
Providence, Rhode Island

C. &. H. Co.

Listed in J C-K 1915-22. Manufacturers of gold, silver and gold-filled knives and jewelry.

CHAPMAN & BARDEN
Attleboro, Massachusetts
(See Barden, Blake & Co.)

C. & B.

CHARTER COMPANY
(See International Silver
Company)

Trademarks used on sterling reproductions of early Colonial silver. Made in the Barbour Silver Co. plant c. 1930-33. When that division was closed, the Charter line was moved to the sterling division in Wallingford. Discontinued about 1942.

BENJAMIN K. CHASE
Rutland, Vermont

Went into business in 1869 as a silversmith and jeweler after serving as a captain in the Union Forces in the Civil War. Advertised gold and silver goods and watches.

JOHN CHATTELLIFR
Newark, New Jersey

Manufacturer of sterling cigar, cigarette and clock cases, razor sets, jewel, match and cigarette boxes, picture frames and watch cases.

CHELTENHAM & CO., LTD.
Sheffield, England
(See National Silver Co.)

CHICAGO SILVER PLATE CO.
(See Elgin-American Mfg. Co.)

SAMUEL CHILD & CO.
Baltimore, Maryland

Listed in Baltimore City Directories 1868-1886 as silverplaters.

CHURCH & ROGERS
(See Rogers Brothers)

LOREY CHURCHILL
Baltimore, Maryland

Listed in Baltimore City Directories 1864–1868 as a silverplater.

CINCINNATI SILVER CO.
Cincinnati, Ohio
(See O. E. Bell Co.)

BENJAMIN CLARK
(See Benedict Mfg. Co.)

FREDERICK H. CLARK
Newark, New Jersey

Listed in J C-K 1915 as manufacturer of sterling silverware. Out of business before 1922.

GABRIEL D. CLARK
Baltimore, Maryland

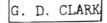

Silversmith in Baltimore 1830–1896, associated with James A. Foxcroft 1831–1839 in the firm of Foxcroft & Clark. Born 1813—died 1896.

CLARK & NOON
Newark, New Jersey

First listed in J C-K as W. F. Cory & Bros., Newark, N. J. in 1896. Clark & Noon are listed as successors in

1915 and not listed after 1922. Makers of sterling silverware and 14 and 18k gold jewelry.

BENJAMIN CLARK SILVER CO.
Ottawa, Illinois
(See Benedict Mfg. Co.)

CLIMAX MESH BAG CO.
Newark, New Jersey

Listed in J C-K in 1915. Out of business before 1922.

COBB, GOULD & CO.
Attleboro, Massachusetts
(See Wallace Silversmiths)
(See Watson Co.)

Founded 1874 in Attleboro, Massachusetts. Succeeded by Watson & Newell in 1894; the Watson Company in 1919 and Wallace Silversmiths in 1955.

HERBERT COCKSHAW, JR.
New York, New York

Listed in 1904 as Howard & Cockshaw; Herbert Cockshaw successor in 1915 and Herbert Cockshaw, Jr. in 1936–37 in the Jobbers' Handbook.

CODDING BROS. & HEILBORN
North Attleboro, Massachusetts

C. B. & H.
STERLING.

In business before 1890. Listed in J C-K in 1896, 1904–1915. Out of business in May 1918. Manufacturers of sterling silver flatware and jewelry.

D. D. CODDING
North Attleboro, Massachusetts

STERLING
D. D. C.

Listed in J C-K in 1896 as manufacturers of sterling silverware. Out of business before 1904.

COHANNET SILVER CO.
Taunton, Massachusetts

Catalog published 1896. Illustrated candlesticks, fern dishes, shaving mugs, tea sets, pickle casters with glass inserts, etc.

L. H. COHEN
New York, New York

Listed in the Jewelers' Weekly 1896 as manufacturers of sterling silverware. Listed in J C-K 1904. Succeeded by L. H. Cohen Co., Inc. between 1909–1915. Last listing was in 1922.

COHEN & ROSENBERGER
New York, New York

Listed in J C-K as Baldwin, Ford & Co. 1896; Ford & Carpenter in 1904 and Baldwin, Ford & Co. 1915–1943. Advertised imitation pearls, novelty jewelry and beads. Listed in sterling silver section until 1943.

S. COHEN & SON
Boston, Massachusetts

A jobbing concern that specialized primarily in plating about 1856.

J. J. COHN
New York, New York

Listed in Jewelers' Weekly, 1896 in sterling section. Also listed in J C-K 1896, leather goods.

L. COHN
Baltimore, Maryland

Listed in 1868-69 Baltimore City Directory as a silverplater.

WILLIAM H. COLE & SONS
Baltimore, Maryland

Listed in 1895 Baltimore City Directory. Advertised plated silverware.

COLONIAL PLATE CO.
Hartford, Connecticut
(See Melrose Silver Co.)

COLONIAL SILVER COMPANY, INC.
Portland, Maine

(On white metal)

(Plated holloware)

Successor to the Stevens Silver Co. in 1899. They were manufacturers of plated silverware. Gold and silver and nickel plating done to order. In business until 1943.

COLONIAL WILLIAMSBURG, INC.
(See Stieff Co.)

COLUMBIA
(See Middletown Plate Co.)

COLUMBIAN SILVER CO.
(See Queen City Silver Co., Inc.)

COMMONWEALTH SILVER CO.
Los Angeles, California

Manufacturers of sterling silverware c. 1920.

COMMUNITY
(See Oneida Silversmiths)

CONCORD SILVERSMITHS, LTD.
(See Ellmore Silver Co., Inc.)

Began as Concord Silver Co., Concord, Massachusetts in 1925. Succeeded by Ellmore Silver Co. c. 1940.

CONNECTICUT PLATE CO.
(See Adelphi Silver Plate Co.)
(See J. W. Johnson)

CONTINENTAL SHEFFIELD
SILVER CO.
Brooklyn, New York
(See Continental Silver Co.)

CONTINENTAL SILVER CO.
New York, New York

The Continental Silver Co. of New York and the Continental Sheffield Silver Co. are related. The former being the sales office of the latter. Listed as manufacturers of plated silver holloware on nickel silver base c. 1920 to 1950.

P. A. COON SILVER MFG. CO.
Syracuse, New York

Manufacturers of plated silverware. Successor to Albert G. Finn Silver Co. between 1904 and 1909. Out of business before 1915.

CORTLAN & CO.
Baltimore, Maryland

Listed in Baltimore City Directories 1868–1870 as silverplaters.

W. F. CORY & BRO.
Newark, New Jersey
(See Clark & Noon)

 **STERLING.**

Not used after 1904

S. COTTLE CO.
New York, New York
(See Howard Sterling Co.)

Established 1865. I. N. Levinson, President. H. S. Morris, Sec'y-Treas. Makers of 14k gold and sterling silver novelties. Not listed after 1920.

S. Cottle invented the machine for making a collar button which became the specialty of Howard & Son about 1880.

COWLES MFG. CO.
Granby, Connecticut
(See International Silver Co.)
(See Rogers Brothers)

Rev. Whitfield Cowles began silverplating in 1843. After he died, his son, William B. Cowles, continued the experiments. In 1845 the Cowles Mfg. Co. was organized with Asa Rogers, James H. Isaacson and John D. Johnson. They used German silver as the base for their silverplated wares. In business only a few years.

COYWELL SPECIALTY CO.
New York, New York

COYWELL
PLATNOID

Listed in 1915 J C-K as manufacturers of sterling silverware. Out of business before 1922.

CRESCENT SILVER CO.
(See Albert G. Finn Silver Co.)

CROMWELL PLATE CO.
Cromwell, Connecticut
(See Barbour Silver Co.)
(See I. J. Steane & Co.)

CROWN GUILD
(See Rockford Silver Plate Co.)

CROWN MFG. CO.
North Attleboro, Massachusetts

C. M. C.

Listed in 1915 J C-K as manufacturers of plated silverware. Out of business before 1922.

CROWN PRINCE
(See G. I. Mix & Co.)

CROWN SILVER CO.
(See American Silver Co.)

CROWN SILVER INC.
New York, New York

The Hasselbring Silver Company, founded in Brooklyn about 1890 by John Hasselbring; the Revere Silver Company, successor to Revere Silversmiths Inc., founded in Brooklyn about 1914 and the Wolfenden Silver Company, successor to J. W. Wolfenden Corporation became divisions of the Crown Silver Inc. in 1955. Manufacturers of sterling silver wares.

CROWN SILVER PLATE CO.
Bristol, Connecticut
(See American Silver Co.)

CROWN SILVER PLATE CO.
New York, New York
(See J. W. Johnson)

CROWN SILVER PLATE CO.
Toronto, Ontario

Listed in J C-K 1909-15. Out of business before 1922.

H. C. CULMAN
Honolulu, Hawaii

H. C.

Listed J C-K 1909. Out of business c. 1917. Manufacturing jewelers. Trademark found on Hawaiian souvenir spoons.

J. F. CURRAN & CO.
New York, New York

Silverplaters c. 1860–1900.

CURRIER & ROBY
New York, New York
(See Elgin Silversmith Co., Inc.)

Successors to George A. Henckel & Co. c. 1940. Now a division of Elgin Silversmith Co., Inc. Manufacturers of sterling silver holloware.

CURTIN & CLARKE
HARDWARE CO.
St. Joseph, Missouri

Listed in J C-K 1909-22 as silverplaters.

CURTIS & DUNNING
Burlington, Vermont

Lemuel Curtis advertised that he made his silver spoons from "silver crowns, without the least alloy." He worked through 1837.

F. CURTIS & CO.
Connecticut
(See American Sterling Co.)
(See Williams Bros. Mfg. Co.)

Frederick and Joseph S. Curtis, brothers who manufactured German silverware, spoons and spectacles in Hartford, moved to Glastonbury. The first notice of the partnership appeared January 24, 1848. Company offices remained at Hartford while manufacturing operations were begun at Curtisville—that section of Glastonbury which today comprises a part of Naubuc. The company name was changed to Curtisville Mfg. Co. "The Memorial History of Hartford County" states that at Curtisville was manufactured the first German Silver in America. The silver-white metal, an alloy of copper, zinc and nickel, was hauled by wagon to Waterbury and there rolled to the desired thickness. (RETROSPECT, A publication of the Historical Society of Glastonbury, No. 10, Feb. 1948.)

H. H. CURTIS & CO.
North Attleboro, Mass.

TRADE MARK

STERLINC.

H. H. C. CO.
(*German Silver Bags.*)

The earliest record found was a Patent Office registration of the trademark in the name of Curtis and Wilkinson, November 3, 1891, to be used on jewelry, table and flatware. The company was sold at auction in May 1915.

Note that the trademark is similar to those of the W. H. Glenny & Company and the Waldo Foundry.

JAMES CURTIS
Chicago, Illinois

Listed in 1954-1855 Chicago Directory as a silverplater.

CURTISVILLE MFG. CO.
Connecticut
(See American Sterling Co.)
(See F. Curtis & Co.)
(See Williams Bros. Mfg. Co.)
(See Thomas S. Vail)

Successor to F. Curtis & Co. of Hartford and Glastonbury. F. Curtis & Co. was reorganized on September 18, 1854 under the name Curtisville Mfg. Co. with Charles Benedict as President and R. F. Fowler, Sec. and Treas. By 1857 the locale was called Curtisville and had its own postmaster. In 1859, Thomas J. Vail assumed the Presidency and the Curtis family no longer appeared in the Hartford listings.

CUVEE SILVER WARRANTED

Known only from name stamped on flatware.

D

A. DAVIS CO.
Chicago, Illinois

R. COIN
R. SPECIAL

Successors to M. C. Eppenstein & Co. before 1904. Out of business shortly afterwards.

DAVIS & GALT
Philadelphia, Pennsylvania

Registered U. S. Patent No. 22,275, January 3, 1893 for manufacture of sterling silverware. Patent Office records show this trademark in use since July 21, 1888. Listed in J C-K 1896-1915. Out of business between 1915-22.

JAMES J. DAWSON CO.
New York, New York

NORTH AMERICA

Listed in J C-K 1904 in plated silverware section. Out of business before 1915.

DAY, CLARK & CO.
Newark, New Jersey; New York, New York

Manufacturers and distributors of sterling and jewelry. The trademark was first used in 1895. Last record found was 1935.

Known only from Denver souvenir flatware. May be a trademark of E. L. Deacon Jewelry Co. of Denver.

E. L. DEACON JEWELRY CO.
Denver, Colorado

E. L. D.
(Souvenir Spoons.)

Listed in J C-K 1909; Eugene L. Deacon, successor before 1915 with address given as Los Angeles, California.

I. N. DEITSCH
New York, New York

Listed in J C-K 1904-15 as manufacturers of sterling silverware. No records after c. 1920.

DEITSCH BROS.
New York, New York

Patent Office records show they were manufacturers of leather articles with sterling silver mountings, September 8, 1896. Listed in J C-K 1896-1922.

DELAWARE SILVER CO.

DELAWARE SILVER CO.

Found on grape design sterling flatware of c. 1895-1900.

DEPASSE MFG. CO.
New York, New York

Manufacturers of sterling silver deposit and gold encrusted glassware. Listed in J C-K 1909-15. Succeeded by Depasse, Pearsall Silver Co. before 1922.

DEPASSE, PEARSALL SILVER CO.
New York, New York

Successors to Depasse Mfg. Co. between 1915-1922. Last record was 1935.

DERBY SILVER CO.
Derby, Connecticut
(See International Silver Co.)

Founded in 1873 by Edwin N. Shelton, Watson J. Miller and Thomas H. Newcomb, silverplaters of holloware. They made decorative wares of sterling silver.

U. S. Patent No. 15,642, June 26, 1888, registered by Watson J. Miller and Henry Berry for M & B sterling trademark to be used on forks, spoons, tea sets, brushes, mirrors and pitchers.

One of the original companies which formed the International Silver Co. in 1898.

Sterling mark not used after about 1895.

ADAM DEUPERT
Baltimore, Maryland

Listed in Baltimore City Directories 1875-1882 as a gold and silversmith (gold leaf).

MISS SARAH B. DICKINSON
Niagara Falls, New York
(See Mrs. Sarah B. Dickinson
Wood)
(See Thomas V. Dickinson)

THOMAS V. DICKINSON
Buffalo, New York
(See Mrs. Sarah B. Dickinson
Wood)

U. S. Patent No. 19,905, registered July 21, 1891 for silver, flat and tableware. The mark is the same as that used by Mrs. Sarah B. Dickinson Wood.

RICHARD DIMES COMPANY
South Boston, Massachusetts

Founded in 1908, according to one account and in 1923 by another. Sold to the King Silver Company in October 1955, which was acquired by Rogers, Lunt & Bowlen (Lunt Silversmiths) soon afterwards. They made sterling silver holloware and flatware and the trademark is registered with the U. S. Patent Office, No. 755,049, by Rogers, Lunt & Bowlen for use on sterling holloware and novelty items.

Manchester Silver Company in 1955 or 1956 acquired the tools, dies and rights to the flatware patterns formerly produced by Richard Dimes.

DIRIGO DISTRIBUTING CO.
New York, New York

DIRIGOLD

Silverplaters c. 1920.

DIRKSEN SILVER FILIGREE CO.
Freeport, Illinois

D. S. F. CO.

Listed in J C-K 1896 as manufacturers of sterling silver filigree articles. Succeeded by Dirksen Silver Co. before 1904 and out of business before 1909.

J. DIXON & SONS
Sheffield, England

STERLING SILVER-

PLATED SILVER

Established in 1806 as silversmiths and electroplaters. They were the leading makers of britannia and silverplated wares imported into this country from the 1830's to the 1860's. Registered U. S. Patent No. 14,806 for the manufacture of silver, nickel-silver, britannia and plated goods, Oct. 11, 1887.

JAMES M. DIXON
Chicago, Illinois

Listed in 1854–55 Chicago Directory as a silverplater.

DOMINICK & HAFF
Newark and New York
(See Reed and Barton)

D. & H.

Traces its beginnings to William Gale & Son silversmiths in New York in 1821. The succession of business names is as follows: Gale & North, 1860; Gale, North & Dominick, 1868 and Dominick & Haff, 1873. From 1871 to 1899 it was a partnership and was incorporated in 1900. They were makers of fine quality sterling holloware and flatware. Noted for the excellent quality and design of many souvenir spoons. In 1928 the company was purchased by Reed and Barton.

One account reports that the business was bought in 1866 by Edward Corning and that the younger Gale was associated with him under the name Gale & Corning until 1869. The present owners were unable to confirm this.

DORANTIQUE
(See Bernard Rice's Sons)

DORST CO.
Cincinnati, Ohio

STERLING SILVER

Successors (?) to Jonas, Dorst & Co. in business 1896. Manufacturers and retailers of sterling and plated silverware, and jewelry. Succeeded c. 1940 by Dorst Jewelry Co. which is still in business.

DOWD-RODGERS CO.
Wallingford, Connecticut

TRADE **D** MARK

Listed in the City Directory 1915/16–1937. Not listed in 1939. Directories published every two years. Jobbers of plated silverware.

THE DUHME JEWELRY CO.
Cincinnati, Ohio

Began as Duhme & Co. in 1839. Became Duhme Jewelry Co. c. 1887–1890. Listed in the City Directories 1896–1907 as dealers in silverware, jewelry, etc.

RUFUS DUNHAM
(See Stevens and Smart)
(See New England Silver Co.)

BRITANNIA

Made britannia and plated ware 1863-1875. In 1877 the company became Rufus Dunham & Sons and continued this same name until 1883 with sons Joseph S., Charles A. and John associated with the firm. In 1894 Joseph S. formed the New England Silver Company.

BENEDICT DUNN
(See Benedict Mfg. Co.)

L. F. DUNN
Niagara Falls, New York

CARBON

Registered U. S. Patent No. 10,765 for the manufacture of knives, forks and spoons, Dec. 4, 1883. Not listed in City Directory (1886 Directory is the earliest available).

DURGIN & BURTT
St. Louis, Missouri
(See F. A. Durgin)

Listed in St. Louis City Directory 1859-60 as manufacturers of silver and plated silverware.

F. A. DURGIN
St. Louis, Missouri

F. A. DURGIN
ST. LOUIS

Founded by Freeman A. Durgin in St. Louis in 1858. The 1859-1860 St. Louis Directory lists him as a member of the firm, Durgin & Burtt. From 1863-1888 he was in business for himself. From 1888-

1911 he was a salesman for the Jaccard jewelry firm. It has not been definitely established that he was actually a manufacturer of silver and plated silverware as he advertised, or whether he was a wholesaler or retailer for others. Much silver, especially flatware, is found with his name.

WM. B. DURGIN CO.
Concord, New Hampshire
(See Gorham Corporation)

DISCOVERY
(*Discontinued.*)

CROMWELL

WATTEAU

FAIRFAX

Founded in 1853 by William B. Durgin who was a silversmith in Concord, New Hampshire about 1850. Makers of sterling silver flatware, gold, silver and plated tableware, jewelry and similar articles (U. S. Patent 20,218, Oct. 13, 1891.) Purchased by Gorham Corporation in 1905 and moved to Providence in 1931.

DUTCH SILVER NOVELTIES
(See Johnson, Hayward &
Piper Co.)

JOSEPH DYAR
Middlebury, Vermont

Advertised from 1822 through 1845 that his table and tea spoons, cream and salt spoons, sugar tongs, thimbles and gold beads were of first quality and workmanship. He was born in 1804 and died in 1851.

E

EAGLE BRAND
(See Simpson, Hall & Miller)

EAGLE SILVER CO.
Providence, Rhode Island

E.S.C.O.

Listed in Providence City Directories 1922-1953 as manufacturers of silver novelties. Owners —Memelaus Sava and Ignatius H. Findan. Manufactured sterling silver cigarette cases, vanity cases, whiskey flasks, match safes, 14k gold inlaid and onyx inlaid wares.

EAGLE STERLING CO.
Glastonbury, Connecticut

Organized in 1895 by William H. Watrous and others to manufacture silverware. Listed in 1896 J C-K in plated silver section. Out of business before 1904.

EASTERN SILVER CO.
(See American Silver Co.)

EASTWOOD-PARK COMPANY
Newark, New Jersey

Manufacturers of exclusive designs in sterling silverware, dresserware, novelties, mesh bags and jewelry for the wholesale trade.

Listed J C-K 1909-1915. Out of business before 1922.

ECKFELDT & ACKLEY
Newark, New Jersey

Listed in 1896 Jewelers' Weekly in sterling silverware section. Listed 1898–1915 J C-K as jewelers. Last record found c. 1935.

1857 WELCH-ATKINS
(See The American Silver Co.)

WM. J. EISENHARDT
Baltimore, Maryland

Listed in Baltimore City Directories 1887–1888 as a silverplater.

M. EISENSTADT JEWELRY CO.
St. Louis, Missouri

Plated silver holloware

M. Eisenstadt Company (Wholesale distributors of silverware and jewelry). Founded in 1853 by Michael Gabriel Eisenstadt. First appeared in St. Louis directory in 1866. From 1904 is listed as M. Eisenstadt Manufacturing Co., and from 1908 on they are listed as manufacturers of jewelry, jobbers of watches and importers of diamonds. In the 1920's, 1930's and 1940's they are listed as M. Eisenstadt Mfg. Co. and they are still in business as M. Eisenstadt, wholesale jewelry.

ELDRIDGE & CO.
Taunton, Massachusetts

Listed in Taunton City Directories from 1800–1884 as silver manufacturers "at Britanniaville, near R. R. crossing Reed & Barton."

ELECTROLYTIC ART METAL CO.
Trenton, New Jersey

Listed in J C-K 1915 with manufacturers of sterling silverware. No record after 1920.

ELEDER-HICKOK CO.
Newark, New Jersey
(See Hickok-Matthews Co.
Silversmiths)

Originally Lebkuecher & Co.; the name was changed by law to F. A. Lester after 1915 and was taken

over by the Eleder Co. in 1918. By 1922 it had become the Eleder-Hickok Co. It merged with the Matthews Company after 1931 to form the Hickok-Matthews Company, manufacturers of sterling silver novelties.

ELGIN-AMERICAN
MANUFACTURING COMPANY
Elgin, Illinois

ELGIN PLATE

STAR CUTLERY CO.
TRIPLE PLATE

ELGIN
TRIPLE 12

ELGIN AMERICAN MFG.CO
WARRANTED

On plated silver knives about 1898.

Began business in 1887. An un-dated Elgin-American catalog in the writer's possession (with illus-trations of souvenirs engraved "Remember the Maine" and desk calendars dated January 1898) in-cludes flatware of plated silver, smoking sets, jewel cases, brace-lets, dresser sets, match safes and novelties.

Registered U. S. Patent No. 103,053, March 16, 1915 for manu-facture of silverware.

Became a division of Illinois Watch Case Company before 1950. Observed their 65th anniversary in 1952. This is the last record found.

ELGIN SILVERSMITH CO., INC.
New York, New York
(See Redlich & Co.)

Founded by two partners, Ludwig & Redlich, and operated under that name until 1892 when Mr. Ludwig sold his interest to Alex Redlich who became sole owner and operated the business until 1920 when he sold his interest to three of his old employees and it became Redlich & Co., Inc. It was taken over by Elgin Silversmith Co., Inc. in 1946. Products are sterling silverware, holloware and 14k goldwares. The Redlich trade-mark has not been changed and is still used by the firm to the pres-ent day. Currier & Roby is now a Division of Elgin Silversmiths.

ELLIS & CO., LTD.
Birmingham, England

Listed in J C-K 1915 to present. Registered U. S. Patent No. 90,691 for use on silver and electroplated articles March 18, 1913. Now known as Ellis Silver Company, Inc., New York.

P. W. ELLIS & CO.
Toronto, Canada

In business before 1890. Listed 1904-1922 J C-K. Importers and wholesalers of watches, clocks, sterling and plated silverware, ivory dresserware, china and cut glass, artware, gold filled, solid gold and platinum jewelry, diamonds, tools, materials and supplies.

ELLMORE SILVER CO., INC.
Meriden, Connecticut
(See Concord Silver Co.)
(See G. H. French & Co.)
(See Frank M. Whiting Co.)

Founded in 1935 as Ellmore Silver Co., and was incorporated soon afterwards. The W. S. Blackinton Co., Frank M. Whiting & Co. and Concord Silver Co. became divisions of the Ellmore Company in the 1940's. The Blackinton Co. and Whiting Company are now independently owned.

Manufacturers of sterling silverware.

EMPIRE ART METAL WORKS
New York, New York

Listed 1909 J C-K in plated silver section.

EMPIRE ART SILVER
(See E. & J. Bass)

EMPIRE SILVER COMPANY
(See Benedict Mfg. Co.)

EMPIRE SILVER PLATE CO.
New York, New York

Listed in 1896 Jewelers' Weekly and J C-K 1896 as manufacturers and importers of plated silver hollowares. Last record in 1924.

EMPRESS WARE
(See New York Stamping Co.)

ENTERPRISE PLATING WORKS
Baltimore, Maryland

Listed in Baltimore City Directories 1894-1916 as silverplaters.

M. C. EPPENSTEIN & CO.
Chicago, Illinois
(See A. Davis & Co.)

R. COIN.

Earliest record found was Patent Office Registration No. 24,525, April 17, 1894 for use on plated silver tableware. Succeeded by A. Davis & Co. c. 1904.

ESSEX SILVER CO.
(See The Wallingford Co.)

EUREKA SILVER PLATE CO.
(See Meriden Silver Plate Co.)

THOMAS EVANS & CO.
Binghamton, New York
(See Geo. W. Shiebler & Co.)

Thomas Evans was a silversmith c. 1850. Listed J C-K 1904 as Theo. Evans & Co.

F

OTTO G. FABER
Baltimore, Maryland

Listed in Baltimore City Directories 1895-1910 as a silversmith,

goldsmith and jeweler. Some of his pieces bear a marked similarity to designs made by Samuel Kirk & Son.

WILLIAM FABER & SONS
Philadelphia, Pennsylvania

Silversmiths and silverplaters 1828-1887.

FAIRCHILD & COMPANY
New York, New York

CHRONOLOGY

Randall & Fairchild	1837
LeRoy W. Fairchild	1843
LeRoy W. Fairchild & Co.	1867
L. W. Fairchild	1873
L. W. Fairchild & Sons	1886
LeRoy Fairchild & Co.	1889
Fairchild & Johnson	1898
Fairchild & Company	1919

F

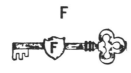

L. W. FAIRCHILD & CO.

FAIRCHILD & JOHNSON CO.

Founded in 1837 as Randall & Fairchild. In 1843, known as LeRoy W. Fairchild; 1867-1873 as LeRoy W. Fairchild & Co.; 1873-1886 as L. W. Fairchild; 1886, L. W. Fairchild & Sons; 1889 it was incorporated as LeRoy Fairchild & Co.; in 1896 Harry P. Fairchild bought out the business and in 1898 he formed the corporation of Fairchild & Johnson. In 1919 it was known as Fairchild & Co., and went out of business c. 1922. Makers of sterling silverware.

FARBER BROS.
New York, New York

Manufacturers and jobbers of plated silver holloware c. 1920–1950.

W. J. FEELEY CO.
Providence, Rhode Island

One account says that the company was founded in 1875 by Michael Feeley. Another says it was established by W. J. Feeley in 1875 and incorporated in 1892. According to this account, W. J. Feeley was born in Providence January 19, 1855 and learned the trade of silversmithing from Knowles & Webster; worked several years as a journeyman before beginning business on his own account.

They were manufacturers of gold and silver ecclesiastical goods. City Directories list the company from 1875 to 1920 as manufacturing jewelers and silversmiths. Listed in 1936–1937 Jobbers' Handbook.

ALBERT FELDENHEIMER
Portland, Oregon

U. S. Patents registered April 28, 1891 and January 1892 for sterling souvenir flatware and jewelry. Became A. & C. Feldenheimer between 1896–1904. Last record c. 1904.

FENNIMAN CO.
New York, New York

Listed J C-K 1915 in sterling silver section. Out of business before 1922.

PETER FERRARI
Baltimore, Maryland

Listed in Baltimore City Directories 1887–89 as a silverplater.

FESSENDEN & COMPANY
Providence, Rhode Island

**925
STERLING
1000**

Established April 1858 by William Fessenden. Makers of sterling silver flatware and holloware. No record after 1922.

MARSHALL FIELD & CO.
Chicago, Illinois

Began business in 1864 as Farwell, Field & Company. In 1865 the company became Field, Palmer & Leiter; Potter Palmer sold out his interests in 1866 and the firm name became Field, Leiter & Company. Marshall Field became sole owner in 1881 and gave the firm its present name.

Marshall Field's was one of the first large department stores to have many articles stamped with trademarks registered for its own use. U. S. Patent No. 146,536, September 6, 1921, was registered for their use on silverware, both sterling and plated.

FILLKWIK CO.
ttleboro, Massachusetts
(See Shields Inc.)

HARVEY FILLEY & SONS
Philadelphia, Pennsylvania

Silver platers c. 1859–c. 1900.

FILLEY & MEAD
Philadelphia, Pennsylvania
(See John O. Mead)

FILLEY, MEAD & CALDWELL
Philadelphia, Pennsylvania
(See John O. Mead)

WILLIAM C. FINCK CO.
Elizabeth, New Jersey

 STERLING

Listed in J C-K 1896-1904. Out of business before 1915. Manufacturers of sterling silverware. Among their products were sterling souvenir spoons.

ALBERT G. FINN SILVER CO.
Syracuse, New York
(See P. A. Coon Silver Mfg. Co.)

TRADE-MARK.

Manufacturers of plated silverware. Founding date not known. Listed J C-K 1904. Succeeded by P. A. Coon Silver Mfg. Co. between 1904-1909.

ALBERT G. FINN SILVER CO.
CRESCENT SILVER CO.

FISHEL, NESSLER & CO.
New York, New York
(See Majestic Mfg. Co.)

Manufacturers of sterling silver and rhinestone-set jewelry, platenoid rhinestone-set jewelry, plated jewelry and card jewelry. Registered U. S. Patent No. 23,016 for use on jewelry, May 16, 1893. Last listing found was 1936-1937.

FLAGG & HOMAN
Cincinnati, Ohio
(See Homan Mfg. Co.)

(Pewter)

FLORENCE SILVER PLATE CO.
Baltimore, Maryland

Listed in Baltimore City Directories 1894-1942 as silverplaters. No City Directories available 1942-1955.

FOOT & COLSON
Chicago, Illinois

Listed in 1854-1855 Chicago Directory as silverplaters. In 1856 Foot was listed as working alone.

E. B. FLOYD
Burlington, Vermont

Worked as late as 1868 in coin silver.

FORBES SILVER CO.
Meriden, Connecticut
(See International Silver Co.)

Organized in 1894 as a department of Meriden Britannia Co. for hollo-ware silverplating. One of the orig-inal companies which formed the International Silver Co.

FORD & CARPENTER
New York, New York
(See Cohen & Rosenberger)

Succeeded Baldwin, Ford & Co. between 1896 and 1904 and were succeeded by Cohen & Rosen-berger before 1915.

FOSTER & BAILEY
Providence, Rhode Island
(See Theodore W. Foster &
Bro. Co.)

Succeeded by Theodore W. Foster & Bro. Co.

THEODORE W. FOSTER &
BRO. CO.
Providence, Rhode Island

F. & B.

Established January 1, 1873 under the name White & Foster. Walter E. White had been listed previously as a jeweler from 1869-1872. The name was later changed to White Foster & Co. and in 1878 when White withdrew, the name became Foster & Bailey. (S. H. Bailey) In May 1898 the company was in-corporated under the name Theodore Foster & Bros., Co. They were among the largest man-ufacturers of jewelry and sterling silver goods in Providence. Among the goods were gold filled, electro-plated and sterling silver vanity cases, cigarette cases, clock cases, ecclesiastical goods, cigar and cigarette holders, knives, medals, pens and pencils, photo frames, dresserware and candlesticks for which U. S. Patent 28,069, April 17, 1896 was registered. This last listing continued until 1951.

J. F. FRADLEY & CO.
New York, New York

TRADE MARK

Established in 1869 and incorporated in 1890. Manufacturers of 14k gold and sterling silver cane and umbrella handles; 14k dresserware and novelties; sterling photo frames, vases, desk accessories and novelties. Listed in J C-K 1896–1922. Last record found 1936–37.

FRANKLIN SILVER PLATE
COMPANY
Greenfield, Massachusetts
(See Lunt Silversmiths)

Incorporated in Greenfield, Massachusetts in 1912. Ceased operations between 1920–22. They were manufacturers of plated silver holloware. The trademark was taken over by Rogers, Lunt & Bowlen (Lunt Silversmiths) c. 1922, but with minor exceptions has not been used.

FRENCH & FRANKLIN
North Attleboro, Massachusetts

Listed in Jewelers' Weekly, 1896 as manufacturers of sterling silverware.

G. H. FRENCH & CO.
North Attleboro, Massachusetts
(See Ellmore Silver Co., Inc.)

Earliest record found c. 1920. Manufacturers of sterling silver novelties, cigarette and vanity cases, cups and tableware. Succeeded by Ellmore Silver Company, Inc. between 1935–43.

FRIED, MILLS & CO., INC.
Irvington, New Jersey

Listed in J C-K 1915 in sterling silver section. Last record found c. 1935.

FRIEDMAN SILVER CO., INC.
Brooklyn, New York
(See Gorham Corporation)

Creators of fine holloware since 1908. Bought by the Gorham Corporation in 1960.

BENJAMIN FROBISHER
Boston, Massachusetts

Benjamin Frobisher was a silversmith and jeweler. Though britannia wares are generally thought not to have been made in this country until 1835 or afterwards, according to the late Carl Dreppard, Frobisher advertised them as early as 1829.

F. S. & S. M.

Known only from sterling souvenir spoon, Souvenir of Luna Park, Coney Island (skyline), copyright 1907.

FUCHS & BEIDERHASE
New York, New York

Founded by Rudolph Fuchs and George B. Beiderhase in 1890. Makers of sterling holloware, cups, napkin rings, dresserware, library articles and novelties. Succeeded by Alvin Mfg. Co. before 1896.

FERD. FUCHS & BROS.
New York, New York

Ferdinand Fuchs & Brothers were listed in J C-K 1896-1915 as makers of sterling silverware. Out of business before 1922.

G

GALE & NORTH
New York, New York
(See Dominick & Haff)

GALE, NORTH & DOMINICK
New York, New York
(See Dominick & Haff)

WM. GALE
New York, New York
(See Gorham Corporation)
(See Graff, Washbourne & Dunn)

W. G. in rectangle; head in a square; tulips in cup-shaped cartouche.

WM. GALE & SON
New York, New York
(See Dominick & Haff)

WM. GALE & SONS
(See Gorham Corporation)
(See Graff, Washbourne & Dunn)

Successor to Wm. Gale. Silversmiths in New York. Succeeded by
Gale, Wood & Hughes.

Wm. Gale & Sons were among
the first American silversmiths to
stamp their solid silver "sterling."

GALE, WOOD & HUGHES
New York, New York
(See Gorham Corporation)
(See Graff, Washbourne & Dunn)

G. W. & H.

Successors to Wm. Gale & Sons.
Members of the firm were William
Gale, Jacob Wood and Jasper W.
Hughes, New York, 1836–1845.
Succeeded by Wood & Hughes.

JOHN GAILLISSAIRE
Baltimore, Maryland

Listed in Baltimore City Directory as silverplater in 1864.

GALT & BRO., INC.
Washington, D. C.

GALT & BRO.

James Galt moved from Georgetown to Alexandria in 1802 and
established his business which included the making of watches, and
later fine silver pieces.

In 1847 James Galt died and
ownership of the business passed
into the hands of M. W. Galt and
William Galt, his sons. Among
their patrons were Abraham Lin-
coln and Jefferson Davis. In 1879
William Galt withdrew from the
firm. The following year M. W. Galt
retired and turned over to Norman
Galt, grandson of the founder, the
responsibility for maintaining the
prestige and respect which the
House of Galt had earned. He was
assisted by Henry C. Bergheimer.

About 1900, Galt and Brother
was chosen to execute a bowl
which was presented to Postmaster Charles Emory Smith for
his efforts in establishing a rural
mail system. This piece of work

brought a special congratulatory note from President Roosevelt in 1902, the one hundredth anniversary of Galt and Brother.

In 1908 Norman Galt died and Henry C. Bergheimer became the first to manage the business without bearing the founder's name. That year they began automobile delivery service. In 1923, Henry C. Bergheimer died and the management was carried on under William H. Wright. In 1934, Galt & Brother was incorporated. Mr.

Wright died in 1940. Since that time Galt's has been headed by Lena M. Black, President.

U. S. Patent No. 19,421, May 5, 1891. Portrait of Christopher Columbus, a copy of M. Maelia's engraved picture of Columbus published by Joseph Delaplaine, Philadelphia and later given to the U. S. Navy Department.

U. S. Patent No. 20,448, December 8, 1891. Landing of Columbus. Facsimile of the famous painting later placed in the U. S. Capitol.

Both trademarks were used on gold, silver and plated silver articles, presumably of the souvenir type.

The George and Martha Washington medallions were registered trademarks for use on souvenir spoons conceived by M. W. Galt. The first of these was a ladle that was an exact facsimile of the Washington ladle preserved in the National Museum, with the addition of the Washington medallion stamped in the bowl.

ALBERT J. GANNON
Philadelphia, Pennsylvania

The Philadelphia City Directory lists Albert J. Gannon as a salesman in 1905; as a silversmith between 1906-1910 and lists Albert J. Gannon Company, silversmiths from 1911-1914. This is the last listing.

GARRETT & SONS
Philadelphia, Pennsylvania

In the 1860's they purchased Reed & Barton wares "in the metal" and operated their own plating establishment.

GEORGE C. GEBELEIN
Boston, Massachusetts

George C. Gebelein was born near Bayreuth, Bavaria, in 1878 and was brought to this country when a year old so his training was entirely American. He was apprenticed at the age of 14 to Goodnow & Jenks. In January 1907, he moved from the joint facilities of The Handicraft Shop of Boston, where he had been since 1904. For

twenty-three years he had a shop of his own at the foot of Beacon Hill.

Besides making fine reproductions and adaptations, he was a collector and dealer in old American and European silver, becoming a recognized authority on silver. He was one of the early recipients of the medal for excel-

lence presented by the Society of Arts and Crafts of Boston. The Williamsburg Communion set is one of his best known productions. His son followed him in the silversmithing craft and after the father's death in 1946, the company was incorporated under family directorship as Gebelein Silversmiths Inc.

GEM SILVER CO.
(See International Silver Co.)

GEM SILVER CO.

Trademark of Wilcox Silver Plate Co. for dresserware and several flatware patterns.

ARTHUR R. GEOFFROY
New York, New York

Listed in J C-K 1896 as manufacturer of sterling silverware. Out of business before 1904. Advertised as maker of wares in sterling silver for the trade only.

GERMAN SILVER
(See Holmes & Edwards)

⊞ GERMAN SILVER ⊕4

GEORGE E. GERMER
Boston, Massachusetts

George E. Germer was the son of a Berlin jeweler and was born in 1868. Even before his apprenticeship, he showed a love of silver. Otto Gericke of Berlin, was his teacher and from him he learned chasing and modeling. He came to the United States in 1893 and for nearly 20 years worked in New York, Providence and Boston. After 1912 he worked independently, producing mostly ecclesiastical silver. During his latter years, he moved his shop to Mason, New Hampshire and produced more silver for churches, some of which is now in museums.

F. S. GILBERT
North Attleboro, Massachusetts

STERLING **G**

Listed J C-K 1904 as manufacturer of sterling silverware. Out of business before 1915.

GINNELL MFG. CO.
Brooklyn, New York

G. MFG. CO.

Listed in J C-K 1915–22 as a manufacturer of sterling silverware and jewelry.

GLASTONBURY SILVER CO.
Chicago, Illinois

GEE-ESCO

Listed in J C-K 1922-1950 as manufacturers of plated silver flatware and holloware. Between 1931-1950 the company name became Glastonbury, Inc.

R. GLEASON & SONS
Dorchester, Massachusetts

Used on plated silver. Attributed to Manhattan Silver Plate Co. in 1904 J C-K.

Began with Roswell Gleason who was a tin worker in 1822. He was first listed as a pewterer about 1830. He was noted for the extremely fine quality of his work. This quality was carried over into britannia work later when the business became one of the largest and most important in Dorchester. After 1850 their products were mostly silverplated. The business closed in 1871.

W. H. GLENNY & CO.
Rochester, New York

Wholesale and retail silverware and jewelry. Note similarity of trademark to that of The Waldo Foundry, Bridgeport, Connecticut, and H. H. Curtis & Co., North Attleboro, Massachusetts.

W. H. GLENNY, SONS & CO.
Buffalo, New York

In business before 1890. Listed in 1896 J C-K. Out of business before 1904. Wholesalers of silverware, including souvenir spoons, stamped with their trademark.

GLOBE ART MFG. CO.
Newark, New Jersey

Listed in J C-K 1915-1922 as manufacturers of sterling silver and plated silverware.

JACOB GMINDER
Baltimore, Maryland

Listed as a silverplater 1867-1901 in Baltimore City Directories.

M. T. GOLDSMITH
Brooklyn, New York

BRITANNIA ARTISTIC SILVER

Established in 1864 by Marcus Goldsmith as Goldsmith Brothers Smelting & Refining Company, Lexington, Kentucky. In 1882, his sons, Moses and Simon, succeeded to the business and in 1884 moved to Chicago. In 1909, the New York branch was opened by Simon. They were known as leaders in smelting and refining gold, silver and platinum. Listed by J C-K as out of business in 1909.

GOLDSMITH'S COMPANY OF CANADA, LTD.
Toronto, Canada

NICKELITE SILVER
SHEFFIELD CUTLERY

Listed in J C-K 1915-1922 in the plated silver section.

GOLDSTEIN & SWANK CO.
Worcester, Massachusetts

Listed in J C-K 1915-1922 as makers of plated ware, jewelers and special order work.

    Became Goldstein, Swank & Gordon before 1936. This is the last record found.

GOLDYN-BRONZ
(See Reed & Barton)

GOODNOW & JENKS
Boston, Massachusetts

Manufacturers of sterling silverware. In business before 1890. George C. Gebelein was an apprentice there in 1893. Went out of business between 1896 and 1909.

GORDON & CO.
Baltimore, Maryland

Listed in Baltimore City Directories as silverplaters 1880-1894. Successors to George B. Gordon who was first listed in 1864. Succeeded by F. S. Gordon.

F. S. GORDON
Baltimore, Maryland

Successors to Gordon & Co. Listed in Baltimore City Directories 1894-1897 as silverplaters. The 1898 and 1899 listings are in the name of Frederick Gordon.

GEORGE B. GORDON
Baltimore, Maryland

Listed in Baltimore City Directories 1864-1879 as silverplaters. Succeeded by Gordon & Co.

GORHAM & CO.
Providence, Rhode Island
(See Gorham Corporation)

Successor to Gorham & Thurber in 1852. Became Gorham Manufacturing Company in 1865 and the Gorham Corporation in 1961.

GORHAM CORPORATION
Providence, Rhode Island

TRADE MARK

STERLING

TRADE-MARK.

STERLING

950-1000 FINE

STERLING
(Sterling silver)

(Plated silver)

* GORHAM
(art bronzes)

(Bronze)

GORHAM
(Gold)

Jabez Gorham, founder of the Gorham Corporation, was born in Providence, Rhode Island in 1792 and at 14 began his seven year apprenticeship to Nehemiah Dodge. After serving this apprenticeship, he formed a partnership with Christopher Burr, William Hadwen, George C. Clark and Harvey G. Mumford about 1815-1818 at which time he purchased his own shop to manufacture small items and became known for his "Gorham chain," unequaled at the time.

With Stanton Beebe he made jewelry until 1831 when Henry L. Webster, formerly with Lewis Cary in Boston, joined the firm to make silver spoons. The firm name was changed to Gorham & Webster. In 1837, the firm was called Gorham, Webster & Price. When Gorham's son, John joined the firm in 1841, the name was changed to Jabez Gorham & Son. John Gorham quickly recognized the advantages of machinery and as a result the Gorham Company was among the first to introduce factory methods to augment hand

A.	1868
B.	1869
C.	1870
D.	1871
E.	1872
F.	1873
G.	1874
H.	1875
I.	1876
J.	1877
K.	1878
L.	1879
M.	1880
N.	1881
O.	1882
P.	1883
Q.	1884
[symbol]	1885
[symbol]	1886
[symbol]	1887
[symbol]	1888
[symbol]	1889
[symbol]	1890
[symbol]	1891
[symbol]	1892
[symbol]	1893
[symbol]	1894
[symbol]	1895
[symbol]	1896
[symbol]	1897
[symbol]	1898
[symbol]	1899
[symbol]	1900
[symbol]	1901
[symbol]	1902
[symbol]	1903
[symbol]	1904
[symbol]	1905
[symbol]	1906
[symbol]	1907
[symbol]	1908
[symbol]	1909
[symbol]	1910
[symbol]	1911
[symbol]	1912
[symbol]	1913
[symbol]	1914
[symbol]	1915
[symbol]	1916
[symbol]	1917
[symbol]	1918
[symbol]	1919
[symbol]	1920
[symbol]	1921
[symbol]	1922
[symbol]	1923
[symbol]	1924
[symbol]	1925
[symbol]	1926
[symbol]	1927
[symbol]	1928
[symbol]	1929
[symbol]	1930
[symbol]	1931

craftsmanship in production of silverware. He designed and made much of the machinery himself if none were available to suit his purposes.

In 1850, three years after Jabez Gorham retired, the company name was Gorham & Thurber. By 1852, it was Gorham & Company. The firm was chartered by the Rhode Island Legislature as the Gorham Manufacturing Company in 1863 and organized as a corporation in 1865. In 1868, they abandoned the coin silver standard (900/1000) and adopted the sterling standard of 925/1000 fine silver. At the same time, the familiar trademark—a lion, an anchor, and a capital G—was adopted for use on all sterling articles. Ecclesiastical wares of gold, bronze, stone, wood and sterling were added in 1885. **L'art nouveau** designs of the talented English artist, William J. Codman, were added under the name "Martelé" in the late 19th century.

Holding companies were chartered in New York during 1906 and 1907 for the purpose of acquiring the Whiting, Durgin and Kerr companies. These corporations in the order of their formation were known as the Silversmiths Stocks Company and The Silversmiths Company. In the reorganization of the Company in 1924, the Silversmiths Company was purchased, its assets taken over and the company dissolved. The Gorham Company then operated as subsidiary divisions, the Whiting Mfg. Co. (moved to Providence in 1925); William B. Kerr Company, (moved to Providence in 1927); and William B. Durgin Company, (moved to Providence in 1931).

About 1913 the Gorham inter-

1932

1933

During 1933 year marks
were discontinued.

January 1941 year marking
was resumed on Sterling
Holloware except lower
priced items.

[1] 1941

The square frame indicates
the decade of the 40's.
The numeral indicates the
year of the decade.

▽ 1950

[1] 1951

The pentagon indicates
the decade of the 50's

The numeral indicates the
year of the decade.

◯ 1960

① 1961

The hexagon indicates the
decade of the 60's.

The numeral indicates the
year of the decade.

CHRONOLOGY

Gorham & Webster	1831–1837
Gorham, Webster & Price	1837–1841
J. Gorham & Son	1841–1850
Gorham & Thurber	1850–1852
Gorham & Company	1852–1865
Gorham Mfg. Company*	1865–1961
Gorham Corp.	1961–present

* Or Lion and Anchor

ests expanded to include the Mt. Vernon Company Silversmiths, Inc., which had resulted from the merging of the Roger Williams Silver Company of Providence, Rhode Island, the Mauser Manufacturing Company of Mt. Vernon, New York and Hayes & McFarland of New York City.

The Alvin Silver Company was acquired in 1928 and its title changed to The Alvin Corporation. Its products are made at the Providence plant though it functions as an organization separate from The Gorham Company.

The Gorham retail store at 5th Avenue and 47th Street in New York merged with Black, Starr and Frost in 1929 under the new firm name of Black, Starr and Frost-Gorham, Inc. In 1940 the name was shortened to Black, Starr & Gorham Inc. In 1962 The Gorham Company sold its interests and the name became Black, Starr & Frost, Ltd.

In 1931 the McChesney Company of Newark, New Jersey was purchased and its tools and dies moved to Providence.

The Quaker Silver Company of North Attleboro, Massachusetts was purchased in 1959, the Friedman Company of Brooklyn New York, in 1960 and Graff, Washbourne & Dunn of New York in 1961.

Flatware year markings have been used since 1868. Letters of the alphabet A through Q were used from 1868 through 1884 at which time symbols were adopted for each year until 1933 at which time they were discontinued. In January 1941, year markings were resumed on sterling holloware, except lower priced items. During the 1940's a square frame indicated the decade and the numeral inside, the year of the decade. A shield was used during the 1950's and a hexagon is being used during the 1960's.

At all periods the Gorham Company has been noted for the fine quality of its die work as well as superior design and fine finishing of all products.

JABEZ GORHAM
Providence, Rhode Island
(See Gorham Corporation)

Founded in 1818 what is now the Gorham Corporation.

JABEZ GORHAM & SON
Providence, Rhode Island
(See Gorham Corporation)

Successor to Gorham, Webster & Price in 1841. Succeeded by Gorham & Thurber in 1850.

GORHAM & THURBER
Providence, Rhode Island
(See Gorham Corporation)

Successor to Jabez Gorham & Son in 1850. Was succeeded by Gorham & Company in 1852.

GORHAM & WEBSTER
Providence, Rhode Island
(See Gorham Corporation)

Successor to Jabez Gorham in 1831. Was succeeded by Gorham, Webster & Price in 1837.

GORHAM, WEBSTER & PRICE
Providence, Rhode Island
(See Gorham Corporation)

Successor to Gorham & Webster in 1837. Succeeded by Jabez Gorham & Son in 1841.

JOHN T. GOSWELL
Baltimore, Maryland

Listed in Baltimore City Directories 1864–1868 as silverplaters.

GOTHAM SILVER CO., INC.
New York, New York

WEAR-WELL

Manufacturers of plated silver holloware c. 1920. Last record found was 1950.

GOULD, STOWELL & WARD
Baltimore, Maryland

James Gould, A. Stowell, Jr., William H. Ward, silversmiths and dealers in jewelry. Advertised silverware made to order. Listed in Baltimore City Directory 1855-1856.

GOULD & WARD
Baltimore, Maryland

James Gould and William H. Ward were successors to Gelston & Gould, silversmiths, c. 1810-1820. Became Gould, Stowell & Ward, c. 1855.

GRAFF, WASHBOURNE & DUNN
New York, New York
(See Gorham Corporation)

Graff, Washbourne & Dunn silversmiths, established in 1899, actually trace their beginnings to William Gale, silversmith in New York in 1833, followed by William Gale & Sons; Gale, Wood & Hughes and Wood & Hughes. They were makers of sterling silver holloware and novelties. The company was purchased by the Gorham Corporation in 1961.

GREEN-SMITH CO.
Denver, Colorado
(See Frederick L. Smith)

F. L. GREGORY
Niagara Falls, New York

Listed in the 1886 Niagara Falls City Directory as makers of silver and plated silverware.

CHARLES W. GRESHOFF
Baltimore, Maryland

Gold and silversmith. Listed in Baltimore City Directories 1888-1898.

FRANCIS A. GRESHOFF
Baltimore, Maryland

Gold and silversmith. Listed in Baltimore City Directories 1864-1885. Succeeded by Francis A. Greshoff & Son in 1887. This listing continued through 1894.

GRIFFON CUTLERY WORKS
New York, New York

Began business before 1904 as Silberstein, Hecht & Company, soon succeeded by A. L. Silberstein and has been Griffon Cutlery Works since 1915.

ED. GRONEBERG
Baltimore, Maryland

Listed in 1855-1856 Baltimore City Directory as a manufacturer and dealer in fine gold jewelry and silverware.

LEWIS GUIENOT
Baltimore, Maryland

Listed in Baltimore City Directories 1870-1877 as a gold and silverplater.

A. T. GUNNER MFG. CO.
Attleboro, Massachusetts

Albert T. Gunner, silversmith, founded the A. T. Gunner Mfg. Co. in 1920. It is a one-man operation today.

H

J. H. FERD. HAHN
Baltimore, Maryland

Listed 1899-1911 Baltimore City Directory as a silverplater and metal worker.

HALL BROS. & CO.
Pittsburgh, Pennsylvania

H. B. & Co.

Wholesale and retail outlet in business c. 1910-1915.

HALL, ELTON & CO.
Meriden, Connecticut
(See International Silver Co.)
(See Maltby, Stevens & Curtiss)
(See Watrous Mfg. Co.)

(German Silver Flatware.)

In 1837 Deacon Almer Hall, William Elton and others formed the firm of Hall, Elton & Co. for the manufacture of German silver flatware and britannia ware. In 1890 the company was purchased by Maltby, Stevens & Curtiss which was in turn purchased by Watrous Mfg. Co. In 1898 they were one of the original companies to become part of the International Silver Co.

Registered U. S. Patent, January 20, 1873 for use on flatware.

CHARLES W. HAMILL & CO.
Baltimore, Maryland

Listed in Baltimore City Directories 1877-1884 as silverplaters.

C. A. HAMILTON
Waterbury, Connecticut
(See Rogers & Hamilton)

U. S. Patent No. 13,289, May 11, 1886 was registered by Charles Alfred Hamilton, president of Rogers & Hamilton, for the manufacture of spoons, knives, forks, ladles, cheese-scoops, tea sets, casters, pitchers, waiters and napkin rings.

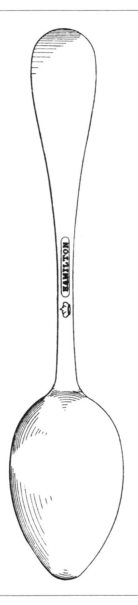

HAMILTON & DIESINGER
Philadelphia, Pennsylvania
(See M. F. Hamilton & Son)

Listed in 1896 Jewelers' Weekly and in 1896 J C-K in sterling silver section. Succeeded by M. F. Hamilton & Son before 1904.

HAMILTON & HAMILTON, JR.
Providence, Rhode Island

★ H & H

★ H & H

Registered U. S. Patent Office, No. 49,473, February 6, 1906.

This manufacturing jewelry business was established January 1, 1871 by R. S. Hamilton, R. S. Hamilton, Jr., and George C. Hunt. They began the manufacture of ladies' jewelry sets, lace pins and gentlemen's chains—all of solid gold. Six months later they began the manufacture of rolled plate chains. They advertised that they were the first makers of gold filled chains. April 27, 1886 they registered a patent for jewelry, chains, trimmings, cuff buttons, bracelets, lockets, cigarette holders and cases, knives and novelties. Listed from 1921–1935 as Hamilton & Hamilton Jr., Inc. Ralph S. Hamilton is still listed as a manufacturing jeweler not associated with a particular firm.

M. F. HAMILTON & SON
Philadelphia, Pennsylvania

Successors to Hamilton & Diesinger before 1904 and out of business before 1909.

HAMILTON MFG. CO.

Known only from name stamped on flatware.

HAMPTON ROADS CUTLERY CO.
Norfolk, Virginia

Listed in J C-K 1915 in plated silver section. Last record c. 1920.

NEWELL HARDING & COMPANY
Boston, Massachusetts

In the 1860's they purchased Reed & Barton wares "in the metal" and operated their own plating establishment.

HARPER & McINTIRE CO.
Ottumwa, Iowa

HAR-MAC

Silverplaters c. 1920.

HARRINGTON & MILLS
Baltimore, Maryland

Listed in Baltimore City Directories 1868-1874 as silverplaters.

R. HARRIS & CO.
Washington, D. C.

Established in 1874-1876. Manufacturing jewelers and silversmiths according to their catalog
E, published c. 1898. No trademark but the company name. Still
in business.

HARRIS & SCHAFER
Washington, D. C.

HARRIS & SCHAFER

Listed in the Washington, D. C.
Directories 1880-1938 as Harris &
Schafer, Jewelers.

Edwin Harris was born in
Charles County, Maryland in 1831.
Educational facilities were limited
at that time, so at a very early age
he went to work in the store of
Galt Bros. of Washington. He was
taken into partnership in 1870 and
remained there in that capacity for
nine years. He then sold his interest and started a store of his own.

Charles A. Schafer, the junior
partner, was born at Boonsboro'
in Washington County, Maryland.
He moved to Washington, D. C.
when ten years of age. He at-
tended both Gonzaga College and
Georgetown University. He entered the employ of Galt Bros. in
1849 and remained with that firm
for thirty years, mastering the
jewelry making and watchmaking
business. When Harris opened his
own store, Schafer chose to join
his as a partner.

Trademarks were registered at
the U. S. Patent Office in 1891 and
1892 for gold, sterling silver and
plated silver flat and tableware.
These trademarks were used on
souvenir silver. It is doubtful if
Harris & Schafer did any manufacturing themselves. They were
noted, however, for the fine quality of silver, jewelry, watches, diamonds, artwares and crystal and
glassware they sold. Much of it
was imported from the finest
houses in Europe.

HARRISON & GROESCHEL
New York, New York

Listed in J C-K 1896 in sterling silver section. Out of business before 1904.

LUCIUS HART
New York, New York

Lucius Hart is listed in New York City Directories 1828-1850. The earlier listings are in connection with Timothy Boardman, pewterer, under the name Boardman & Hart. By 1850 the Boardman name was dropped and the listing was Lucius Hart, Britannia Ware Manufacturer. After 1863 the listing was Lucius Hart & Company. During the 1860's Hart bought many of Reed & Barton's wares "in the metal" and operated his own plating establishment in New York.

HARTFORD SILVER PLATE CO.
Hartford, Connecticut
(See Barbour Silver Co.)
(See International Silver Co.)
(See I. J. Steane Co.)

Listed in Hartford City Directories from 1882 through 1894. Each listing accompanied by a half or full page advertisement.

The 1882 listing says they were manufacturers of fine electroplated holloware. Incorporaters: James G. Batterson, E. N. Welch, Henry C. Robinson, W. H. Post, Jonathan Goodwin, James L. Howard and Rush P. Chapman.

They advertised "Everything in silver plate." Absorbed by Barbour Silver Co. in 1893 which became part of the International Silver Co. in 1898.

HARTFORD STERLING COMPANY
Philadelphia, Pennsylvania
(See I. J. Steane Co.)
(See Tennant Company)
(See Phelps & Cary Co.)

The upper trademark is identical to those of The Tennant Co. and Phelps & Cary Co., with the exception of the initials in the shield.

Successors (?) to the Tennant Co., New York, c. 1901.

The Philadelphia City Directories list the Hartford Sterling Company from 1901-1924. In 1901 and 1902 the listing refers to foreign plated ware. Subsequent listings are for plated ware. The 1907-1912 Directory lists Isaac J. Steane (probably Isaac J. Steane, Jr.), president, Arthur B. Wells, secretary and Jacob S. Hecker, treasurer.

HARVEY & OTIS
Providence, Rhode Island

Manufacturing jeweler and silversmith. Listed J C-K 1896–1965.

H-O

HASKELL, BEECHER & CO.
Baltimore, Maryland

Listed in Baltimore City Directories 1885–1886 as silverplaters.

HENRY C. HASKELL
New York, New York

Listed in J C-K in sterling silver
and jewelry sections 1896–1904.
Out of business before 1915.

JOHN HASSELBRING
Brooklyn, New York
(See Crown Silver Inc.)

Founded about 1890 by John
Hasselbring. Purchased by Crown
Silver Inc. about 1954-1955 and
is now a division of that company
in New York. Their products are
silver peppermills, bar accessories, silver trimmed salad bowls
and silver trimmed cutlery.

Another trademark, containing
a deer head, has been reported
but not found.

HAVONE CORPORATION
New York, New York

Listed J C-K 1915 in sterling silver
section. Patents and trademarks
taken over by Elgin-American Mfg.
Co., Elgin, Illinois.

Elgin-American manufactures
match boxes, vanity, photo and
cigarette cases, belt buckles, cuff
links, traveling clocks, photo
lockets and knives.

HAWTHORNE MFG. CO.
New York, New York

Manufacturer of sterling silverware. Listed in J C-K 1904 as out
of business.

HAYDEN MFG. CO.
Newark, New Jersey
(See G. W. Parks Co., Inc.)

Listed in J C-K 1896–1904 as manufacturers of sterling silverware and jewelry. Succeeded by G. W. Parks Co., Inc. before 1909.

WILLIAM W. HAYDEN CO.
Newark, New Jersey

Listed in J C-K 1904 in sterling silver section. Out of business before 1909.

HAYES & MCFARLAND
Mount Vernon, New York
(See Gorham Corporation)
(See Mt. Vernon Silversmiths, Inc.)

In 1903 merged with the Mauser Manufacturing Company of New York and the Roger Williams Silver Company of Providence, Rhode Island to form the Mt. Vernon Silversmiths Company which was purchased by the Gorham Corporation in 1913.

J. R. HAYNES
Cincinnati, Ohio

Listed in Cincinnati City Directories 1850–1859 as a silversmith who operated a silverware factory.

C. E. HAYWARD COMPANY
Attleboro, Massachusetts
(See Walter E. Hayward Co., Inc.)

HAYWARD & SWEET
Attleboro, Massachusetts
(See Walter E. Hayward Co., Inc.)

WALTER E. HAYWARD CO., INC.
Attleboro, Massachusetts

Hayward

HAYWARD

Established in 1851 as Thompson, Hayward & Co., in Mechanicsville. Charles E. Hayward and Johnathan Briggs became partners in 1855. Charles E. Hayward was one of seven children of Abraham Hayward, captain of a privateer during the War of 1812. When Charles was 17 he was apprenticed to Tifft & Whiting to learn jewelry making.

The Hayward and Briggs partnership was dissolved in 1855 and Walter E. Hayward became associated with his father under the name of C. E. Hayward Co.

In 1887 the younger Hayward accepted George Sweet as a partner and the firm became Hayward & Sweet Company. The firm name became Walter E. Hayward Co. before 1904. Frank J. Ryder and Charles C. Wilmarth, both already associated with the firm, purchased the company in 1908.

Ryder bought out Wilmarth's interest in 1917 and remained sole owner until incorporation in 1921. Frank J. Ryder, Sr. died in 1943 and three years later his son, Frank, Jr., became president and part owner; acquiring full ownership in 1949. They are still in business manufacturing religious items of sterling silver and gold and gold-filled jewelry.

H. B. & H. A. 1
(See Holmes, Booth & Haydens)

HEER BROS. CO., INC.
Baltimore, Maryland

Listed in the Baltimore City Directories 1927-1928 as manufacturers of silverware.

HEER-SCHOFIELD CO.
Baltimore, Maryland
(See Schofield Co., Inc.)

HEINTZ ART METAL SHOP
Buffalo, New York

Listed in J C-K 1915-1922 in the plated silver section. Became Heintz Bros. Mfg. before 1935. This is the last listing found. Manufacturers of art metal goods and novelty jewelry.

HEIRLOOM
(See Oneida Silversmiths)

HEMILL SILVERWARE INC.
New York, New York

SHEFFIELD H. S. CO.

Manufacturers (?) or silverplaters c. 1920-1930.

THE HEMMING MFG. CO.
Montreal, Canada

Listed in J C-K as manufacturers of sterling silverware and jewelry c. 1909. Out of business before 1915.

GEORGE A. HENCKEL & CO.
New York, New York
(See Currier & Roby, Inc.)

Manufacturers of small articles in sterling silver for the trade only. Listed in J C-K 1909-1922. Succeeded by Currier & Roby, Inc. before 1943.

HENNEGEN, BATES & COMPANY
Baltimore, Maryland

HENNEGEN, BATES
& CO.

Listed in Baltimore City Directories 1890-c. 1930 as jewelers and silversmiths. Company name found stamped on many sterling silver articles.

HERBST & WASSALL
Newark, New Jersey

Listed J C-K 1904-1922 as manufacturers of sterling silver goods, 14k gold ware and novelties. Last record found was 1931.

HEIRLOOM STERLING
Oneida, New York
(See Oneida Silversmiths)

GEORGE E. HERRING
Chicago, Illinois

YOUREX

Registered U. S. Patent No. 59,353 January 8, 1907 for use on imitation silverware. Out of business before 1915.

HIBBARD, SPENCER, BARTLETT & CO.
Chicago, Illinois

Trademark registered May 15, 1906 (No. 52,721) to be used on plated silver holloware, flatware and tableware. Used continuously since April 1, 1905. Application filed by A. M. Graves, secretary.

Trademark registered on August 7, 1906 (No. 55,072) to be used on jewelry, solid and plated, precious metalware—silver and plated silver holloware. Used continuously since May 1884. Application filed by A. C. Bartlett, president.

HICKOK MATTHEWS COMPANY
Newark, New Jersey
(See Eleder-Hickok Co.)
(See Lebkueker & Co.)

(On novelties)

(On holloware)

Formed by the merger, between 1931-1943 of the Eleder-Hickok Company, manufacturers of sterling silver novelties and the Matthews Company (incorporated in 1907). They are manufacturers of sterling holloware and presentation pieces.

Purchased in 1965 by Wolfgang K. Schroth from David M. Warren, Jr., president and owner.

Mr. Schroth was born in Frankfort, Germany and received his training under August Bock and Emil Woerner. He formed his own silver company there, but came to this country in 1955 and joined Tiffany and Company as their silversmith. In 1961 he joined Hickok-Matthews as manager and silversmith. One of the country's foremost silversmiths, Mr. Schroth lectures extensively on that subject.

GEORGE W. HICKOK & CO.
Santa Fe, New Mexico

"Manufacturers of filigree spoons and everything in the filigree line." CENTURY MAGAZINE, April 1892. Montezuma spoon marked "Copyrighted".

HICKS SILVER CO.
(See A. R. Justice Co.)

H. M. HILL & CO.
Lynn, Massachusetts

Registered U. S. Patent No. 19,221, March 24, 1891 for manufacture of sterling souvenir flatware. Out of business before 1922.

M. FRED HIRSCH CO., INC.
Jersey City, New Jersey

M. F. H. Co.

In business c. 1920-1945 as manufacturers and jobbers of sterling silverware.

HIRSCH & OPPENHEIMER
Chicago, Illinois

Manufacturing jeweler. Special order work. Listed J C-K 1904-1922.

CHARLES E. HOCHHAUS
Baltimore, Maryland

Listed in Baltimore City Directories 1874-1879 as a silverplater.

F. B. HOFFMAN & CO.
Baltimore, Maryland

Listed in Baltimore City Directories 1870-1871 as silverplaters.

FREDERICK S. HOFFMAN
Brooklyn, New York
(See Clarence B. Webster)

Listed in J C-K 1896 in sterling silver section. Other sources indicate that these trademarks were used also on 14 and 18k gold and silver novelties and on silver mountings for leather goods. Succeeded by Clarence B. Webster before 1904.

HOLBROOK MFG. CO.
Attleboro, Massachusetts

Founded by Harry R. and Charles L. Holbrook. Listed in Attleboro City Directories from 1905-1916 as manufacturers of special machines and novelties.

HOLBROOK & SIMMONS
(See Thornton & Company)

H. & S.

JOHN HOLIDAY
Baltimore, Maryland

Listed in Baltimore City Directory in 1872 as a silverplater.

HOLMES, BOOTH & HAYDENS
Waterbury, Connecticut

**H. B. & H. A. 1.
SHEFFIELD PLATED CO.
STERLING SILVER PLATE CO.
UNION SILVER PLATE CO.**

Organized by Israel Holmes in 1853 to roll brass. They made plated silver copper sheets for photography which produced a better and less expensive photograph than copper plate.

During the Civil War they made brass buttons for both military and civil uniforms, brass fittings and kerosene lamps. After the war they went into the nickel-silver business and turned out huge quantities of knives, forks and spoons for silverplating.

Succeeded by Rogers & Hamilton c. 1886.

HOLMES BROS. & CO.
Baltimore, Maryland

Listed in Baltimore City Directories 1877-1890 as silverplaters.

HOLMES & EDWARDS SILVER CO.
Bridgeport, Connecticut
(See International Silver Co.)

XIV

Founded in 1882 by George C. Edwards and C. E. L. Holmes. Through contract for silver inlay process, patented by Warner Bros. of Syracuse, N.Y., in 1887, they became leaders in the field of inlaid silver flatware. Registered patent December 15, 1885 for production of imitation silverware, plated silver and other tableware. One of the original companies to become part of the International Silver Co. in 1898.

ROLLED PLATE, HOLMES & EDWARDS   **INLAID**   HE

ORIENTAL   **HESCO**

MEXICAN CRAIG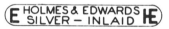

EDWARDS

B. S. CO.

XIV. HOLMES & EDWARDS   **VIANDE**

STRATFORD SILVER PLATE CO.

STRATFORD SILVER CO.   **STRATFORD PLATE**

Ⓔ**Sterling Inlaid**   Ⓔ HOLMES & EDWARDS SILVER – INLAID HE

STRATFORD SILVER CO AXI   **HOLMES & EDWARDS**
                               INLAID

STRATFORD SILVERPLATE

HOLMES NICKEL PLATE CO.
Baltimore, Maryland

Listed in 1886 Baltimore City Directory as silverplaters.

HOLMES PLATING WORKS
Baltimore, Maryland

Listed in Baltimore City Directories 1895-1896 as silverplaters. Successor to Robert Holmes.

ROBERT HOLMES
Baltimore, Maryland

Listed in 1894 Baltimore City Directory as a silverplater.

HOLMES & SON
Baltimore, Maryland

Listed in Baltimore City Directories 1896-1940 as silverplaters.

HOLMES & TUTTLE MFG. CO.
Bristol, Connecticut
(See American Silver Co.)
(See Bristol Brass & Clock Co.)
(See International Silver Co.)

HOLMES & TUTTLE

H. & T. MFG. CO.

Organized by Israel Holmes in 1851. Made plated silver knives, forks and spoons. Taken over by Bristol Brass & Clock Co., in 1857 and operated as their silverware department until 1901 when it became the American Silver Company which was bought by International Silver Co. in 1935.

WILLIAM HOLMES
Baltimore, Maryland

Listed in Baltimore City Directories 1865-1876 as a silverplater.

HOMAN MANUFACTURING
COMPANY
Cincinnati, Ohio

Established in 1847 by Henry Homan and Asa F. Flagg.

The Cincinnati City Directories of 1842-1843 and 1846 list Asa F. Flagg as a britannia manufacturer. An English potter, he went to Cincinnati to form a partnership with Homan for the manufacture of pewter. Flagg was so devoted to his work that he was known locally as "Pewter" Flagg.

Under the firm name Homan & Co. (pieces are also found marked Flagg & Homan), they made britannia ware until Flagg's retirement in 1854.

**HOMAN & COMPANY
CINCINNATI**

(For other trademarks see Homan Silver Plate Co.)

M. Miller joined the firm and remained a co-partner until the death of Henry Homan in 1865.

Homan's widow, Margaret, with their sons, Frank (who died in 1880), Louis and Joseph T., managed the firm until her retirement in 1887.

About 1864 the company gradually changed from the manufacture of pewter, britannia and German silver to electro-plated silverware. They also advertised that they did gold plating.

Their regular products were

ecclesiastical wares, registered U. S. Patent 27,974, March 17, 1896, (chalices, patens, beakers, tankards, baptismal bowls, alms dishes and candlesticks); Ohio-Mississippi river boat equipment (bowls, pewter plates, beakers, trenchers, chargers, tea sets and swivel lamps); bar equipment and articles for domestic use (tea and coffee sets, cups, ewers and basins, warming pans, pitchers, jugs, sugar sifters, pewter combs, spectacle frames, clockweights and buttons).

Around 1896 the name of the firm was the Homan Silver Plate Company which was succeeded by Homan Manufacturing Company between 1904 and 1915. No listing found after c. 1942.

HOMAN SILVER PLATE COMPANY
Cincinnati, Ohio
(See Homan Manufacturing Company)

(*Nickel Silver.*)

(*Church Goods.*)

(*Popular Price Goods.*)

GEO. E. HOMER
Boston, Massachusetts

(Souvenir   Spoons.)

In business before 1890. Listed in J C-K in sterling silver section 1896-1922. Homer's-Jewelers in business 1954 in same block but relationship not confirmed.

HOPE SILVER CO.
(See Geo. W. Parks Co.)

HOPEWELL SILVER COMPANY
(See Reed & Barton)

Hopewell Silver Co.

HOPKINS & BRIELE
Baltimore, Maryland

Listed in Baltimore City Directories 1879-1886 as gold and silversmiths.

J. SETH HOPKINS & CO.
Baltimore, Maryland

Listed in Baltimore City Directories 1887-1888 under plated silverware.

HORTON & ANGELL
Attleboro, Massachusetts

Manufacturers of gold and silver goods. Listed J C-K 1896. Founded 1870. Now called Horton Angell.

E. V. HOUGHWOUT & COMPANY
New York, New York

In the 1860's they purchased Reed & Barton wares "in the metal" and operated their own plating establishment.

HOUSATONIC MFG. CO.
New Haven, Connecticut

Registered trademark No. 40,725 on July 7, 1903 for use on tableware, spoons, knives, forks, table tongs of plated ware. Used continuously in their business since April 1, 1902. Edgar A. Russell, Treasurer.

HOWARD & CO.
New York, New York

HOWARD & CO.

HOWARD & CO.

Established   as   silversmiths
c. 1866. Last listing 1922.

HOWARD & COCKSHAW CO.
New York, New York
(See Herbert Cockshaw, Jr.)

HOWARD CUTLERY CO.
New York, New York

(*Knives.*)

(*Hollowware.*)

Manufacturers of plated silver
knives and holloware. Successor
to E. Magnus before 1896. Out of
business before 1909.

HOWARD & SON
Providence, Rhode Island
(See Howard Sterling Co.)
(See Parks Bros. & Rogers)

The trademark is similar to that
used by Parks Bros. & Rogers—a
four-leaf clover partially encircled
by the word "sterling" in a horse-
shoe arrangement.

Registered U. S. Patent No.
15,614, June 19, 1888 for useful
or ornamental articles made of
solid silver.

HOWARD STERLING CO.
Providence, Rhode Island
(See S. Cottle)

TRADE MARK
1776

Established January 1, 1878 as
H. Howard & Co., with Hiram
Howard, A. J. Scherrieble and
Arnold Nicoud.

   January 1, 1879, Arnold Nicoud
withdrew and a limited partnership was formed with Sterns
Hutchins. The firm name was
Howard & Scherrieble until the
expiration of the limited partnership on January 1, 1884, when
Hutchins retired and Stephen C.

Howard, son of the senior member
of the firm was admitted as a
partner. On February 5, 1884,
Scherrieble withdrew and the firm
name was changed to Howard &
Son.

   In 1892 it was listed as Howard
Sterling Company and by 1915
was listed as out of business.

   Lever cuff and collar buttons
were among the specialties. One,
in particular, the "Sensational"

collar button, was made by a
machine invented for the purpose
by S. Cottle.

   They also made silverware, both
table and ornamental. Patent No.
24,713, May 15, 1894. Around
1893 they shared the same address with Parks Bros. & Rogers
and Hamilton & Hamilton, Jr.
though no relationship has been
established. Their trademark is
similar to Parks Bros. & Rogers.

H. & T. MFG. CO.
(See American Silver Co.)

H. G. HUDSON
Amesbury, Massachusetts

Trademarks in 1896-1904 editions of J C-K were parts of the designs used on the souvenir spoons sold by H. G. Hudson honoring John Greenleaf Whittier, "the Quaker Poet," who moved to Amesbury in 1836 after serving in the Massachusetts legislature. U. S. Patent Office also registered No. 19,959, August 4, 1891, for the manufacture of flatware, spoons, knives, forks and ladles. It is doubtful that Hudson did the manufacturing himself as numerous examples of these spoons bear the mark of the Durgin Company, now a Division of The Gorham Company.

WALTER HUNOLD
Providence, Rhode Island

First listed in Providence City Directory in 1903 as Walter

Hunold. About 1920 listed as Nussbaum & Hunold (B. Nussbaum, W. Hunold, J. Nussbaum), manufacturing jewelers. From 1921-1925 the listing was Walter Hunold. This is the last listing.

GEORGE J. HUNT
Boston, Massachusetts

George J. Hunt was born in Liverpool, England in 1865, serving the usual seven years' apprenticeship in one of the leading silversmith concerns of that city. In 1885 he came to the United States and worked in several silver factories. In 1905 he opened his own shop in Boston. His real love was teaching others the craft of silversmithing and this became his major interest. He was also a jeweler.

HURLY SILVER CO.
Scriba, New York
(See Benedict Mfg. Co.)

Purchased by Benedict Silver Co. in 1894.

J. H. HUTCHINSON & CO.
Portsmouth, New Hampshire

OLD CONSTITUTION

Registered U. S. Patent No. 19,770, June 30, 1891, for use on spoons,

forks, bells, plates and holloware of sterling silver and plated silver. This drawing of "Old Constitution" is the trademark registered. It is doubtful if Hutchinson company actually manufactured any of the silverware. Souvenir spoons sold by him bear the Durgin Company mark. Out of business before 1915.

WM. HUTTON & SONS, LTD.
Sheffield, England

Silversmiths, cutlers and electroplaters established in 1800. Limited since 1893 in which year

they absorbed Fanell, Elliott & Co. Made sterling silverware, nickel spoons and forks and steel cutlery. Last listing in 1922.

Registered U. S. Patent 40,657, June 23, 1903 for silver and plated silver tableware.

I

IMPERIAL SILVER PLATE CO.
(See A. F. Smith Co.)

INDEPENDENCE BRAND
(See American Silver Co.)

INDIANA BRAND
(See Anchor Silver Plate Co.)

J. T. INMAN & CO.
Attleboro, Massachusetts

They were listed in J C-K 1896–1922 as manufacturers of sterling silver and plated silver cigarette cases, link buttons, buckles, vanity cases, dorines (powder boxes), bar pins, cuff and collar pins and souvenir goods.

GOLDEYE

STERLING.

Listed in the Attleboro City Directories 1892-1944 as manufacturing jewelers with James McNerney as owner. Listed from 1944-1963 with Roy W. Inman.

When the Watson Company went out of business about 1955,

the Inman Company bought some of the souvenir spoon dies (The Wallace Company took over the old Watson business). These dies were used by the Inman Company until 1964 when Whiting & Davis Co. purchased the company and integrated the complete manufacturing facilities into its own plant.

INTERNATIONAL SILVER CO.
Meriden, Connecticut

 STERLING

INTERNATIONAL
SILVER COMPANY

 STERLING

 STERLING

 STERLING

Wilcox

 INTERNATIONAL SILVER COMPANY

I.S.CO.   **INTERNATIONAL SILVER CO.**

INTERNATIONAL S. CO.   **INTERNATIONAL**

           I.S. CO.

 STERLING

           INSICO

⚓ ROGERS ⚓ STERLING   **R. & B.**

INTERNATIONAL SILVER COMPANY

The International Silver Company was incorporated in 1898 by a number of independent New England silversmiths whose family backgrounds began with the earliest American settlers. International Silver has become not only world renowned for the quality of its fine silver, it has also become the world's largest manufacturer of silverware.

The history of International Silver Company and its predecessors is a history of America's silversmithing. Early records of this industry started with Ashbil Griswold who set up his pewter shop in Meriden, Connecticut, soon expanding his business to include britannia ware. Meriden became the center of pewter, britannia ware and coin silver manufacturing through the efforts of Griswold and other independent makers who joined together to finance the Yankee peddlers responsible for selling and bartering these wares.

About the same time, the growing demand for coin silver led the three Rogers brothers, Asa, Simeon and William, to open their workshop in Hartford, Connecticut. The high cost of coin silver, as well as its impractical nature for constant use, led to experimentation in the new process of electroplating spoons and forks with pure silver.

In 1847 they perfected this process and marketed their first silverware under the firm name of Rogers Bros. Their fine workmanship and high quality material soon established the name of the 1847 Rogers Bros. line throughout the country. This reputation is maintained today.

Britannia, more brilliant, harder and more resistant to wear than pewter, was replacing pewter in many American homes. Several small factories in Meriden turned to the production of this new ware, most of which was marketed by Horace C. and Dennis C. Wilcox under the name of H. C. Wilcox & Co. The Meriden Britannia Company which followed in 1852, offered German silver holloware and flatware for silverplating by 1855.

In 1862, the Rogers brothers, who had been making and selling plated silver ware in Hartford, were moved to Meriden and added to the Meriden Britannia Company. Their 1847 Rogers Bros. trademark was an important addition.

Other silversmiths, who had set up small shops in Connecticut, soon realized they could all work more efficiently and supply the demands of the public better by combining into one organization. The scope of the Meriden Britannia Co. had become international with the establishment of London and Canadian branches and sales offices in New York, Chicago and San Francisco. The Meriden Britannia Co. was the leading spirit in the formation of The International Silver Company in November 1898.

Among the many independent companies which became part of The International Silver Company, either directly or indirectly through Meriden Britannia Co., were the American Silver Co., Bristol, Conn. established in 1901; Barbour Silver Co., Hartford, 1892; Derby Silver Co., Birmingham, 1873; Forbes Silver Co., Meriden, 1894; Hall & Elton Co., Wallingford, 1837; Holmes & Edwards Silver Co., Bridgeport, 1882; Holmes & Tuttle, Bristol, 1851; International Silver Co. of Canada, Ltd., Inc., 1922; La Pierre Mfg. Co., Newark, 1895; Maltby, Stevens & Curtiss, Shelton, 1879; Manhattan Silver Plate Co., Brooklyn, 1877; Meriden Britannia Co., Meriden, 1852; Meriden Britannia Co., Ltd., Hamilton, Ont., 1879; Meriden Silver Plate Co., Meriden, 1869; Middletown Plate Co., Middletown, 1864; Norwich Cutlery Co., Norwich, 1890; Parker & Casper, Meriden, 1867; C. Rogers & Bros., Meriden, 1866; Rogers Cutlery Co., Hartford, 1871; W. Rogers Mfg. Co., Ltd., Niagara Falls, 1911; Rogers Bros., Hartford, 1847; Rogers & Bro., Waterbury, 1858; Rogers & Hamilton Co., Waterbury, 1886; Rogers, Smith & Co., Hartford, 1854; Simpson, Hall, Miller & Co., Wallingford, 1866; Simpson Nickel Silver Co., Wallingford, 1871; Standard Silver Co. of Toronto, Co., Ltd., 1895; Watrous Mfg. Co., Wallingford, 1896; E. G. Webster & Son, Brooklyn, 1886; E. G. Webster & Bro., Brooklyn, 1863; Webster

Mfg. Co., Brooklyn, 1859; Wilcox Britannia Co., Meriden, 1865; Wilcox Silver Plate Co., Meriden, 1867; Wilcox & Evertsen, New York, 1892 and William Rogers Mfg. Co., Hartford, 1865.

By 1900, the Meriden-Wallingford area of Connecticut had become a center for silver craftsmanship. Almost the peak of production was reached shortly before World War II.

Today the International Silver Co. is not only the world's largest manufacturer of fine tableware, it makes a broader variety of products than any other silverware manufacturer. These include institutional and ecclesiastical wares. The Hotel Division specializes in flatware and holloware designed for use by hotels, restaurants, airlines, railways, steamships and institutions.

It is one of the few silver manufacturing companies to maintain an historical library where extensive research is done on the silver industry.

SILVER PLATED WARE

ALBANY SILVER PLATE	KENSICO
AMERICAN SILVER CO.	KENSINGTON SILVER PLATE
AMSILCO	MANOR PLATE
ATLAS SILVER PLATE	N. E. S. P. CO.
AVON SILVER PLATE	NEW ENGLAND SILVER PLATE
B. S. CO.	NO-TARN
CARV-EZE	OLD COMPANY PLATE
CROWN SILVER CO.	R. & B.
DEERFIELD SILVER PLATE	R. C. CO.
EASTERN SILVER CO.	ROGERS CUTLERY CO.
1847 ROGERS BROS.	ROGERS & HAMILTON
1865 WM. ROGERS MFG. CO.	ROYAL PLATE CO.
GEM SILVER CO.	SILVERWELD (knives)
H. & T. MFG. CO.	SOUTHINGTON COMPANY
HOLD-EDGE	STRATFORD PLATE
HOLMES & EDWARDS	STRATFORD SILVER CO.
HOLMES & TUTTLE	STRATFORD SILVER PLATE CO.
I. S. CO.	SUPERIOR
INDEPENDENCE TRIPLE	VIANDE
INLAID	WILCOX SILVER PLATE CO.
INSICO	WORLD
INTERNATIONAL	WM. ROGERS & SON
INTERNATIONAL SILVER CO.	WM. ROGERS MFG. CO.

INTERNATIONAL SILVER
COMPANY OF CANADA, LTD.
Hamilton, Ontario
(See International Silver Co.)

Began with the establishment of the Meriden Britannia Co. Ltd. at Hamilton, Ontario in 1879. Organized to take care of the Canadian business of the International Silver Co. Was incorporated in 1925.

INTERNATIONAL-COMMONWEALTH
SILVER CO.
New York, New York

POPPY
(Deposit Ware.)

Listed in J C-K 1915–1922 as successor to International Silver Deposit Works, founding date unknown.

J

A. JACOBI
Baltimore, Maryland
(See Jenkins & Jenkins)

Founded in 1879 as manufacturing silversmiths. Company name changed to Jacobi & Co. in 1890.

JACOBI & COMPANY
Baltimore, Maryland
(See Jenkins & Jenkins)

Successors to A. Jacobi in 1890; reorganized as Jacobi & Jenkins in 1894.

JACOBI & JENKINS
Baltimore, Maryland
(See Jenkins & Jenkins)

Successors to Jacobi & Co. in 1894; succeeded by Jenkins & Jenkins in 1908.

Members of the firm were A. Jacobi, W. Armour Jenkins and W. F. Jacobi. In 1895 they advertised that they were "the only silversmiths in Maryland making and retailing their own work exclusively—all articles of sterling silver."

JENKINS & JENKINS
Baltimore, Maryland

Successors to Jacobi & Jenkins in 1908. Originally founded by A. Jacobi in 1879; changed to Jacobi & Company in 1890; reorganized as Jacobi & Jenkins in 1894 and succeeded by Jenkins & Jenkins in 1908.

The tools and dies were purchased c. 1915 by Schofield Company, Inc. of Baltimore, manufacturers of silverware and jewelry.

Not connected with the present J. Jenkins' Sons Company, Inc. of Baltimore.

JENNINGS & LAUTER
New York, New York

Listed in J C-K 1896 as Reeves & Sillcocks; succeeded by Reeves & Browne before 1904; by Browne, Jennings & Lauter before 1915 and by Jennings & Lauter before 1922. Listed in sterling silver section.

JENNINGS SILVER CO.
Irvington, New Jersey

J.S.C.

Manufacturers and jobbers of sterling and plated silver holloware. Listed J C-K 1915–1943.

C. C. JOHNSON
Chicago, Illinois

Listed in 1854–1855 Chicago Directory as a silverplater.

E. S. JOHNSON & CO.
New York, New York

Listed in 1896–1922 J C-K in sterling silver and jewelry sections.

JOHNSON & GODLEY
Albany, New York

Samuel Johnson and Richard Godley listed in Albany City Directories 1843–1850 as producing factory-made silver. Their marks consisted of the two surnames in addition to "pseudo hallmarks."

JOHNSON, HAYWARD & PIPER CO.
New York, New York

DUTCH SILVER NOVELTIES

Listed in J C-K 1904–1915 in plated silver and jewelry sections. Were probably distributors.

J. W. JOHNSON
New York, New York

CONNECTICUT PLATE CO.
(Hollowware.)

CROWN SILVER PLATE CO.
(Flatware.)

ROYAL PLATE CO.
(Flatware.)

Founded in 1869 by J. W. Johnson who had as a boy worked for J. A. Babcock & Co. in the plating shop. Johnson was an agent for the Middletown Plate Company after working for Babcock.

By 1919, the J. W. Johnson company was operated by the founder's son, Harry F. Johnson, still under the same name.

They were jobbers who specialized in plating and were also wholesalers of plated silverware. Last listed in 1950.

J. H. JOHNSTON & CO.
New York, New York

C. B. M. C.
C. P. F.
DUPICATE WEDDING PRESENTS

The earliest record found for this company was July 30, 1878, when they were listed under sterling silver and plated ware, jewelry and miscellaneous. Out of business before 1915.

JONES, BALL & POOR
(See Shreve, Crump & Low Co., Inc.)

JOHN B. JONES CO.
(See Shreve, Crump & Low Co., Inc.)

JONES, LOW & BALL
(See Shreve, Crump & Low Co., Inc.)

JONES, SHREVE, BROWN & CO.
(See Shreve, Crump & Low Co., Inc.)

JONES & WARD
(See Shreve, Crump & Low Co.,
Inc.)

J. S. C.

J. S. C.

Attributed in the 1904 J C-K to a Division of the International Silver Company. Not confirmed by International.

A. R. JUSTICE CO.
Philadelphia, Pennsylvania

(Pearl Handled Knives.)

HICKS SILVER CO.
(Hollowware.)

MEDFORD CUTLERY CO.
(Pearl Handled Knives.)

RIVERTON SILVER CO.
(Hollow and Flatware.)

The Philadelphia City Directories list the A. R. Justice Company from 1881 (hardware) through 1935-1936. The 1882 listing is in the name of Alfred R. Justice, cutlery. In 1885, the names of F. Millwood & Herbert M. Justice are added. In 1886 is the first reference to plated ware. The 1892 listing is A. R. Justice & Company (with C. Arthur Roberts added to those mentioned), silverware and cutlery. By 1895 there is reference only to silverware and plated ware and in 1899 the reference is to silversmiths. In 1910-1911 silverware and cut glass are mentioned. Further listings mention only silverware.

JUSTIS & ARMIGER
Baltimore, Maryland

JUSTIS & ARMIGER
TRIPLE PLATE
BALTIMORE

First listed in the Baltimore City Directory in 1891 as manufacturers of silverware, solid and plated. Succeeded by James R. Armiger in 1893.

K

KANN BROS. SILVER CO.
Baltimore, Maryland

Listed in Baltimore City Directories 1899-1913. Successors to Kann & Sons Mfg. Co., silverplaters.

KANN & SONS
Baltimore, Maryland

Silverplaters of spoons. Not listed in Baltimore City Directories until 1877, but advertisements say "Established 1870." Succeeded by Kann & Sons Mfg. Co. in 1886.

KANN & SONS MFG. CO.
Baltimore, Maryland

Listed in Baltimore City Directories in 1886-96 as silverplaters. Successors to Kann & Sons.

E. M. KARMEL & CO.
Brooklyn, New York

Listed J C-K 1915-1922 in sterling silver section.

J. KATZ & CO.
Baltimore, Maryland

Listed in Baltimore City Directories 1901-1904 as silversmiths.

C. F. KEES & CO.
Newark, New Jersey

Successor, before 1904, to Henry I. Leibe Mfg. Co. and were succeeded by Archibald, Klement Co. c. 1909. They were manufacturers of sterling silver and gold lorgnettes and related items.

KELLEY & MACBEAN
New York, New York

Listed in the 1900 Niagara Falls City Directory as makers of silver and plated silverware.

MRS. ANNIE KENNEY
Baltimore, Maryland

Listed in Baltimore City Directories 1867-1873 as a gold and silversmith.

CHARLES KENNEY
Baltimore, Maryland

Listed in Baltimore City Directories 1867-1868 as a silverplater.

AMBROSE KENT & SONS, LTD.
Toronto, Ontario

Established in 1867 as Kent Bros. Merged with Fairweather Ltd. in 1946 and became Kent-Fairweather, Ltd. Kent sold out in late 1953 and the firm name reverted to Fairweather, Ltd. No silverware is sold there now.

KENT & STANLEY CO., LTD.
Providence, Rhode Island

STERLING.

Listed in Providence City Directories 1889-1897 as manufacturers of silver souvenir articles. Patent No. 24,618, May 1, 1894 registered for these. Advertisement in City Directory says "rolled plate and silver chains a specialty."

WM. B. KERR & CO.
Newark, New Jersey
(See Gorham Corporation)

AMERICAN BEAUTY

Established by William B. Kerr in Newark, New Jersey in 1855. Makers of flat and tableware, gold dresserware and jewelry. Used **fleur-de-lis** trademark in 1892. Purchased by the Gorham Corporation in 1906 and moved to Providence, Rhode Island in 1927.

KEYSTONE SILVER CO.
Philadelphia, Pennsylvania

(On plated silver)

(On sterling silver)

Manufacturing silversmiths since 1914. Makers of reproductions in silver and gold; original designing; ecclesiastical goods and restorations.

L. KIMBALL & SON
Haverhill, Massachusetts

The business was established by Leverett Kimball in 1840. In 1850 and 1851 Mr. Kimball advertised "burning fluid, lamps, etc." In 1879 his ads were for Christmas gifts. In 1891 his ad in the City Directory states "makers of Hannah Duston (also spelled Dustin) and the Bradford Academy souvenir spoons."

Registered U. S. Patent No. 19,222, March 24, 1891. The firm name is listed until 1927, with F. C. Davis and J. D. Folsom, proprietors and called silversmiths, jewelers and opticians.

KIMBALL & RESTAURICK
Boston, Massachusetts

K. & R.

Listed in sterling silver section of 1904 J C-K as out of business.

KING SILVER CO.
Boston, Massachusetts
(See Lunt Silversmiths)

Founded in 1955. They purchased the Richard Dimes & Co. c. 1956, and in turn were acquired by Lunt Silversmiths about 1957.

SAMUEL KIRK & SON, INC.
Baltimore, Maryland

ORGANIZATIONAL TITLES

Kirk & Smith	1815–1820
Samuel Kirk	1821–1846
Samuel Kirk & Son	1846–1861
Samuel Kirk & Sons	1861–1868
Samuel Kirk & Son	1868–1896
Samuel Kirk & Son Co.	1896–1924
Samuel Kirk & Son, Inc.	1924–present

In August 1815, 22 year old Samuel Kirk opened his small shop in Baltimore and founded the oldest surviving silversmithing firm in the United States.

He was born in Doylestown, Pennsylvania in 1793. Through both parents he was descended from English silversmiths of the 17th century: Joan Kirke, registered in Goldsmith's Hall, England 1696–1697 and Sir Francis Child, Lord Mayor of London in 1669 and founder of the Child Banking House.

At 17, Samuel was apprenticed to James Howell, silversmith of Philadelphia and on completing his apprenticeship moved to Baltimore.

In 1815, Samuel Kirk and John Smith entered into a partnership which continued until 1820. In 1846, Samuel Kirk's son, Henry Child Kirk, became a partner and the firm name was changed to Samuel Kirk & Son. In 1861, Charles D. and Clarence E. Kirk also entered the business and the name was changed to Samuel Kirk & Sons. After the Civil War, the two younger brothers left the firm and the name reverted to Samuel Kirk & Son.

After the death of Samuel Kirk in 1872, his son continued alone until 1890, when his only son, Henry Child Kirk, Jr., joined as a partner, retaining the firm name, Samuel Kirk & Son. In 1896, Henry Child Kirk, Sr. formed a corporation and remained as active head until his death in 1914 when his son succeeded as president. Each of these early representatives of the Kirk family served an apprenticeship in the craft and qualified as working silversmiths. Kirk silver continues to be made under the direct supervision and guidance of a member of the Kirk family.

It was Samuel Kirk who introduced the intricate and often imitated Repousse style of ornamentation to America in 1828. It is often referred to as "Baltimore silver."

Kirk's tradition for fine craftsmanship has brought many famous people to its shop. It is not surprising that when the White House dinner service was in need of repair, Kirk's was selected to renovate the five hundred and fifty pieces of gold flatware that had been in use for state banquets since the administration of President Monroe.

Many famous trophies and presentation pieces have been designed by Kirk's. The most ambitious was the forty-eight piece dinner service commissioned for the old Cruiser **Maryland** in 1905 and now on exhibit at the State House at Annapolis. Nearly two hundred scenes and pictures present a panorama of Maryland's illustrious history.

Kirk silver has always reflected the trends of decorative design. Early pieces were made in the chaste and simple lines of the Georgian era. The China trade is reflected in delicate Oriental lines, and the elaborate ornamentation of the Victorian age produced some magnificent pieces. Contemporary simplicity produces pieces remarkably like those of the very first made by Samuel Kirk.

New techniques, progressive research and new designs have been added to Kirk silver, but, their firm produces prestige merchandise. They pride themselves that hand crafting techniques are still essential in the production of Kirk sterling.

YEAR	BALTIMORE ASSAY MARK	DOMINICAL LETTERS
1814		B
	ASSAYER'S AND MAKER'S MARKS	
1815		A
1816		GF
1817		E
1818		D
1819		C
1820		A OR B
1821		G
1822		F
1823		E
1824		D OR C
1825 1826 1827	no example	B A G

In the absence of any example of the assayer's marks for the years 1825 to 1827 and because of the great number of examples in existence bearing the 1824 marks, it is generally conceded that the 1824 marks were continued through the years 1825, 1826 and 1827.

YEAR	ASSAYER'S AND MAKER'S MARKS	DOMINICAL LETTERS

1828 — F OR E

1829 — D

1830 — C

ASSAY MARKS AND DOMINICAL LETTERS WERE NOT USED AFTER 1830

1830 to 1846

1846 to 1861

S.KIRK&SON 11OZ

SK & SON   S.KIRK & SON 1015

11·OZ

1861 to 1868

S.KIRK & SONS 10.15

S.KIRK&SONS 11OZ

1868 to 1898

S KIRK & SON   925/1000

1880 to 1890

S.KIRK&SON

S.Kirk & Son   11OZ

YEAR	KIRK'S MAKER'S MARKS

1896 to 1903 flatware

S.KIRK&SONCO $925/1000$

S.KIRK& SON CO $\dfrac{925}{1000}$

1903 to 1924 holloware

S.Kirk & SonCo.   925

S.Kirk&SonCo. $925/1000$

1907 to 1914 flatware

S.KIRK & SON CO $925/1000$

S.Kirk&SonCo $925/1000$

1903 to 1907 holloware

KirkCo $925/1000$ S Kirk&SonCo $\dfrac{925}{1000}$

S Kirk& SonCo $925/1000$ S.Kirk&Son Co

1925 to 1932 holloware

S.Kirk&Son Inc. STERLING

1927 to 1961 flatware

PAT. S.KIRK& SON STERLING

1932 to 1961 flatware

S.KIRK & SON STERLING

1932 to 1961 holloware

S.KIRK & SON STERLING

S.Kirk&Son   STERLING

1959 to 1961 flatware

S.KIRK&SON STERLING©

H. A. KIRBY
Providence, Rhode Island

Retailer of silverware and jewelry. Established in 1886 as Kirby, Mowry & Co. Incorporated in September 1896. Advertised solid gold and diamond jewelry, ear rings, scarf pins, brooches, studs, collar buttons and rings. In 1905 the listing was H. A. Kirby Co. and this listing was continued until the death of Henry A. Kirby in 1920.

KIRBY KRAFT
(See Middletown Silver Co.)

JULIUS KIRSCHNER & CO.
New York, New York

JULCKO
(Mesh Bags.)

Listed J C-K 1915–1943. Wholesalers of plated silverware and mesh bags.

C. KLANK & SONS
Baltimore, Maryland
(See Schofield & Co., Inc.)

ORGANIZATIONAL TITLES

Klank & Bro.	1872–1891
Conrad Klank & Sons	1892
C. Klank & Sons Mfg. Co.	1893–1894
C. Klank & Sons	1895–1911

First listed in the Baltimore City Directory in 1872–1873 as Klank & Bro., silverplaters. From 1874–1892 they were listed as silversmiths. Conrad, Frederick W. and George H. Klank were listed as members of the firm.

In 1892 the firm name became Conrad Klank & Sons, silversmiths, with Conrad, Frederick and George H. Jr., listed as members of the firm. The 1893 listing was C. Klank & Sons Mfg. Co., with Conrad listed as manager.

In 1895 the listing was C. Klank & Sons, the members of the firm remaining the same until 1899 when the members were listed as Conrad, F. William, and Herbert Klank and James L. McPhail. This listing continued until 1905 when James L. McPhail, who had also been listed as a member of the firm of A. G. Schultz & Co. during the same period, was no longer listed at either. In 1905 or 1906 C. Klank & Sons was purchased by Heer-Schofield, later Schofield & Co. though it continued to be listed under its own name through 1911.

KLANK MFG. CO.
Baltimore, Maryland

Listed in 1892 Baltimore City Directory as silversmiths and silverplaters. George H. Klank, manager.

WILLIAM KLANK
Baltimore, Maryland

Listed in Baltimore City Directories 1895-1899 as a silversmith. Not at the same address as C. Klank & Sons.

KNICKERBOCKER SILVER CO.
Port Jervis, New York

Manufacturers of plated silver holloware. Established before 1896 as Knickerbocker Mfg. Co. Name changed to Knickerbocker Silver Co. before 1904. Last record found was 1935.

Not used after c. 1900

JACOB KNIPE
Baltimore, Maryland

Listed in Baltimore City Directories 1864-1880 as a silverplater.

WM. KNOLL & CO.
New York, New York

Listed J C-K 1904 in sterling silver section. Out of business before 1915.

J. B. & S. M. KNOWLES CO.
Providence, Rhode Island

Manufacturers of sterling silver only. Organized in 1852. U. S. Patent No. 38,096, April 15, 1902 for spoons to be marked **RED CROSS.** Out of business between 1904 and 1909.

RED CROSS

KOECHLIN & ENGLEHARDT
Newark, New Jersey

Earliest record found U. S. Patent 56,499, registered October 2, 1906 for use on sterling and plated silver flat and holloware. Out of business before 1915.

GUSTAVE F. KOLB
New York, New York

Manufacturers (?) of sterling silver c. 1920.

KOONZ MFG. CO.
Greenfield, Massachusetts

Listed J C-K 1915 as manufacturers of sterling silver. Out of business before 1922.

CHARLES KRAEMER
Baltimore, Maryland

Listed in Baltimore City Directory 1882 as a silversmith.

CHARLES M. KRAMER
Baltimore, Maryland

Listed in Baltimore City Directory in 1885 as a silverplater.

KRAUS & JANTZEN
New York, New York
(See Kraus, McKeever & Adams)

KRAUS, KRAGEL & CO.
New York, New York
(See Kraus, McKeever & Adams)

KRAUS, McKEEVER & ADAMS
New York, New York

First listed in 1896 as Kraus, Kragel & Co.; in 1904 as Kraus &

Jantzen and in 1922 as Kraus, McKeever & Adams. Trademarks used on sterling silver frames for handbags; 14k gold mountings and sterling silver mountings for leather articles.

KRIDER & BIDDLE
Philadelphia, Pennsylvania
(See Peter L. Krider Co.)

PETER L. KRIDER CO.
Philadelphia, Pennsylvania

Peter L. Krider was a silversmith in Philadelphia c. 1850; became Krider & Biddle, which was succeeded by Peter L. Krider Co. before 1896.

KRONHEIMER &
OLDENBUSCH CO.
New York, New York

Listed in J C-K 1909–1922 in plated silver section.

LEONARD KROWER & SON, INC.
New Orleans, Louisiana

Established before 1896 as Leonard Krower, wholesalers and jobbers of sterling silver, plated silver, platinum, optical goods, medals, watches, clocks, pearls, diamonds, cut glass and gold jewelry. Listed in J C-K 1943 as Leonard Krower & Son and were incorporated before 1950. Acquired by the Gordon Jewelry Corporation in 1965.

THE FRANK KURSH & SON CO.
Newark, New Jersey

 Sterling

Listed in J C-K 1904 in sterling silver section. Out of business before 1915.

Trademark identical to Shoemaker, Pickering & Co.

L

FERDINAND C. LAMY
Saranac Lake, New York

Registered trademark in U. S. Patent Office No. 21,899, October 25, 1892 for use on spoons, forks, knife handles, etc. of souvenir type. Listed in J C-K as out of business before 1922.

LANDERS, FRARY & CLARK
New Britain, Connecticut

AETNA WORKS
LANDERS, FRARY &
CLARK

UNIVERSAL
(used after 1897)

**LANDERS FRARY & CLARK
ÆTNA WORKS**

Landers, Frary & Clark began as a partnership in 1842 with George M. Landers and Josiah Dewey; became Landers & Smith Mfg. Co. in 1853 and Landers, Frary & Clark in 1865. They purchased the Meriden Cutlery Co. in 1866. Their newly-built Aetna Works held this cutlery division. The factory burned in 1874 and was immediately rebuilt. They are still manufacturers of silverware, electric appliances, cutlery and miscellaneous hardware.

In 1954 they purchased the Dazy Corp.

R. LANGE
Baltimore, Maryland

Listed in Baltimore City Directory 1864 as a silverplater.

RALPH LANGE
Baltimore, Maryland

Listed in Baltimore City Directories 1872–1889 as a silverplater.

RUDOLPH LANGE
Baltimore, Maryland

Listed in Baltimore City Directories 1884–1885 as a silverplater at the same address as R. Lange who was listed in 1864.

LA PIERRE MFG. CO.
Newark and New York
(See International Silver Co.)

(Used before 1896)

Established about 1895. Specialized in manufacturing of sterling
novelties, dresserware and silver
deposit wares. Bought by International Silver Co. in 1929 and
moved to Wallingford, Connecticut.

LA SECLA, FRIED & CO.
Newark, New Jersey

Listed J C-K 1909-1915 in sterling
silver section. Out of business before 1922.

LEBKUECHER & CO.
Newark, New Jersey
(See Eleder-Hickok Co., Inc.)
(See Hickok Matthews Company
—Silversmiths)

Name changed by law to F. A.
Lester. Taken over by The Eleder
Co. in 1918. By 1922 it became the
Eleder-Hickok Co., Inc.

LEBOLT & CO.
Chicago, Illinois

Registered trademark in U. S.
Patent Office No. 70,833-y, October 6, 1908 for manufacture of
silverware and jewelry. Listed
J C-K 1915-1922.

LEDIG MFG. CO.
Philadelphia, Pennsylvania

Listed in J C-K 1896 in plated silver section. Out of business before 1904.

(Solid Plated and Composition Ware.)

HENRY L. LEIBE MFG. CO.
Newark, New Jersey
(See Archibald, Klement)
(See C. F. Kees Co.)

KARL F. LEINONEN
Boston, Massachusetts

Karl F. Leinonen, born in Turku,
Finland in 1866. Served the regular seven year apprenticeship

there. He came to the United
States in 1893 and worked in a
commercial repair shop in Boston.
In 1901, when Arthur A. Carey,
president of the Boston Society of
Arts & Crafts, financed the opening of the Handicraft Shop, where

a large number of silversmiths had
bench space, he placed Leinonen
in charge. He was still in this position in 1932. His son, Edwin, became his assistant.

Now listed in the Boston Directory as Karl F. Leinonen & Sons.

THE LENAU CO.
Attleboro Falls, Mass.

L STERLING.

Listed in J C-K in sterling silver section in 1896. Out of business before 1904.

LEONARD MFG. CO.
Chicago, Illinois (?)

Manufactured plated silver spoons to commemorate the World's Columbian Exposition in Chicago, 1892.

LEONARD, REED & BARTON
Taunton, Massachusetts
(See Reed & Barton)

LEONARD, REED & BARTON
(On britannia)

JOSEPH LESHER
Victor, Colorado

REFERENDUM

Joseph Lesher, a Victor real estate and mining man picked the world's greatest gold mining district as the place to distribute his eight-sided silver dollars which he manufactured in a campaign for the free coinage of silver.

One of the rarest items sought by American numismatists, the silver pieces have achieved real value. But in 1900 and 1901, when Lesher was having the coins minted in Denver, they had a value of $1.25 and were issued to merchants to be handed out and redeemed in merchandise. From the high silver content of the coins, Lesher could not have made any money on the arrangement.

No more than 3,500 of the coins were minted. There was a total of 18 varieties, each differing in some minor detail.

The first dies were made by Frank Hurd of Denver. Later dies were made by Herman Otto. The first type, issued in 1900, was 35 mm. across and was stamped one ounce silver, value $1.25. One side had the words, **Jos. Lesher, Referendum Souvenir;** the other side, **A Commodity, Will Give in Exchange for Currency Coin or Merchandise at Face Value.** In order to avoid trouble with the U. S. Government Lesher made his dollars eight-sided, but that did not help. Only a few days after the first coin was issued, government agents called on Lesher to see the dies. Lesher handed them over and then, he reported to the newspapers later, "they pulled out a sack in which they put the dies and walked away, and I never saw them again." The government agents claimed that the silver pieces had the function of coins and were contrary to law. Lesher appealed to Senator Teller for help. Teller took it up with the secretary of the treasury and it was finally agreed that, with certain changes in the design of the coin, the minting could continue.

The second set was issued for exchange of merchandise at A. B. Bumstead. Others were issued for various firms bearing the legend, Trade Mark Reg. U. S. Patent Office No. 36,192, April 9, 1901 Design Patent April 16, 1901. They also bear the altered inscription "Jos. Lesher's Referendum Silver Souvenir Medal."

F. A. LESTER COMPANY
(See Eleder-Hickok Co., Inc.)
(See Hickok Matthews Company
   Silversmiths)
(See Lebkuecher & Co.)

LEVITT & GOLD
New York, New York

Listed in J C-K 1915-1922 in sterling silver section. The trademark was also used on platinum and gold novelties. Listed c. 1935 as Levitt & Co. (?)

CHAS. J. LEWARD
New York, New York

TRADE MARK.

Listed J C-K in 1896 in sterling silver section. Out of business before 1904.

LEWIS BROS.
New York, New York

Listed in 1896-1904 J C-K as manufacturers of sterling silver novelties and jewelry. Address was the same as S. M. Lewis & Co. Out of business before 1915.

S. M. LEWIS & CO.
New York, New York

**S. M. L. & CO.
STERLING**

Listed 1896 J C-K in sterling silver section. Out of business before 1904. Address was the same as Lewis Bros.

LIEBS SILVER CO., INC.
New York, New York

Listed in J C-K 1915 as Liebs Co.; became Liebs Silver Co., Inc. before 1922. The last record found was 1931. Manufacturers of sterling silver holloware.

J. ARTHUR LIMERICK
Baltimore, Maryland

Listed in Baltimore City Directories 1903-1904 as successor to Jacob Gminder who began plating silver in 1867.

WILLIAM LINK CO.
Newark, New Jersey

Listed J C-K 1896 as William Link; later Link, Angell & Weiss; succeeded by Link & Angell c. 1900; listed in 1915 as Wm. Link Co. Manufacturers of sterling and jewelry.

WILLIAM LINKER
Philadelphia, Pennsylvania

Registered trademark in U. S. Patent Office, No. 55,945, August 21, 1906 for gold and silver flatware, holloware and tableware. Out of business between 1909 and 1915.

LIPPIATT SILVER PLATE AND
ENGRAVING CO.
New York, New York

Samuel F. B. Morse, inventor of the telegraph, was President of the Lippiatt Silver Plate and En-

graving Co. The company controlled the licensing of a special process for finishing silver. They also used this process for making plated silverware.

They registered a trademark in the U. S. Patent Office, November 1, 1870 for silver and plated ware. Out of business before 1904.

P. H. LOCKLIN & SONS
New York, New York

Manufacturers c. 1920–1930 of sterling silverware, vases, candlesticks, salt and pepper shakers, umbrella handles, canes, riding crops, muffineers, novelties, cigar and cigarette holders, and articles of other materials mounted in 14 and 18k white gold and platinum.

MILLIE B. LOGAN
Rochester, New York

U. S. Patent No. 20,375 registered for Millie B. Logan on November 17, 1891 for gold and silver tableware. Listed in J C-K 1896 among manufacturers of souvenir silverware. Rochester city directory lists her as a manufacturer of ladies' fashionable hair work, hair jewelry, etc., from 1871–c. 1908.

H. LORD & CO.
Savannah, Georgia
(See Black, Starr & Frost Ltd.)

In business c. 1805. Partners were Hezekiah Lord, Cornelius Paulding and Isaac Marquand.

LOTT & SCHMITT, INC.
New York, New York

Listed J C-K 1915 in sterling silver section. Out of business before 1922.

LOW, BALL & CO.
(See Shreve, Crump & Low Co., Inc.)

DANIEL LOW & CO.
Salem, Massachusetts

WITCH

Established in 1867 by Daniel Low as a small jewelry store. Low's reputation as a source of unusual gifts and fine gold and silver articles soon earned a reputation for the store and the confidence of his patrons.

In 1887, when souvenir spoons were being introduced in European cities, Daniel Low took a trip abroad and brought back the idea of making a Witch spoon as a souvenir of Salem and the Witchcraft tradition. His son, Seth F.

Low, designed the first Witch spoon. It was made by the Durgin Division of The Gorham Mfg. Co. Its immediate popularity and that of the second Witch spoon which followed shortly afterwards, were largely responsible for the souvenir spoon craze that swept across the country shortly before 1900.

In 1896 Seth F. Low became a partner in the business. In September 1, 1907 the business was incorporated under the name Daniel Low & Co., Inc. so that it might be carried on without interruption.

Aware that most of the goods purchased in his store were for gifts, Daniel Low decided to reach out beyond the confines of his own city and in 1893 first published a small catalog to establish a mail order business. Since then the Daniel Low Year Book has become a national institution.

JOHN J. LOW & CO.
(See Shreve, Crump & Low Co., Inc.)

MRS. LUCKEY
Pittsburgh, Pennsylvania

Woman silversmith who worked in Pittsburgh between 1830 and 1840.

LUDWIG, REDLICH & CO.
(See Elgin Silversmith Co., Inc.)

Registered trademark in U. S. Patent Office No. 21,423, July 5, 1892 for solid silverware and tableware.

LUNA METAL
(See Rowley Mfg. Co.)

LUNT SILVERSMITHS
Greenfield, Massachusetts
(See Franklin Silver Plate Company)
(See Rogers, Lunt & Bowlen)

LUNT STERLING

Lunt Silversmiths began with the formation of the A. F. Towle & Son Co. in 1883 in Newburyport, Massachusetts. The company was moved to Greenfield in 1890 and operated until 1902.

George C. Lunt took charge of the engraving department of the A. F. Towle & Son Co. and in 1902 was instrumental in the organization of Rogers, Lunt & Bowlen Co. Rogers, Lunt & Bowlen Co. has operated in Greenfield since then under the same corporate name. In 1935 they began using as a tradename the title LUNT SILVER-

SMITHS and to trademark their products LUNT STERLING, but the corporation name remains the same. George C. Lunt died in 1952 and Denham Lunt is now president of the company.

The Franklin Silver Plate Company of Greenfield, Massachusetts was taken over between 1920–1922. With minor exceptions their trademarks have not been used.

About 1957 the King Silver Company of Boston, including the trademark and assets of the Richard Dimes Co., was added to the firm.

Lunt sterling is noted for fine craftsmanship and good taste in design.

W. H. LYON
Newburgh, New York

Listed in the Newburgh City Directory 1891–1920. His advertisement in the directory stated that Lyon, the Jeweler was sole manufacturer of the Washington Headquarters Souvenir Spoon, in Tea, Coffee, Orange and Sugar Spoons, also

Butter Knives, etc. The trademark was the representation of the building known as "George Washington's Newburg[h] N. Y. headquarters." Registered in U. S. Patent Office, No. 18,906, January 17, 1891.

LYONS SILVER PLATE CO.
(See Manhattan Silver Plate Co.)

M

J. S. MACDONALD
Baltimore, Maryland

J. S. MACDONALD CO.
Baltimore, Maryland

Listed in Baltimore City Directories 1911-1921 under plated silverware. Successors to J. Stuart MacDonald who began business in 1887.

MACOMBER MFG. CO.
Providence, Rhode Island

MM Co.

Manufacturers of plated silverware c. 1910.

R. H. MACY & CO.
New York, New York

Chatsworth

(On plated silver)

Founded by Rowland Hussey Macy of Nantucket Island who went to sea as a whaler when he was only fifteen. At Macy's store he is spoken of as **Captain Macy**—a slight exaggeration.

Nantucketers still speak of "that Macy boy who went to New York and made out all right—even though he did become an off-islander."

He engaged in several business ventures. First, in Boston, where he operated a thread and needle shop—a short-lived venture. His next store was Macy & Company, run in partnership with his brother in Marysville, California, where they were drawn by the Gold Rush.

The family moved back to Massachusetts and in Haverhill he opened the Haverhill Cheap Store.

Finally, in the fall of 1858 he opened his first New York store on 6th Avenue, just below 14th Street.

Macy had some unusual ideas in advertising and believed strongly in the value of this advertising. A distinctive characteristic of this was the introduction of a trademark—a red rooster—used after June 1851 in the Haverhill Store. In New York he adopted a five-pointed red star in 1862 or 1863.

Silverware was first sold in the store in 1874 and was supplied by L. Straus & Sons, wholesalers. Like other large department stores, Macy's had goods marked with their private brands and trademarks.

E. MAGNUS
New York, New York
(See Howard Cutlery Co.)

D. J. MAHONY
New York, New York

M

Listed in J C-K in 1896 in sterling silver section. Out of business before 1904.

MAJESTIC MFG. CO.
New York, New York

Listed in J C-K in 1896 in sterling silver section. Out of business before 1904.

The 1904 J C-K attributes similar trademark to Fishel, Nessler & Co.

MAJESTIC SILVER COMPANY
New Haven, Connecticut

MAJESTIC

Founded in 1910 as The Regal Silver Manufacturing Company by M. L. Baker, who, at 86, is still with the company. Present president is Milton Baker, son of the founder.

From 1910 till 1942 they manufactured silverplated flatware. In the late 1920's the production of stainless steel flatware was begun.

In the early 1930's a separate related firm, The Regal Specialty Mfg. Co., began the manufacture of silverplate and stainless steel flatware. At the end of World steel flatware. At the end of World War II silverplated flatware was discontinued and now only stainless steel flatware is made.

In late 1945, through internal corporate changes, The Majestic Silver Co. emerged as the parent company and The Regal Specialty Co. continued as the subsidiary.

MALACCA PLATED
(See G. I. Mix & Co.)

MALTBY, STEVENS &
CURTISS CO.
Wallingford, Connecticut
(See International Silver Co.)

(On plated silver)

(On sterling silver)

Successor to Maltby, Stevens & Company's spoon factory, Birmingham, Connecticut, the new

company was headed by Elizur Seneca Stevens, Chapman Maltby and John Curtiss. They bought and occupied the old Hall, Elton & Co. plant and manufactured flatware for plating about 1890. In 1896 the company was purchased by the Watrous Mfg. Co., which was one of the original companies to become a part of International Silver Co. in 1898.

MANCHESTER MFG. CO.
Providence, Rhode Island
(See Baker-Manchester Mfg. Co.)
(See Manchester Silver Co.)

Manufacturers of sterling silver fancy flatware, holloware and novelties. Baker-Manchester Mfg. Co. listed in 1922 J C-K as successors.

MANCHESTER SILVER CO.
Providence, Rhode Island

Founded in 1887 by William H. Manchester, descendent of an English family of silversmiths. Operations started on Stewart Street under the name W. H. Manchester & Co. They moved to Chestnut Street where Mr. Manchester was associated with a Baker family. From 1904 until 1914-1915, the company name was Manchester Mfg. Co. Manchester moved his operation to the present location on Pavilion Avenue in 1914 or 1915, while the Bakers continued for a time on Chestnut Street under the name Baker-Manchester Co. William Manchester was no longer connected with this operation.

William Manchester had an associate by the name of MacFarland. On his retirement, Frank S. Trumbull, of an industrial family from Connecticut, took his place. When Mr. Manchester and his son retired, the business was owned solely by Frank S. Trumbull until 1947, when E. B. McAlpine and his son, George Wescott McAlpine acquired an interest. Following the death of Mr. Trumbull in 1954 the McAlpine family acquired the entire stock.

Their products are sterling silver flatware and holloware. Everything is marketed under the slogan, "If it's Manchester, it's Sterling."

In 1955 or 1956 they acquired the tools, dies and rights to the flatware patterns formerly produced by Richard Dimes Co.

W. H. MANCHESTER & CO.
Providence, Rhode Island
(See Manchester Silver Co.)

Manufacturers of sterling silver fancy flatware, holloware and novelties.

MANDALIAN & HAWKINS
North Attleboro, Massachusetts
(See Mandalian Mfg. Co.)

M & H

Founding date unknown. Succeeded by Mandalian Manufacturing Company before 1922.

MANDALIAN MFG. CO.
North Attleboro, Massachusetts

DEBUTANTE

Successors to Mandalian & Hawkins before 1922. Last record found in 1935. Manufacturing jewelers and jobbers.

MANHATTAN SILVER PLATE CO.
Lyons, New York
(See International Silver Co.)

Identical to a mark used by Roswell Gleason. Perhaps erroneously attributed to Manhattan Silver Plate Co. in 1904 J C-K.

Incorporated in 1877. Moved from Brooklyn to Lyons, New York in 1904. One of the original companies to become part of International Silver Co. in 1898.

Manhattan trademark not used after 1904.

MANNING, BOWMAN & CO.
Meriden, Connecticut

(Not used after 1898)

E. B. Manning, Middletown, Connecticut was a britannia ware maker from 1850-1875.

Thaddeus Manning and Manning, Bowman & Company were listed in the Connecticut Business Directory of 1866 as britannia ware manufacturers. The company was founded in 1857 and incorporated in 1887.

Company records do not show just when the manufacture of plated silver products began, but, they are listed in J C-K from 1896-1915 with trademarks for plated silver. One clue lies in the fact that they won an award at an exhibition of the American Institute of New York in 1869 for plated silverware.

Best known for their manufacture of electrical appliances, the Manning-Bowman Company is now a Division of the McGraw-Edison Company, Boonville, Missouri.

MAPPIN & WEBB, LTD.
Sheffield, England

TUSCA

Silversmiths and electroplaters. By appointment to several members of the Royal family and foreign rulers. Early in the 80's bought the old business of Stephen Smith & Son's (formerly Smith & Nicholson), of Covent Garden, London. Became limited in 1899.

MARCEL NOVELTY CO.
New York, New York

Listed in J C-K 1896-1904 in sterling silver section. Out of business before 1915.

FRED I. MARCY & CO.
Providence, Rhode Island

Listed J C-K in 1896 in sterling silver section. Out of business before 1904.

MARION PLATE CO.
(See Bernard Rice's Sons)

MARQUAND & BROTHER
New York, New York
(See Black, Starr & Frost, Ltd.)

In business 1814-1831. Partners were Isaac Marquand and Frederick Marquand.

MARQUAND & COMPANY
New York, New York
(See Black, Starr & Frost, Ltd.)

In business 1834-1839. Partners were Frederick Marquand, Josiah P. Marquand and Erastus O. Tompkins. Famed silversmiths and jewelers.

MARQUAND, HARRIMAN & CO.
New York, New York
(See Black, Starr & Frost, Ltd.)

In business c. 1809-1810. Partners were Isaac Marquand, Orlando Harriman and Cornelius Paulding.

MARQUAND & PAULDING
Savannah, Georgia
(See Black, Starr & Frost, Ltd.)

Founded c. 1801 and in business until 1810. Partners were Isaac Marquand (who had been apprenticed to his uncle, Jacob Jenning, Norwalk, Connecticut) and Cornelius Paulding.

MARQUAND, PAULDING & PENFIELD
Savannah, Georgia
(See Black, Starr & Frost, Ltd.)

In business c. 1810-1816. Partners were Isaac Marquand, Cornelius Paulding and Josiah Penfield.

MARSHALL-WELLS HARDWARE CO.
Duluth, Minnesota

Began as the Chapin-Wells Hardware Company in 1886. In 1893, Albert M. Marshall, a Saginaw, Michigan merchant bought out the Chapin interest and the company became the Marshall-Wells Co., hardware wholesalers. Old city directory advertisements indicate that the company first distributed only tools, hardware, cutlery and saddlery. Later their merchandise included everything that could be classified as hardware. It was the largest hardware wholesale distributor in the Northwest and Canada.

November 24, 1908 a trademark, No. 71,473, was registered in their name for silverplated knives, forks and spoons. In an advertisement from the **Zenith Magazine,** their monthly publication, it was noted that cutlery was stamped "manufactured exclusively for Marshall-Wells" and bore the Zenith trademark. Branch jobbing houses were located in Winnipeg (1900), Portland (1901), Spokane (1909), Edmonton (1910), Aberdeen, Seattle, Great Falls, Billings, Minneapolis and Vancouver, B. C. They also had warehouses in Moosejaw, Sasketchewan and Calgary, Alberta.

In May 1955, the trustees of the A. M. Marshall estate sold the controlling interest to Ambrook Industries of New York. At that time Marshall-Wells was the largest wholesale hardware operation in the world.

In 1958, Marshall-Wells and Kelly-How, Thompson, a Midwest

hardware distributor merged and in August of that same year the company was sold to Coast-to-Coast stores, and in 1959 Marshall-Wells closed its main office and warehouse in Duluth and moved to New York City.

A 1963 newspaper clipping indicated that the Marshall-Wells Co. of Duluth was still in business, having purchased a St. Louis, Missouri furniture company, but no longer operated as a wholesale hardware distributor.

MARYLAND SILVER CO.
Baltimore, Maryland

Listed in Baltimore City Directories 1906–1908 as silversmiths.

MARYLAND SILVER PLATE CO.
Baltimore, Maryland

Listed in Baltimore City Directories 1889–1899 under plated silverware.

MATHEWS & PRIOR
New York, New York

Founding date unknown. Listed in J C-K in 1904 in sterling silver section as out of business.

MATTHEWS COMPANY
Newark, New Jersey
(See Hickok Matthews Company
—Silversmiths)

(On sterling holloware)

Incorporated in 1907. Merged with Eleder-Hickok Company between

1931–1943 to become Hickok-Matthews Company. Was purchased in 1965 by Wolfgang K. Schroth and is now known as Hickok Matthews Company—Silversmiths, Montville, New Jersey.

THE MAUSER MANUFACTURING COMPANY
New York, New York

Listed in J C-K since 1896 as manufacturers of sterling silver only. Also makers of silver-mounted cut glass, novelties, holloware and dresserware.

The diamond-enclosing-an-M trademark is still listed under Mt. Vernon Company Silversmiths.

In 1903 The Mauser Mfg. Co. merged with the Hayes & McFarland Company of Mount Vernon, New York and the Roger Williams Silver Company of Providence, Rhode Island to form the Mt. Vernon Company Silversmiths, Inc. which was purchased by the Gorham Corporation in 1913.

FRANK T. MAY CO.
New York, New York and
Rutherford, New Jersey

Listed in J C-K in 1904–1943.

Manufacturers and distributors of sterling silver bags, 14k vanity and ladies' cigarette cases and novelties and jewelry.

JOSEPH MAYER & BROS.
Seattle, Washington
(See E. J. Towle Mfg. Co.)

MAYO & CO.
Chicago, Illinois

Listed in J C-K in 1896 in sterling silver section. Out of business before 1904.

THE McCHESNEY CO.
Newark, New Jersey
(See Gorham Corporation)

Manufacturers of sterling silver c. 1920. Purchased by the Gorham Corporation in 1931. The tools and dies were moved to Providence, Rhode Island.

DAVID H. McCONNELL
New York, New York

SO. AM.

Earliest record found was registration of U. S. Patent No. 32,828, May 9, 1899 for use on plated flatware. Out of business before 1915.

JOHN M. McFARLANE
(See Shreve, Crump & Low Co., Inc.)

WALTER H. McKENNA & CO., INC.
Providence, Rhode Island

Established in 1915 as manufacturers of 14k and 10k gold, sterling silver and gold filled jewelry. Also make sterling baby spoons. Still in business in 1965.

MEALY MANUFACTURING
COMPANY
Baltimore, Maryland

HAND WROUGHT

First listed in the Baltimore City Directory in 1900 as John W. Mealy Son & Company, jewelers. In 1906 John W. was listed as president; Edward H. as treasurer and Charles A. as secretary. In 1908 Allan B. Crouch was listed as secretary and Charles A. as treasurer.

In 1909 Crouch is no longer listed. The company name was listed through 1930. There is a gap in directories from 1930-1935, after which there is no further listing.

All of these listings are under the head of silversmiths. This listing, in addition to the type of trademark, indicates handwrought silver was made.

JOHN O. MEAD
Philadelphia, Pennsylvania

Britannia ware manufacturer of Philadelphia, John O. Mead, laid the foundation for the important 19th century industry of electroplating silver.

Around 1830–1835 Mead was in charge of the silverplating and gilding work at the N. P. Ames Manufacturing Company of Chicopee, Massachusetts, using the old mercury and acid process.

He went to England to learn the new technique in Birmingham and continued his experiments on his return. Reputedly the first successful American electro-silver plater around 1840–1859.

In 1845 he formed a partnership in Hartford, Connecticut with William and Asa Rogers under the name of Rogers & Mead. This company was soon dissolved.

Mead returned to Philadelphia in 1846 and re-established his business under the name John O. Mead, later Mead & Sons, then Filley & Mead (or Filley, Mead & Caldwell) while William and Asa Rogers founded the firm of Rogers Bros. Mead & Sons had an extensive business. Their plant employed more than two hundred workmen and they turned out about fifty different designs in tea sets alone. Much of their ware was supplied "in the metal" by Reed & Barton, the plating being done in the Mead plant.

MECHANICS STERLING COMPANY
Attleboro, Massachusetts
(See Watson Co.)

Flatware.
MECHANICS STERLING CO.

Listed as sterling manufacturer in Jewelers' Weekly 1896. Mark is identical to Watson-Newell, now part of Wallace Silversmiths—a division of Hamilton Watch Co.

MEDFORD CUTLERY CO.
(See A. R. Justice Co.)

THE MELROSE SILVER CO.
Hartford, Connecticut

COLONIAL PLATE CO.

Listed in J C-K in 1904. Out of business before 1909.

MERIDEN BRITANNIA CO., LTD.
Hamilton, Ontario

Established in 1879 for the production of 1847 Rogers Bros. silverplate, sterling silver flatware, silverplated nickel silver and white metal holloware. Merged with International Silver Co. of Canada, Ltd. about 1912.

MERIDAN BRITANNIA COMPANY
Meriden, Connecticut
(See International Silver
Company)

1847

(Nickel Silver, Silver Soldered Holloware.)

(Standard White Metal
Holloware.) (Plated Ware.)

1847 ROGERS BROS.

(Spoons, Forks, Knives, etc.)

(Nickel Silver, White Metal Mounted Holloware.)

(Solid Steel, Silver Plated Knives.)

MERIDEN BRITᴬ CO.

(Spoons, Forks, Knives, etc.)

1847 ROGERS BROS. ⚙ XII ₜᵣᵢₚₗₑ ˣ⁵

STERLING

NICKEL SILVER.

WHITE METAL.

MADE AND
GUARANTEED BY

∗∗∗ROGERS BROS.

STERLING

(Holloware.)

STERLING FINE
(Flatware.)

Organized in December 1852 by Horace C. and Dennis C. Wilcox of H. C. Wilcox & Co. Other founders were Isaac C. Lewis of I. C. Lewis & Company; James A. Frary of James A. Frary & Company; Lemuel J. Curtis; William W. Lyman of Curtis & Lyman and John Munson.

Organized for quantity production, their first products were britannia hollowares. By 1855 they were also offering plated silver holloware and flatware and German silver articles. Pearl handled wares were added about 1861.

In 1862 the Rogers brothers who had been making and selling plated silver forks, spoons and other wares were moved to Meriden. Their 1847 Rogers Bros. trademark was an important addition to the Meriden Britannia Company.

In 1896 they ceased stamping their products "Quadruple" plate.

The Meriden Britannia Company officers were among the leaders in the formation of the International Silver Company in 1898.

MERIDEN CUTLERY COMPANY
South Meriden, Connecticut

MERIDENCUTLERY CO.

(On carving knives with sterling silver blades)

MERIDEN CUTLERY CO.

This firm began in 1834, when G. and D. N. Ropes manufactured cutlery in Maine. A few years later, A. R. Moen of New York manufactured table cutlery in Wethersfield, Connecticut. The business was acquired by Julius Pratt & Co. of Meriden who continued it for about two years. In 1845, these two firms were consolidated as Pratt, Ropes, Webb & Co. Mr. Ropes erected a factory in Hanover where the business continued until 1855, when the joint stock company Meriden Cutlery Company was formed. One of their specialties was pearl handled cutlery which usually carried the date 1855.

The company was purchased by Landers, Frary & Clark in 1866 which is still in business.

These two trademarks were used on carving knives with sterling silver blades c. 1900.

MERIDEN JLY. MFG. CO.
Meriden, Connecticut

(On plated silver)

Listed in J C-K 1915. Became Meriden Jewelry Co. before 1922. Manufacturers of sterling silver and plated silver cigarette cases, fancy pieces and flatware.

MERIDEN SILVER PLATE CO.
Meriden, Connecticut
(See International Silver Co.)

Organized in 1869 by Charles Casper and others. George R. Curtis was president. One of the original companies to become part of the International Silver Company in 1898.

(*On Cheaper Grade.*)

EUREKA SILVER PLATE CO.
MERIDEN SILVER PLATE CO.

MERIDEN STERLING CO.
Meriden, Connecticut

Listed in J C-K 1896 in the sterling silver section. Out of business before 1904.

MERMOD & JACCARD
JEWELRY CO.
St. Louis, Missouri

Established in 1829 by Louis Jaccard who was joined by A. S. Mermod in 1845. In 1848, D. C. Jaccard, relative of Louis Jaccard, joined. In 1865 Goodman King became associated with the firm. In 1901 they absorbed the E. Jaccard Jewelry Co. and Merrick, Walsh & Phelphs Jewelry. In 1905 the name of King was added to the firm name.

In 1917 they became part of Scruggs, Vandervoort & Barney but retain their identity as a separate corporate body.

MERRILL BROS. & CO.
New York, New York

Merrill Brothers & Company was listed in J C-K 1896 as manufacturers of sterling silver and pewter. By 1922 the name was The Merrill Co., Inc. and it became The Merrill Shops before 1931.

MERRY & PELTON SILVER CO.
St. Louis, Missouri
(See Pelton Bros. Silver Plate Co.)

(Hollowware.)

SECTIONAL PLATE XII
STANDARD PLATE 4
TRIPLE PLATE 12
(Flatware.)

(Hollowware.)

Listed J C-K 1904 as manufacturers of plated silver holloware and flatware. Out of business before 1909. Not listed in St. Louis City Directories which were checked back to 1840.

MERWIN-WILSON CO., INC.
New Milford, Connecticut

Company established by the Merwin brothers in 1912 as successors to Bennett Merwin Silver Company. Shortly afterwards one brother was killed.

Roy (?) Wilson joined the remaining Merwin. The company made pewter reproductions and plated silver prize cups and trophies until 1935 when they sold out to Robert Oliver who operated under the name of Danforth Company. The company and its molds have changed hands several times since that time and are thought to be in use now in the manufacture of pewter reproductions in Woodbury, Connecticut.

METALLURGIC ART CO.
Baltimore, Maryland

Listed in Jewelers' Weekly as manufacturers of sterling silverware in 1896.

First listed in the Baltimore City Directory in 1895 as Victor G. Bloede, Carl Schon, jewelry manufacturers. In 1896 the listing is Metallurgic Art Company. In 1900 Bloede and Carl Schon, Jr. are listed as members of the firm.

In 1901 the Metallurgic Art Company is no longer listed. Bloede is listed as president of Victor G. Bloede, Manufacturing Chemists. Schon is not listed at all.

METAL PRODUCTS CORP.
Providence, Rhode Island

MPRD

Manufacturers of plated silverware c. 1920. Out of business before 1922.

METROPOLITAN SILVER CO.
(John Toothill)
New York, New York

Listed in J C-K in 1896–1904 in plated silver section. Out of business before 1915.

MEXICAN CRAIG
(See Holmes & Edwards Silver Co.)

MEXICAN SILVER
(See Holmes & Edwards Silver Co.)

MEYER & WARNE
Philadelphia, Pennsylvania

Silverplaters c. 1859–1880?

MIAMI SILVER CO.
Cincinnati, Ohio

Listed in City Directories 1903–1912 as silverplaters.

MIDDLESEX SILVER CO.
(See Middletown Silver Co.)

MIDDLETOWN PLATE CO.
Middletown, Connecticut
(See International Silver Co.)

COLUMBIA

SUPERIOR

Organized in 1864 as makers of silverplated holloware. Were among the original companies which formed the International Silver Co. in 1898.

This trademark adopted about 1866.

MIDDLETOWN SILVER CO.
Middletown, Connecticut

MIDDLETOWN SILVERWARE

Listed in J C-K in 1909–1922 as manufacturers of plated silverware. Last record found was 1936.

(On britannia)

(On nickel silver)

MIDDLESEX SILVER CO.

(on plated nickel silver)

MILDRED QUALITY SILVER PLATE
(See National Silver Co.)

MILFORD SILVER CO.

Known only from name stamped on souvenir flatware.

THE MILLER JLY. CO.
Cincinnati, Ohio

M STERLING

Listed in J C-K 1915 in the sterling silver section and in jewelry. Last listing in 1922.

WM. J. MILLER
Baltimore, Maryland

Listed in Baltimore City Directories 1904–1920 as a silversmith.

MITCHELL & POOL
Baltimore, Maryland

Listed in Baltimore City Directory in 1889 as silverplaters. Succeeded by B. Pool & Company in 1894.

G. I. MIX & CO.
Yalesville, Connecticut

CROWN PRINCE
MALACCA PLATED
THE COLUMBIA

"In 1848 Charles Parker and Garry I. Mix began the manufacture of Britannia and German silverware, continuing until 1854, when Mix retired to establish himself in business at Yalesville. Parker and Jeralds (Thomas and Bennet) continued at the old place as the Parker Mfg. Co. In 1857 the old mill and factory buildings were destroyed by fire and a new factory erected.

In 1876 the Parker Mfg. Co. discontinued the manufacture of German silverware, but the production of Britannia spoons has since been carried on, in a limited way, by Bennet Jeralds.

G. I. Mix & Co. at Yalesville, are extensive manufacturers of Britannia goods . . . In 1886 steam power—50 horse—was added to the water motor, and the capacity for production was increased." HISTORY OF NEW HAVEN COUNTY CONNECTICUT, Vol. 1. Edited by J. L. Rockey.

JAMES MIX
Albany, New York

JAMES MIX

The James Mix who designed the James Mix "Albany" souvenir spoon c. 1890 may have been a descendent of James Mix, silversmith in Albany, New York, 1817–1850. His son, James Mix, Jr., was listed in the Albany City Directories as a manufacturing jeweler, 1846–1850.

M. M. CO.
(See Macomber Mfg. Co.)

JACOB A. MOLLER
New Rochelle, New York

Listed in 1907 New Rochelle City Directory as a silversmith. No other listing.

MONARCH SILVER CO.
(See Knickerbocker Silver Co.)
(See Standard Silver Co.)

MONTAUK SILVER CO.
(See J. W. Johnson)

MONTGOMERY BROS.
Los Angeles, California

The Los Angeles City Directories list James Montgomery as watchmaker and jeweler from 1883–1886. The first listing for Montgomery Bros. (Jas. A. and Geo. A.) is for the year 1888. The same listing is carried for 1890. No distinction made between retailers and manufacturers in the directories.

On October 27, 1891, Montgomery Bros. registered Patent No. 20,270 for the manufacture of gold, silver and plated articles, flatware and jewelry. Their trademark is listed in J C-K souvenir section.

MONUMENTAL PLATING WORKS
Baltimore, Maryland

Listed in Baltimore City Directories 1887–1912 as silverplaters. Wm. Focke, proprietor.

MOORE BROS.
Attleboro, Massachusetts

M.B.

Listed in Attleboro City Directories as manufacturing jewelers with John F. and Thomas H. Moore as owners from 1907-1916 and John F., Thomas H. and Charles E. Moore from 1916-1940.

MOORE & HOFMAN
Newark, New Jersey
(See Schmitz, Moore & Co.)

Successors to Schmitz, Moore & Co. between 1915-1922. Succeeded by Moore & Son (?) before 1943.

Manufacturers of sterling silver dresserware, vanity and cigarette cases, tableware and novelties.

MOORE & LEDING, SILVERSMITHS
Washington, D. C.

Listed in the Washington, D. C. City Directories from 1882 to 1902. Listed as Moore & Leding, 1882-1899, jewelers. Listed as Robert Leding (successor to Moore & Leding) 1900-1902, jeweler.

Moore & Leding marketed the "Washington City" and "Mount Vernon" souvenir spoons, both made by The Gorham Company. These two spoons were patented in 1890 and 1891, respectively, and were put on the market shortly after the first Witch spoon designed for Daniel Low Company.

MT. VERNON COMPANY
SILVERSMITHS, INC.
Mount Vernon, New York
(See Gorham Corporation)

Founded in 1903 through the merger of the Hayes & McFarland Company of Mount Vernon, the Mauser Mfg. Company of New York and Roger Williams Silver Company of Providence, Rhode Island.

Purchased by the Gorham Corporation in 1913.

MULFORD, WENDELL & CO.
Albany, New York

Their history can be traced to William Boyd, silversmith (b. 1775-d. 1840) who entered into partnership with Robert Shepard in 1810, under the name Shepard & Boyd (c. 1810-1830). They were succeeded by Boyd & Hoyt (c. 1830-1842); Boyd & Mulford (c. 1832-1842) and Mulford, Wendell & Co. c. 1843.

John H. Mulford and William Wendell, are listed as silversmiths, as are their predecessors.

Mulford and Wendell were also jobbers who did silverplating about 1855. They published an illustrated catalog in 1859.

MULHOLLAND BROS. INC.
Aurora, Illinois

Successor to Aurora Silver Plate Company between 1915-1922. Continued the manufacture of plated flatware and holloware until 1934 when they went out of business. D. E. Mulholland, president; W. S. Mulholland, vice president.

S. F. MYERS & CO.
New York, New York

In business about 1860 as specialists in plating. (U. S. Patent, February 8, 1887) for jewelry and silverware, plated silver and clocks.

MYRICK, ROLLER & HOLBROOK
Philadelphia, Pennsylvania

In business before 1890. Out of business before 1904. Trademark found on souvenir spoons.

N

NAPIER-BLISS CO.
Meriden, Connecticut
(See Napier Co.)

Successor to E. A. Bliss Co. about 1915. Succeeded by the Napier Company in 1920.

NAPIER COMPANY
Meriden, Connecticut

NAPIER CO.

NAPIER

The present Napier Company began as Carpenter & Bliss, established in North Attleboro, Massachusetts, in 1875. Succeeded by E. A. Bliss Co., Meriden, Connecticut in 1883; became the Napier-Bliss Co. about 1915 and the Napier Company in 1920.

Manufacturers of sterling and plated silver novelties, jewelry and silverware.

Registered U. S. Patent No. 144,870, July 19, 1921 for jewelry.

NASCO
(See National Silver Company)

NASSAU LIGHTER CO.
New York, New York

Listed J C-K in sterling silver section in 1915. Out of business before 1922.

NATIONAL CUTLERY CO.
(See Rockford Plate Silver Co.)

NATIONAL SILVER COMPANY
New York, New York

MILDRED QUALITY
SILVER PLATE

Manufacturers of sterling and plated silverware. Began with Samuel E. Bernstein who was first in business in New York in 1890. Became the National Silver Company before 1904.

Cheltenham & Company, Ltd., Sheffield, England, became a division of National Silver Company before 1950; the F. B. Rogers Silver Company was added in February 1955 and in 1956 they purchased the Ontario Manufacturing Company of Muncie, Indiana.

NATIONAL SILVER DEPOSIT
WARE CO., INC.
New York, New York

Listed in J C-K 1922-1950. Manufacturers of silver and gold encrusted glassware, desk sets, ornamental serving trays and silver plated holloware.

T. E. NEILL CO.
Brooklyn, New York

TENCO

NEVADA SILVER METAL
(See Standard Silverware Co.)

NEVIUS COMPANY
New York, New York

Registered a trademark, No. 48,036, December 5, 1905 for table utensils made of sterling silver. The application was filed by Benjamin C. Nevius, treasurer, who stated that the trademark had been used continuously by them since 1897.

Out of business before 1915.

NEW AMSTERDAM SILVER CO.
New York, New York
(See Knickerbocker Silver Co.)

NEW ENGLAND CUTLERY CO.
(See American Silver Co.)

NEW ENGLAND SILVER CO.
Deering, Maine

NEW ENGLAND SILVER CO.
QUADRUPLE PLATE.

Founded in 1894 by Joseph S. Dunham, son of Rufus Dunham. Joseph had formerly been associated with Stevens, Smart & Dunham.

NEW ENGLAND SILVER PLATE CO.
(See Adelphi Silver Plate Co.)
(See American Silver Co.)
(See Bristol Brass & Clock Co.)

NEW YORK SILVER DEPOSIT CO.
Jersey City, New Jersey

Began as New York Silver Deposit Company, founding date unknown. Suceeded by Imperial Art Ware before 1915 and out of business before 1922.

NEW YORK STAMPING CO.
Brooklyn, New York

(*Housefurnishing Goods.*)

Listed in J C-K in 1915–1922 in plated silver section.

NEWBURYPORT SILVER CO.
Keene, New Hampshire

nSco
(*Sterling Silver Ware.*)

N. S. C.

(On plated silver)

Listed in the City Directory of Keene, New Hampshire 1905–1914. John Currier, Pres., Geo. E. Stickney, Treas., Caleb Stickney, Mgr. Makers of sterling silver, flat and holloware.

Founded by Caleb Stickney about 1904–1905. He was once associated with the Towle Silver Company in Newburyport, Massachusetts, but left it to start his own business in Keene.

The business was not successful and failed within a few years.

WILLIAM F. NEWHALL
Lynn, Massachusetts

First established as a jewelry business by Stephen Cyrus Newhall in 1872. William Frederick Newhall entered the employ of his brother at that time and in 1885, after the death of Stephen, William succeeded to the business. In 1907 he took into partnership his eldest son, Fred Clinton Newhall. The company name became W. F. Newhall & Sons, Inc. before 1922.

Stephen is listed in the Lynn City Directories as a clock repairer,

watchmaker and jeweler. William is listed as a clerk, jeweler and optician. Newhall's did special order work, enameling, engraving, die sinking and gold and silver-plating.

The 1896–1922 editions of J C-K carry a trademark (No. 19,751, June 23, 1891 for flat and tableware) that is the handle of a spoon with an old woman and a cat. Newhall's sold many souvenir spoons. Some, at least, carry the Durgin Co. trademark.

There is no record of the shop after 1957.

E. NEWTON & CO.
New York, New York

STERLING **N**

Listed in J C-K 1896–1904 in the sterling silver section. Out of business before 1915.

NIAGARA SILVER CO.
New York, New York
(See Oneida Silversmiths)
(See Wm. A. Rogers, Ltd.)

R. S. MFG. CO.
COIN SILVER METAL
EXTRA ᶜᴼᴵᴺ ˢᴵᴸᵛᴱᴿ PLATE
EXTRA ᶜᴼᴵᴺ ˢᴵᴸᵛᴱᴿ No. 12 PLATE

NICHOLS BROS.
Greenfield, Massachusetts

NICHOLS BROS.
Greenfield, Mass.
12 dwt.

Listed in 1896 Jewelers' Weekly as manufacturers of plated silverware.

NIEDERER & MOORE
Baltimore, Maryland

Listed in Baltimore City Directory in 1885 as a silversmith.

GEBRUEDER NOELLE
Luedenscheid, Germany

(Knives, Forks, Spoons.)

Registered trademark U. S. Patent Office, No. 11,800, December 16, 1884 for knives, forks and spoons. Also, No. 50,984, April 3, 1906 for knives, forks and spoons of britannia.

Listed in J C-K 1896–1922 in the plated silver section. No record after 1922.

NORTH AMERICA
(See James J. Dawson Co.)

NORTHERN STAMPING & MFG. CO.
Seattle, Washington
(See E. J. Towle Mfg. Co.)

NORWICH CUTLERY COMPANY
Norwich, Connecticut
(See International Silver Company)

Organized and wholly owned by William H. Watrous, of Rogers Cutlery Company, Hartford, Connecticut.

Made cutlery for plating from about 1890. Did not use a trademark because they sold their products to other silver manufacturers.

One of the original companies to become part of the International Silver Company in 1898.

WILLIAM NOST CO., INC.
New York, New York

William Nost was a silversmith in New York before 1915. Succeeded by William Nost Company, Inc. before 1922. They made sterling silver holloware.

NOVELTY PLATING WORKS
Baltimore, Maryland

Listed in the Baltimore City Directories 1890-1915 as successors to Schrier & Protze who began silverplating in 1888.

Anton Protze listed as proprietor 1893-1898. Louis Liepman, proprietor 1899-1915.

NOYES BROTHERS
New York, New York

Wholesalers of silverware and novelties. Begun in New York in 1892 by Pierrepont and Holton Noyes, sons of John Humphrey Noyes, founder of the Oneida Community.

This partnership was dissolved after about two years with Holton going into the restaurant business and Pierrepont Noyes returning to Niagara Falls to develop the Oneida Community silver company.

BENJ. D. NUITZ
Baltimore, Maryland

Listed in 1893 Baltimore City Directory under plated silverware.

NUSSBAUM & HUNOLD
Providence, Rhode Island
(See Walter Hunold)

NUSSHOLD

O

OHIO SILVER PLATE CO.
(See Queen Silver Co.)

OLD ENGLISH BRAND, B.
(See American Silver Co.)

OLD NEWBURY CRAFTERS, INC.
Newburyport, Massachusetts

Incorporated in 1916 by silver-smiths of long experience. It has been producing and distributing fine handwrought silverware and holloware continuously since that date.

At the present time, the company is the largest producer of handwrought silver in the United States.

In 1964 they purchased the Worden-Munnis Co., founded in Boston in 1940 and are now producing their sterling holloware line.

Each craftsman at Old Newbury Crafters has a personal signature mark that is stamped on each piece of silver flatware.

Personal Signature Marks of the

Fletcher S. Carter

Chester A. Dow

James F. Harvey

Robert H. Lapham

Gayden F. Marshall

Daniel S. Morrill

Roger R. Rowell

Reynolds F. Senior

George R. Woundy

In use as of June, 1965

N. & D. ONDERDONK
New York, New York

N. & D. O.

N. & D. Onderdonk were silver-smiths working in New York c. 1800. They are listed in J C-K in the sterling silver section. Out of business before 1904.

ONEIDA SILVERSMITHS
Sherrill, New York

J. ROGERS & CO.
A.1. NICKEL SILVER NO. 210
CARBON
N. F. SILVER CO., 1877
SILVER METAL
210 NEARSILVER
U. S. SILVER CO.
ALPHA PLATE
COMMUNITY
COMMUNITY PLATE
DURO PLATE
N. F. NICKEL SILVER
NIAGARA FALLS CO., 1877
O. C.
O. C. LUSTRA
ONEIDA
ONEIDA COMMUNITY DIAMOND
    PLATE
ONEIDA COMMUNITY PAR PLATE
ONEIDA COMMUNITY RELIANCE
    PLATE
ONEIDA COMMUNITY SILVER
    PLATE
REX PLATE
RELIANCE
RELIANCE PLATE
TRIPLE PLUS
TUDOR PLATE
ONEIDACRAFT

John Humphrey Noyes and a little association of men first began their experiment in communal living at Oneida Creek about 1848.

Their first products were canned fruits and vegetables which found a ready market. Later their chief support came from the manufacture of steel traps.

In 1877 the Oneida Community embarked on the manufacture of tableware. The Wallingford branch made ungraded, tinned, iron spoons in two patterns called "Lily" and "Oval." These two iron spoons were the direct ancestors of the whole line of Community Plate.

By 1878 the mill was turning out steel spoon blanks sold for plating to the Meriden Britannia Company. In 1880 the factory was moved to Niagara Falls.

Their first silverware could not compete with higher quality silver made by other companies. A decision was made to turn out a better quality and better designed line. Their new design, called "Avalon" was exhibited in 1901 as the Buffalo Exposition.

In January 1902 the new line of Community Plate was introduced, but, was not immediately successful. A complete change in advertising methods in high-priced, large-circulation magazines proved enormously effective. It was the first "pretty girl" advertising in America and not only affected the sales of their silver, it also had a profound effect on the whole advertising business. Between 1912-1914 the whole silverware plant was moved from Niagara Falls to Sherrill, New York.

In 1926 they opened a plant, the Kenwood Silver Company, in Sheffield, England and in 1929 bought Wm. A. Rogers, Ltd. Besides the main Wm. A. Rogers, Ltd. plant, they acquired four other factories and their brands; 1881 Rogers; Simeon L. & George H. Rogers Company and Heirloom.

One March 1, 1935, the company name was changed to Oneida, Ltd., and is now commonly known as Oneida Silversmiths.

In 1965 they adopted as their symbol of excellence the Roman cube "tessera hospitalis," which was placed in the hands of a visitor as a pledge of hospitality and friendship. Oneida's tessera is a cube of solid silver, engraved with the company name on all planes.

NEIDA STERLING
ee Oneida Silversmiths)

Oneida Sterling

NTARIO MFG. CO.
uncie, Indiana
ee National Silver Company)

Founded 1897. Succeeded by National Silver Company in 1956. Manufactured plated silverware.

RANK N. OSBORNE
ew York, New York

XIX CENTURY
HEIRLOOM

No. 23,729 October 24, 1893
For jewelry, spoons, forks, ladles, cutlery, etc.

HEIRLOOM

No. 23,730 October 24, 1893

Listed in J C-K 1904-1915. May have been wholesale jeweler or distributor.

Also used other trademarks on jewelry sold at the Chicago Columbian Exposition, 1892-1893.

No record after 1915.

WIATT & WARNER
rtland, Oregon

O. & W.

Listed in the Portland City Directory for 1894 and 1895 only. Listed under sterling silver section of the 1896 edition of the J C-K as out of business in 1896. No information in the Portland newspaper index.

P

THE PAIRPOINT CORPORATION
New Bedford, Massachusetts

PAIRPOINT
FLAT 1880 WARE.
BEST
(*Flatware.*)

BRISTOL PLATE CO.

(*Hollowware.*)

TRADE   MARK.

(*Hollowware.*)

Organized in 1880 and became one of the country's largest manufacturers of plated silverware.

In 1894, the Mount Washington Glass Company became part of the Pairpoint Mfg. Co.

In 1900, financial difficulties of both companies led to their merging to form the Pairpoint Corporation. Only the glass working part continued under various firm names. Finally, all operations ceased in 1958.

PAIRPOINT MFG. CO.
New Bedford, Massachusetts
(See The Pairpoint Corporation)

PALMER & BACHELDER
Boston, Massachusetts

In the 1860's they purchased Reed & Barton wares "in the metal" and operated their own plating establishment.

PALMER & OWEN
Cincinnati, Ohio

Listed in Cincinnati City Directories 1850-1859 as silversmiths who operated a silverware factory.

PALMER & PECKHAM
North Attleboro, Massachusetts

P & P
STERLING.

Listed in J C-K 1896. Out of business before 1904.

PARKER & CASPER BRITANNIA CO.
(See Parker & Casper)

PARKER & CASPER CO.
Meriden, Connecticut
(See International Silver Co.)
(See Wilcox Silver Plate Co.)

Organized by Charles Casper, John E. Parker, Edmund Parker, Phillip S. Pelton and Samuel L. Dodd, Jr. Incorporated August 6, 1866 with Samuel Dodd, president, under the name Parker & Casper Britannia Co. In May 1867 it became Parker & Caspar Co.

They were specialists in silver-plated holloware.

The business was sold in 1869 to the Wilcox Silver Plate Co. which became part of International Silver Co. in 1898.

PARKS BROS. & ROGERS
Providence, Rhode Island
and New York

Established in 1892 by Geo. W. Parks, W. C. Parks and E. I. Rogers. Manufacturing jewelers.

Their trademark is similar to that of the Howard Sterling Co. About 1893 they occupied the same building as Howard Sterling Co. and Hamilton & Hamilton, Jr., though no relationship has been established.

Not listed after 1930.

C. W. PARKS COMPANY
Providence, Rhode Island

HOPE SILVER CO.

(On plated silver)

(On sterling silver)

Successors to Hayden Mfg. Co. before 1909. Listed in J C-K in 1909–1915 as manufacturers of sterling and plated silver. Out of business before 1922.

PAUL REVERE SILVER CO., INC.
Boston, Massachusetts

PAUL REVERE

Registered trademark U. S. Patent No. 85,612, March 5, 1912 for plated silverware. Out of business before 1922.

PAYE & BAKER MFG. CO.
North Attleboro, Massachusetts

Successors to Simmons & Paye before 1891. Their first products were souvenir spoons of sterling silver. They also made plated silver table novelties, holloware and Dutch silver reproductions.

Last record found was c. 1935.

GEO. W. PAYSON & CO.
Baltimore, Maryland

Listed in Baltimore City Directory in 1904 as a silversmith.

PELTON BROS. SILVER PLATE CO.
St. Louis, Missouri
(See Merry & Pelton Silver Co.)

**TRIPLE PLATE 12
SECTIONAL PLATE XII
STANDARD PLATE 4**
(*Flatware.*)

(*Hollowware.*)

Listed in St. Louis City Directories 1872-1900 as manufacturers of plated silverware.

J. PENFIELD & COMPANY
Savannah, Georgia
(See Black, Starr & Frost, Ltd.)

In business from 1820-1828 Partners were Josiah Penfield Moses Eastman and Frederick Marquand.

PEQUABUCK MFG. CO.
(See American Silver Co.)

W. H. PFEIFFER
Niagara Falls, New York

Listed in the 1890 Niagara Falls City Directory as maker of silver and plated silverware.

PHELPS & CARY CO.
New York, New York
(See Hartford Sterling Co.)
(See The Tennant Co.)

STERLING
TRADE MARK

Listed in J C-K 1904 in sterling silver section as out of business Trademark identical to that of Hartford Sterling Co. and The Tennant Co. except for initials in shield.

PHILADELPHIA
SILVERSMITHING CO.
Philadelphia, Pennsylvania

Listed in J C-K in sterling silver section 1915-1922. Last record found was c. 1935.

PHILADELPHIA PLATE CO.

Attributed in **Century of Silver,** to a Division of the International Silver Company. Not confirmed by them.

THOMAS PHILE
Baltimore, Maryland

Listed in Baltimore City Directories 1871-1872, 1879-1887 as a whitesmith.

ALBERT PICK & CO.
Bridgeport, Connecticut

Manufacturers of plated silver flatware and holloware. Successors to the E. H. H. Smith Silver Company in 1920. Last appeared in the Bridgeport City Directory in 1927.

PILGRIM
(See Friedman Silver Co., Inc.)

PITTSBURGH SILVERWARE CO.
Pittsburgh, Pennsylvania

Listed in the Pittsburgh City Directories from 1884 through 1887.

The 1884 directory lists it as the Pittsburgh Silverware Installment Company.

The 1885, 1886 and 1887 directories list it as the Pittsburgh Silverware Company.

The 1887 directory gives the last listing as follows: Pittsburgh Silverware Company, 511 Market St., Manufacturers' Agents for Fine Electro-Plated Ware, Silverware, watches, jewelry leased on easy payments. F. R. Jones, Manager. No trademark shown.

PITTSBURGH SILVERWARE
INSTALLMENT COMPANY
Pittsburgh, Pennsylvania
(See Pittsburgh Silverware Co.)

Listed in the Pittsburgh City Directory 1884.

GUSTAVUS & POHLMAN
Baltimore, Maryland

Listed in Baltimore City Directories 1903–1904 as a silversmith.

POMPEIAN GOLD
(See Weidlich Bros. Mfg. Co.)

POOL & CO.
Baltimore, Maryland

Listed in Baltimore City Directories 1899–1915 as successors to B. Pool & Co.

B. POOL & CO.
Baltimore, Maryland

Listed in Baltimore City Directories 1894–1898 as silverplaters. Successors to Mitchell & Pool who were first listed in 1889. Succeeded by Pool & Co. in 1899.

POOLE & ROCHE
(See Poole Silver Co., Inc.)

POOLE SILVER CO.
Taunton, Massachusetts

(On sterling silver)

(Quadruple Plate.)

POOLE SILVER CO.
TAUNTON, MASS
NICKEL SILVER

SHEFFIELD PLATE

(On plated silver)

Founded in 1893 in Taunton, Massachusetts with a small two-room factory as manufacturers of plated silverware. Originally called Poole & Roche. Mr. Poole bought out his partner Mr. Roche and was sole owner until his death when his three sons took over the active management. In 1946 they retired and sold the company to an investment group headed by Sidney A Kane of Providence, Rhode Island The company has grown rapidly.

In 1946 a sterling silver department was added and in 1964 a brass division.

Today the company operates the Poole Silver Company for plated holloware, the Bristol Silver division, founded in 1950, for popular priced plated holloware as well as the above.

POOLE STERLING CO., INC.
(See Poole Silver Co., Inc.)

POPE'S ISLAND MFG.
CORPORATION
New Bedford, Massachusetts

Incorporated in 1890 on the island from which it took its name. Horse bits and harness trimming were manufactured at these works. As the company was listed among manufacturers of silverplated wares by the J C-K 1896 until 1915, some of these trappings must have been plated silver.

PORTER BRITANNIA & PLATE
COMPANY
Taunton, Massachusetts

Organized in 1859. E. W. Porter of Reed & Barton, became superintendent of the new company. Their products were similar to those made by Reed & Barton. In business at least until 1866.

THE POTOSI SILVER CO.
Birmingham, England

(*White Metal.*)

Founded by Levi and Salaman who were electro-platers and silversmiths in 1870. They absorbed the Potosi Silver Company in 1878.

It was succeeded by Barker Bros. Silversmiths, Ltd., Unity Works, Birmingham, England between 1915 and 1922.

On October 19, 1886 they registered a U. S. Patent for plated silver on white metal.

The Potosi Silver Company name was probably derived from the Potosi Mine, discovered in 1545 in the area that was later to be named Bolivia.

. C. POWELL
New York, New York

P 🦉

Listed in J C-K in sterling silver section in 1909 as out of business.

PREMIER CUTLERY INC.
New York, New York

Elk

Manufacturers of plated silver cutlery c. 1920.

PREMIER SILVER CO.
Brooklyn, New York

Manufacturers of sterling silverware c. 1920.

PRESTO CIGARETTE CASE CORP.
North Attleboro, Massachusetts

Manufacturers of gold, sterling and plated silver cigarette cases c. 1920-1930.

J. N. PROVENZANO
New York, New York

(On Knives.)

In business before 1896. Distributors (?) of sterling silverware, gold and platinum seed pearl and gun metal goods.
Not listed after 1904.

PROVIDENCE SILVER PLATE CO.
(See Aurora Silver Plate Co.)

PROVIDENCE STOCK CO.
Providence, Rhode Island

TRADE MARK.

Listed in J C-K in 1896-1904 in sterling silver section. Subsequent listings are under jewelry and watch attachments, chains, fobs and bracelets. Last record found was 1950.

PRYOR MFG. CO., INC.
Newark, New Jersey

Listed in J C-K in 1915 in sterling silver section.
Consolidated with B. M. Shanley, Jr., Co. between 1915-1922.

PUTNAM & LOW
(See Shreve, Crump & Low Co., Inc.)

Q

QUAKER SILVER CO., INC.
North Attleboro, Massachusetts
(See Gorham Corporation)

QUAKER
VOGUE

Makers of sterling silver holloware. Founded in North Attleboro, Massachusetts about 1930. Purchased by the Gorham Corporation in 1959.

QUEEN CITY SILVER CO., INC.
Cincinnati, Ohio

Manufacturers of plated silver
holloware c. 1888. Last record
found was 1931.

R

HARRY S. RAINS
New York, New York

LA MILITAIRE

Silverplaters c. 1920.

RAND & CRANE
Boston, Massachusetts

HOLMES

First record found was U. S. Patent registration for HOLMES
trademark, May 5, 1891 to be

used on solid and plated souvenir
spoons and forks.

The company was listed in J C-K
1896–1922, but the HOLMES
trademark was not used after
1903.

C. RAY RANDALL & CO.
North Attleboro, Massachusetts

STERLING CRR

Manufacturers of sterling silver,
10k gold and gold-filled bar pins,

brooches, necklaces, belt buckles,
scarf pins, links and pin sets.

Listed in J C-K 1915–1922. Last
record found was 1935.

RANDALL & FAIRCHILD
(See Fairchild & Co.)

RANDALL HALL & CO.

Known only from name stamped
on flatware.

DAVID REAY, JR.
Baltimore, Maryland

Listed in Baltimore City Directories 1865–1873 as a silverplater.

REDDALL & CO., INC.
Newark, New Jersey

Listed as John W. Reddall & Co. in 1896 Jewelers' Weekly.

Listed in J C-K 1896–1904 in sterling silver section. Out of business before 1909.

REDFIELD & RICE
New York, New York
(See Bernard Rice's Sons)

Founded in 1867. Later Bernard Rice's Sons.

REDLICH & CO.
New York, New York
(See Elgin Silversmith Co., Inc.)

REED & BARTON
Taunton, Massachusetts
(Registered July 29, 1890)

𝕿𝖗𝖆𝖉𝖊 𝕸𝖆𝖗𝖐

𝕾𝖙𝖊𝖗𝖑𝖎𝖓𝖌

TRADE MARK

STERLING

HOPEWELL
SILVER CO.

(Registered July 29, 1890)

(On sterling silver)

Viking Brand

REED & BARTON
(Nickel Silver Flatware and Hollowware.)

REED **&** **BARTON**

TRADE   MARK

(White Metal Hollowware.)

GOLDYN-BRONZ

(On plated silver)

Isaac Babbitt and William W. Crossman, both of Taunton, Massachusetts, formed the partnership of BABBITT & CROSSMAN in 1824 that led to what is now Reed & Barton.

Babbitt had opened a small jewelry store in 1822. The small workshop in the back held his attention more than selling jewelry and repairing watches. Aware of the public's preference for the new britannia ware, he often discussed its properties with his friend, William Porter, who was also a jeweler.

Early in 1824, after much experimenting, Babbitt hit upon the right combination for producing this new alloy.

William Crossman completed his apprenticeship in the jewelers trade; became dissatisfied with his job in Castleton, Vermont and returned to Taunton.

Babbitt and Crossman decided to pool their resources and experience in a partnership to manufacture britannia ware, though they did not abandon the jewelry store.

They entered this new industry just at the time when mechanization put many establishments, that continued hand-wrought production, out of business. Because of the uncertainty of their ability to produce and market britannia, they also turned out a great deal of pewter.

Their business prospered so that in 1826 they were able to build a new shop on Fayette Street, equipped with steam power. New machinery was made by Nathaniel Leonard of Taunton. Babbit was superintendent; William W. Porter, foreman and it is assumed that Crossman managed the jewelry store and sales of the new factory products.

By 1827, with business increasing, more capital was needed so William Allen West bought into the business and a new partnership was formed under the name BABBITT, CROSSMAN & COMPANY. The jewelry store was apparently sold at this time.

On February 18, 1829, Isaac Babbitt sold his interest in the partnership and Zephaniah A. Leonard bought a one-third interest. The new company of CROSSMAN, WEST & LEONARD was formed.

On August 18, 1830 this partnership was dissolved and a joint-stock company, the TAUNTON BRITANNIA MANUFACTURING COMPANY was formed.

On February 16, 1833 the TAUNTON BRITANNIA MANUFACTURING COMPANY was reorganized. When it failed in November 1834, only three people had faith to continue. They were the company agent, Benjamin Pratt; Henry Reed, a spinner and his friend, Charles E. Barton, the solderer.

Barton, brother-in-law of William Crossman, had moved to Taunton from Warren, Rhode Island and started to work in 1827 at the age of 19 as an apprentice.

Henry Good Reed was the son of a family prominent in Taunton for five generations.

Knowledge of britannia manufacturing was their chief asset. To this, Benjamin Pratt contributed his experience in salesmanship. Once again, April 1, 1835, the TAUNTON BRITANNIA MANUFACTURING COMPANY was under new management.

Reed & Barton rented a few of the tools and equipment of the old company while Pratt sold what he could and tried to collect money owed to the company. By the end of 1836, the business had survived and made slight gains. Horatio Leonard transferred to his son, Gustavus, all rights, title and the stock and tools of the business. Soon afterwards an agreement was drawn up that left ownership of the factory itself in the Leonard family and granted to Reed & Barton one-third ownership each in the tools of the company as well as one-third interest in profits. The Taunton Britannia Manufacturing Company remained in legal existence only in the capacity of a landlord. The operating company was known as LEONARD, REED & BARTON and on February 20, 1837 began business under the new name.

The year 1837 was not an auspicious one for a struggling business. More than 600 banks closed their doors. Nine-tenths of the factories of the eastern states were said to have closed. Once again, they managed to survive.

By 1840, Henry Reed and Charles Barton purchased Leonard's interest in the company. Leonard continued to work for the company as salesman-treasurer and the Leonard, Reed & Barton mark was used on some company wares. However, when the company applied for a renewal of their trademark registration, they claimed that the name "REED & BARTON" had been used since August 26, 1840. Possibly both marks were used from 1840 to 1847.

By 1848, Reed & Barton were turning their attention to plated silverware.

The transition from the 1837 Reed & Barton shops to the 1859 factory was gradual, but, inevitable. Specialization emerged through necessity for business growth. New marketing methods were introduced and were extremely successful.

The 1850's, with its demands far exceeding the producing capacities of some large companies, gave rise to a confusing competitive situation. Started by the Meriden Britannia Company, which purchased large quantities of wares from other manufacturers, other companies soon followed. This often placed the manufacturer in the position of competing with his own goods. Goods manufactured by Reed & Barton might be sent to Hartford for a coating of Rogers Bros. silver plate and a Rogers Bros. stamp, and appear in the market in competition with the Reed & Barton plated line.

In the middle 1860's jobbers, and retailers, who operated their own plating shops purchased two-thirds of the factory output. They purchased quantities of wares "in the metal," plated them and sold them with their own trademarks. Practically none of the britannia or plated silver makers could supply a complete line. Reed & Barton and the Meriden Britannia Company offered the greatest assortment, yet Reed & Barton bought most of its flatware from Rogers & Brother and the Hartford Manufacturing Company. They produced little of their own flatware except for the hotel trade until the 1860's. Flatware of almost all manufacturers turned up in many different catalogs and with many trademarks. Rogers & Brother, on the other hand, in 1865 was one of Reed & Barton's largest customers for holloware. That is why it is not unusual to find identical pieces of flatware and holloware bearing the trademarks of either company.

The depression of 1866 and 1867 brought about the failure of many jobbing concerns, a large number of whom abandoned plating and confined themselves to wholesale business.

The extension of the market for solid silver services led Reed & Barton into its production in 1889.

On September 13, 1867, Charles Barton died with Henry Reed at his bedside. In 1868 a new partnership, consisting of Henry Reed, Henry Fish and George Babrook who had long been active in marketing, was formed. Each assumed a third interest. The name of the firm continued unchanged. In February, 1888, the company was incorporated.

As early as 1903 Reed & Barton began to reproduce colonial pewter ware which for more than thirty years was popular and a financial success.

Sterling flat and holloware replaced plated ware in more and more homes so that by 1904 sterling had become the largest selling line produced.

In 1911 a moderately low-priced line was marketed under the name Reed Silver Company. It passed out of existence in 1913 because the ware did not come up to the standard expected of the Reed & Barton name.

In 1913 the Hopewell Silver Company was formed to market a high-quality line of small items. They also put out a line of Lenox china with silver and gold deposit. Both lines failed by 1918.

In 1928 Reed & Barton purchased the Dominick & Haff Company of Newark, New Jersey.

In the 1930's the Viking brand of plated holloware was brought out and terminated in 1941 with the revival of a demand for quality wares.

In 1950 the Webster Company became a subsidiary.

REED, BARTON & COMPANY
Taunton, Massachusetts

Set up in 1886 for electroplating. This short-lived enterprise was managed by Edward Barton, son of Charles Barton, and a Waldo Reed, no relation of Henry Reed, but a son-in-law of Charles Barton. They attempted to capitalize on the reputation of the established Reed & Barton name. Bought out in 1892 by Reed & Barton.

REED SILVER COMPANY
(See Reed & Barton)

REEVES & BROWNE
Newark, New Jersey
(See Jennings & Lauter)

REEVES & SILLCOCKS
New York, New York
(See Jennings & Lauter)

THE REGAL SILVER MFG. CO.
New Haven, Connecticut
(See Majestic Silver Co.)

(Used 1910 to present)

REGAL SPECIALTY
MANUFACTURING COMPANY
(See Majestic Silver Company)

REICHENBERG-SMITH CO.
Omaha, Nebraska
(See A. F. Smith)

IMPERIAL SILVER PLATE CO.

RENOMMÉE MFG. CO.
Newark, New Jersey

R. M. CO.

Listed in J C-K 1896–1904 in sterling silver and jewelry sections.

RENTZ BROS.
Minneapolis, Minn.

< STERLING >

Listed in 1896 Jewelers' Weekly as manufacturers of sterling silverware. Also importers of jewelry. Last record found was c. 1935.

REVERE SILVER CO.
Brooklyn, New York
(See Crown Silver, Inc.)

Successor c. 1960 to Revere Silversmiths, Inc., and now a Division of Crown Silver, Inc., New York. Manufacturers of sterling holloware.

JOSEPH T. RICE
Albany, New York
(See Mulford & Wendell)

Silversmith 1813-1853. John H. Mulford was apprenticed to him.

BERNARD RICE'S SONS
New York, New York

DORANTIQUE
(Copper and Brass Novelties.)

Founded in 1867 in New York as Redfield & Rice. A merger of the Apollo Silver Company, Redfield & Rice and Shepard & Rice formed Bernard Rice's Sons before April 18, 1899, as Patent Office records show the registration of No. 32,722, for a trademark to be used on plated silverware, under Bernard Rice's Sons name.

They specialized in plated silver holloware, shaving stands, mirrors and dresser sets. Out of business before 1959.

RICHFIELD PLATE COMPANY
(See Homan Manufacturing Company)

RICHTER MFG. CO.
Providence, Rhode Island

Manufacturers and importers of sterling silver deposit ware, novelties, and cut glass c. 1915-1920.

JOHN H. RILEY
Baltimore, Maryland

Listed in Baltimore City Directories 1876-1883 as a gold and silversmith (gold beater).

GOTTLIEB RITTER
Baltimore, Maryland

Listed in Baltimore City Directories 1895-1899 as a silversmith. Succeeded by Ritter & Sullivan in 1900.

RITTER & SULLIVAN
Baltimore, Maryland

TRADE ⟨R&S⟩ MARK

Gottlieb Ritter listed in Baltimore City Directories as a silversmith 1895-1899. Joined by Wyndham A. Sullivan in 1900 in the firm of Ritter & Sullivan which continued in business until 1915.

RIVERTON SILVER CO.
(See A. R. Justice)

CHAS. M. ROBBINS
Attleboro, Massachusetts

(Flatware.)

(On plated silver)

(Used before 1900)

(Used c. 1900–1926)

(Present mark)

(On sterling silver)

What is now The Robbins Company was born during the election year of 1892.

Charles M. Robbins, the company's founder, became so interested in the presidential campaign that he designed and produced campaign buttons for his favorite candidate in his own simple shed workshop. This was the start of a business which now has more than 20 general product lines.

At one time, The Robbins Company's jewelry enameling department was the largest in the world.

Principal products today are emblems, service and safety awards, badges, commemorative materials, medallions, insignia, religious and organization jewelry, advertising specialties, souvenirs, premiums and costume jewelry.

Charles Robbins was joined in 1904 by Ralph Thompson, who acquired ownership of the company in 1910. In 1912, the Robbins Company was formed.

David M. Jordan, who joined the firm in 1950 as general manager, is president today.

In October, 1961, Robbins acquired a wholly owned Canadian subsidiary, Stephenson, Robbins Company, Ltd., Montreal, Canada.

In July, 1963, The Robbins Company became a wholly owned subsidiary of Continental Communications Corporation of New York. The new owners sold the Canadian subsidiary in 1964.

ROCHESTER STAMPING CO.
Rochester, New York

Silverplaters c. 1920.

ROCKFORD SILVER PLATE CO.
Rockford, Illinois
(See Sheets-Rockford Silver Plate
Co.)

ROCKWELL SILVER CO.
Meriden, Connecticut

Founded in 1907. Listed in J C-K in 1915–1965. Manufacturers (?) of sterling silverware, china, glassware and silver depositware.

RODEN BROS., LTD.
Toronto, Ontario

STERLING SILVER

ELECTRO PLATE

In business at least as early as 1891 as Roden Bros. Listed J C-K 1904–1922. Became Roden Bros., Ltd. between 1904–1915. Distributors or jobbers (?) of sterling silverware, plated silver, novelties and cut glass.

JOSEPH RODGERS & SONS
Sheffield, England

✳ ✠

(On sterling silver)

RODGERS

(On plated silver)

Cutlers, silversmiths and electroplaters for more than two centuries. Also manufacturers of

silver and plated wares. Their trademark was probably the oldest in continuous use, being granted in 1682. Registered trademark U. S. Patent Office, No. 16,478, April 9, 1889. No record after 1922.

ROEDER & KIERSKY
New York, New York

R. & K.

STERLING.

Listed in J C-K in 1896 in sterling silver section.

ASA ROGERS, JR. & CO.
(See Rogers Brothers)

Successors to Rogers & Cole on June 4, 1832 when John A. Cole retired from the firm. The business

was bought by William Rogers July 28, 1838.

ROGERS & BRITTIN
West Stratford, Connecticut

 UNXLD

Trademark registered May 4, 1880
by Rogers & Brittin, West Stratford, Connecticut for britannia,
plated silver and solid silverware.
Out of business before 1904.

(Britannia, Silver Plated and Solid Ware.)

ROGERS & BROTHER
Waterbury, Connecticut
(See Rogers Brothers)

(Hollowware.)

★ **ROGERS & BRO., A 1.**
  (Best Quality Flatware.)

R. & B.
  (Second Quality Flatware.)

★ **ROGERS & BROTHER,**
  (H. H. Knives.)

★ **ROGERS & BROTHER, 12**
  (No. 12 Steel Knives.)

★ **R & B**
  (Pearl Knives.)

**ROGERS & BRO.—GERMAN SIL-
VER**
  (German Silver Flatware, Unplated.)

MANOR PLATE
(on low priced line)

Established by Asa, Jr. and Simeon
Rogers in 1858. One of the origi-
nal companies that became part of
International Silver Co. in 1898.

ROGERS BROS.
(See Rogers Brothers)

In 1847, Asa Rogers, Jr., with his
brothers produced and distributed
plated silver spoons carrying the
ROGERS BROS. trademark.

ROGERS BROS. MFG. CO.
(See Rogers Brothers)

Organized 1853, by William and
Asa Rogers, Jr. Simeon Rogers became a stockholder in a few
months. Consolidated with Rogers,
Smith & Co., October 1, 1861 because of financial difficulties.

ROGERS BROTHERS

In 1820 William, the eldest, left the parental farm to become an apprentice to Joseph Church, jeweler and silversmith in Hartford, Connecticut.

In 1825 William became Church's partner in making coin silver spoons stamped, CHURCH & ROGERS. Before 1835, Asa, Jr. and Simeon Rogers were both associated with the firm. William also stamped spoons with his individual (EAGLE) WM. ROGERS (STAR) mark during this time (1825-1841). His spoons are noted for their symmetrical outline, pleasing proportions and fine finish.

Early in 1830 Asa, Jr. formed a partnership with John A. Cole. in New Britain, ROGERS & COLE, to manufacture coin silver flatware.

When Cole retired on June 4, 1832 the name of the firm was changed to ASA ROGERS, JR. & CO. with William Rogers as a partner.

In 1834 William left the company and Asa, Jr. continued the business alone, moving to Hartford. William continued his partnership with Church while associated with Asa, Jr. in New Britain. This partnership continued until August 2, 1836 when William moved to his own shop, under the name WILLIAM ROGERS. He was probably the first in this country to advertise and manufacture tableware of sterling silver as it had been the general practice to use coin silver.

On July 23, 1838 William bought the spoon manufactory of Asa, Jr. In 1841 Asa, Jr. advertised that he was once again making spoons.

Simeon learned the trade in William's business and in 1841 was admitted as a partner in the jewelry and silverware store, WM. ROGERS & CO., with the new mark, (EAGLE) WM. ROGERS & CO. (STAR) stamped on their coin silver spoons.

About 1843-1844 Asa, Jr. experimented with electroplating in association with Wm. B. Cowles and James H. Isaacson and on November 13, 1845 the COWLES MFG. CO. in Granby was formed to manufacture German and silverplated spoons, forks, etc. Stockholders were Wm. B. Cowles, Asa Rogers, Jr., Jas. H. Isaacson and John D. Johnson. In 1846 Asa, Jr., William and Isaacson left COWLES MFG. CO. and it went out of business a few years later.

In 1845, William and Asa, Jr. in partnership with J. O. Mead, manufactured electroplated silverware in Hartford as ROGERS & MEAD until 1846.

Early in 1847 Asa, Jr., having returned to Hartford, in cooperation with his brothers, produced and distributed silverplated spoons carrying the ROGERS BROS. trademark. Advertisements of this period read as if WM. ROGERS & CO. (composed of William and Simeon) were the producers.

ROGERS BROS. were unable to handle their increasing volume of business, so in 1853 a new company was organized—ROGERS BROS. MFG. CO. William and Asa, Jr. were large stockholders; Wil-

liam was president. Simeon did not join the firm except as a stockholder a few months later.

In 1856 William Rogers left ROGERS BROS. MFG. CO. and with George W. Smith, manufacturer of silverplated holloware, organized ROGERS, SMITH & CO. with William as president. On October 1, 1861 ROGERS BROS. MFG. CO. and ROGERS, SMITH & CO. were consolidated with William as president.

In 1862 the MERIDEN BRITANNIA CO. bought the tools and dies of the company. William joined MERIDEN BRITANNIA CO. to direct production of the 1847 ROGERS BROS. line.

In 1865 William became an organizer and partner in the WILLIAM ROGERS MFG. CO. Associated with him was his son, William Rogers, Jr. They manufactured plated silverware. Asa, Jr. and Simeon, still stockholders in ROGERS BROS. MFG. CO., established ROGERS & BROTHER CO. in Waterbury in 1858. It was incorporated the following year.

Asa, Jr., with his nephew, William H. Watrous, in 1871 organized the ROGERS CUTLERY CO. in Hartford. Frank Wilson Rogers, brother of William Rogers Jr., was secretary and a director. They manufactured silverplated flatware and became part of INTERNATIONAL SILVER CO. in 1898. William, Asa, Jr. and Simeon were all employed by MERIDEN BRITANNIA CO. when they died.

C. ROGERS & BROS.
Meriden, Connecticut
(See International Silver Co.)

C‑B‑ROGERS‑&‑CO

C. ROGERS & BROS., A 1.

Organized February 26, 1866 by Cephas B. Rogers, Gilbert Rogers and Wilbur F. Rogers when they bought the stock in trade of "one Frary,"—probably James A. Frary who had died in December 1865.

Their first products were casket hardware and furniture trimmings. Their use of "C. Rogers & Bros." trademark on silverplated spoons resulted in court action. They were permitted to use the trademark and continued to do so until the concern was bought by International Silver Co. in 1903. Their products were considered an imitation of the original Rogers brothers and none of their trademarks were ever used by International.

ROGERS & COLE
(See Rogers Brothers)

Organized in 1830 by Asa Rogers, Jr. and John A. Cole in New Britain to manufacture coin silver flatware. Out of business June 4, 1832.

ROGERS CUTLERY CO.
(See Rogers Brothers)

R. C. CO. Al PLUS

ROGERS CUTLERY CO.

ROGERS CO

Founded in 1871. Consolidated with Wm. Rogers Mfg. Co., Hartford, Connecticut in 1879.

Frank Willson Rogers, usually known as F. Willson Rogers, son of William Hazen Rogers and brother of Wm. Henry Rogers (who called himself Wm. Rogers, Jr.) was secretary and a director of Rogers Cutlery Co. and also of Wm. Rogers Mfg. Co. when the two companies consolidated.

One of the original companies to become part of the International Silver Co. in 1898.

F. B. ROGERS SILVER CO.
Taunton, Massachusetts

Founded 1883 in Shelburne Falls, Massachusetts. Moved to Taunton in 1886, at which time it was incorporated. Successors to West Silver Co. before 1896. Still in business.

Other trademarks refer to "Sheffield" silver on copper.

Became a division of National Silver Co. in February 1955.

ROGERS & HAMILTON CO.
Waterbury, Connecticut
(See International Silver Co.)

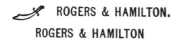

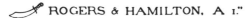

ROGERS & HAMILTON

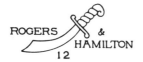

HAMILTON

Rogers & Hamilton Co. was incorporated February 14, 1886 and produced silverplated flatware, taking over the spoon business of Holmes, Booth & Hayden and occupying their building for eight or ten years. President and a stockholder was Charles Alfred Hamilton, who had traveled for Rogers & Brother, Waterbury, for some time. William H. Rogers was made secretary and was a stockholder. Undoubtedly asked to join the company for the use of his name as he was not a silversmith, but was a cigar dealer in Hartford.

One of the original companies to become part of International Silver Co. in 1898.

HENRY ROGERS, SONS & CO.
Montreal, P. Q.

Listed in J C-K in 1909 in plated silver section. No record after c. 1915.

J. ROGERS SILVER CO., INC.
(See Oneida Silversmiths)

ROGERS, LUNT & BOWLEN CO.
Greenfield, Massachusetts
(See Lunt Silversmiths)

ROGERS & MEAD
(See Rogers Brothers)

In 1845, William and Asa Rogers, Jr. in partnership with J. O. Mead, manufactured electroplated silverware in Hartford under the name Rogers & Mead. This partnership was dissolved in 1846.

ROGERS SILVER PLATE CO.
Danbury, Connecticut

Listed in J C-K from 1896 through 1922. Founded by Nathaniel Burton Rogers in association with his brothers Cephas B. and Gilbert H. Rogers, who, with another brother, Wilbur F., were principals in the firm of C. Rogers & Bros. of Meriden, Connecticut which later became a part of the International Silver Co.

Rogers Silver Plate Company manufactured silver-plated novelties—candlesticks,   book-ends, pincushions, etc. After the death of the founder, the assets of the company were purchased by Cephas B. (II), who was a manufacturer of electric lighting fixtures and lamps. He continued the manufacture of novelties under his own name until his retirement in the early 1950's.

SIMEON L. & GEO. H. ROGERS CO.
Hartford, Connecticut
(See Oneida Silversmiths)

ACORN

In business 1900. Acquired by Wm. A. Rogers Limited in 1918. Purchased by Oneida in 1929.

SIMEON L. & GEO. H. ROGERS CO.
S. L. & G. H. ROGERS CO.
S. L. & G. H. R. CO.
ROGERS

ROGERS, SMITH & CO.
(See Rogers Brothers)

Organized January 1, 1857 by William Rogers, Sr. and George W. Smith. They consolidated October 1, 1861 with Rogers Bros. Mfg. Co. because of financial difficulties.

August 12, 1862, the flatware division was sold to the Meriden Britannia Company and the Rogers brothers went to work for them.

Edward Mitchell, formerly with Rogers, Smith & Co. bought the holloware division and on November 6, 1862 organized the Rogers Smith Co. of New Haven for the manufacture of holloware.

(Old Mark.)

On January 13, 1863, the Meriden Britannia Company bought the holloware division of the Rogers Smith & Co. of New Haven. The business continued in New Haven.

In June 1865 the plating shop of the Rogers Smith & Co. of New Haven was moved to Meriden and consolidated with that of the Meriden Britannia Co. on January 1, 1866.

New Mark)

On May 22, 1876, the Meriden Britannia Co. directors voted to bring the business of Rogers Smith & Co. to Meriden on January 1, 1877.

There is merchandise in existence with trademarks bearing the names of Hartford, used from 1857 to 1862; New Haven, 1862 to 1877; West Meriden from 1877 until the early 1880's (when the term West Meriden went out of general use, and Meriden, which was used from that time until about 1918).

R. S. & CO.

WILLIAM ROGERS
(See Rogers Brothers)

(On coin silver)

WM. A. ROGERS, LTD.
(See Oneida Silversmiths)

(Highest Grade Flatware.)

(Half Plate Flatware.)

(Silver Plate on Brass Base.)

(12 Dwt. Knives and Forks.)

(12 Dwt. Knives and Forks.)

(Special Knives and Forks Plated with 16 Dwt. Silver.)

(Light Plate Knives and Forks.)

WM.A.ROGERS A.I.®

NIAGARA SILVER CO.
R. S. MFG. CO.
BUSTER BROWN

R. S. MFG. CO.

(Highest Grade Hollowware.)

WARREN SILVER QUADRUPLE PLATE COMPANY
NEW YORK
(Medium Grade Hollowware.)

1877 N.F. Co.

Successor to Niagara Silver Co. before 1904. They acquired Simeon L. and George H. Rogers Co. in 1918.

Were purchased by Oneida Silversmiths in 1929.

According to Oneida records, Wm. A. Rogers, Ltd. was an Ontario corporation with offices in New York City and factories in Niagara Falls, New York and North Hampton, Massachusetts. The company began making plated silverware in 1894.

The (R) Rogers (R) trademark was first used about 1901. The Warren Silver Plate Co. trademark first used in 1901 was apparently derived from the fact that the New York office was at 12 Warren St.

The 1881 (R) Rogers (R) trademark was first used by Wm. A. Rogers, Ltd. c. 1910.

The Niagara Silver Co. and 1877 N. F. Silver Co. are discontinued trademarks which Oneida acquired through the purchase of Wm. A. Rogers, Ltd.

WILLIAM ROGERS & CO.
(See Rogers Brothers)

Organized in 1841 by William Rogers with his brother, Simeon Rogers who had been apprenticed to him. They used the mark (Eagle) Wm. Rogers & Co. (Star) on their coin silver spoons.

WILLIAM ROGERS, JR.
(William Henry Rogers)
(See Rogers Brothers)
(See Simpson, Hall, Miller & Co.)

⚹ Wm Rogers ★

The original William Hazen Rogers had two sons, William Henry Rogers, and Frank Willson (sometimes spelled Wilson) Rogers. William Henry changed his name to William Rogers, Jr. in order to be more closely associated with his father's well known name.

In 1868, Wm. Rogers, Jr., together with his father, made a contract with the Meriden Britannia Company for 10 years. Upon the death of his father, in 1873, the contract was to continue with the son until the expiration—which was in March of 1878. Wm. Rogers, Jr. was not successful in renewing the contract with the Meriden Britannia Co., but in that year he did make a 15 year contract with Simpson, Hall, Miller & Co. to superintend their flatware manufacturing and with his permission to use on the silverplated flatware the trademark Eagle Wm. Rogers Star. The contract with Simpson, Hall, Miller & Co. terminated in 1893 and Wm. Rogers, Jr. died in 1896.

The trademark is a very active one today on moderately priced flatware.

WILLIAM ROGERS MFG. CO.
Hartford, Connecticut
(See Rogers Brothers)

WM. ROGERS MFG. CO.
⚓ ROGERS ⚓
HARTFORD. CONN.

Organized 1865 by William Hazen Rogers and his son, Wm. Rogers, Jr. (William Henry Rogers). Were one of the original companies to form the International Silver Co. in 1898.

ROGERS BRAND
SILVER PLATED WARE.
THE BRAND WITHOUT A RIVAL
ANCHOR

1846 ⚓ ROGERS ⚓ AA

⚓ ROGERS ⚓
1865. WM. ROGERS M'F'G. CO.
WM. ROGERS & SON.

**R. C. CO.
ROGERS NICKEL SILVER
ROGERS CUTLERY CO.**

⚓ W. R. & S.

R.C. CO.

WM. ROGERS MFG. CO., LTD.
Niagara Falls, Ontario

Bought by Wm. Rogers Mfg. Co. (Division of International Silver Co., Meriden, Connecticut in 1905.)

WM. G. ROGERS

(Flatware.)

Trademark registered U. S. Patent No. 36,147, January 1, 1901 for silverware, knives, forks and spoons. Listed 1904-1915 in J C-K in plated silver section.

WILLIAM H. ROGERS
Hartford, Connecticut

(Silver and Silver Plated Ware.)

Trademark registered U. S. Patent Office, No. 16,007, November 13, 1888 for silver and plated silverware. Out of business before 1915.

WILLIAM H. ROGERS
CORPORATION
Plainfield, New Jersey

Listed in J C-K in 1904 in plated silver section. No record in U. S. Patent Office.

J. W. ROSENBAUM & CO.
Newark, New Jersey

Listed J C-K in 1909-1915 in plated silver section. Out of business before 1922.

FRANCIS ROSENDORN
Baltimore, Maryland

Listed in Baltimore City Directories 1864-1869, 1883-1886 as a silverplater.

CHARLES ROUSH
Baltimore, Maryland

Listed in 1891 Baltimore City Directory under plated silverware.

ROWLEY MFG. CO.
Philadelphia, Pennsylvania

LUNA METAL

(Seamless Nickel Silver Hollow Ware.)

Listed in J C-K in 1909 in plated silver section. Out of business before 1915.

ROYAL MFG. CO.

Known only from name stamped on flatware, 1890-1900 period.

ROYAL METAL MFG. CO.
New York, New York

Listed in J C-K in 1909 in plated silver section. Out of business before 1915.

ROYAL PLATE CO.
(See American Silver Co.)
(See J. W. Johnson)

R. S. MFG. CO.
(See Niagara Silver Co.)

C. F. RUMPP & SONS
Philadelphia, Pennsylvania

Carl Frederich Rumpp, born in Nuertingen, Germany, arrived in this country in 1848 at the age of 20. He brought with him little else but an appreciation of this country and its opportunities, the tools of his trade and a determination to make the best leather goods his thorough apprenticeship had taught him.

Only 25 years after its founding in 1850, the fame of the company had spread through the country and is still considered the standard by which leather goods are judged. Many desk sets, belts, writing cases and travel cases they manufacture are fitted with sterling silver mountings.

RUSSELL HARRINGTON
CUTLERY CO.
Southbridge, Massachusetts

(Used 1881)

J. RUSSELL & CO.
GREEN RIVER WORKS

The present Russell Harrington Cutlery Company was formed in 1932 through the merger of the Harrington Cutlery Co. and the John Russell Co.

Founded in 1834 by John Russell, descendent of an old New England pioneer family, it was first known as J. Russell & Company Green River Works.

The company became well known for an expression used on

1834 J. RUSSELL & CO.

"*Professional*" **Pattern**

the American frontier in the two decades preceding the Gold Rush to California in 1849. This expression, "Up to the Green River," had two meanings—one referred to quality when traders boasted that their goods were "Up to Green River" knives; the other was used when hand-to-hand combat settled personal differences and onlookers shouted, "Give it to him—up to the Green River"—the trademark found near the hilt. (This is the Bowie knife of Texas fame.)

John Russell retired from the firm in 1868, at which time it was incorporated under the name John Russell Mfg. Co. In 1873, it was reorganized and the name was changed to John Russell Cutlery Co. Under this name, in 1881, then located in Turners Falls, they registered a patent for making plated silver knives.

John Russell was the son of the silversmith, also named John Russell, who served his apprenticeship under Isaac Parker.

The Parker-Russell Silver Shop in Old Deerfield, Massachusetts, is a tribute to Isaac Parker and the first John Russell. Through Parker and his apprentice, American silver craftsmanship can be traced by way of Russell & Ripply, J. Russell Cutlery, Towle & Sons and Rogers, Lunt & Bowlen to Lunt Silversmiths.

JOHN RUSSELL CUTLERY CO.
Turners Falls, Massachusetts
(See Russell Harrington Cutlery Co.)

S

SAART BROS. COMPANY
Attleboro, Massachusetts

Successors to W. H. Saart Co.

Founded by William H. Saart, with his brothers, Albert and Herman. Probably in existence for some time prior to its incorporation in 1906. Frank E. Nolan became principal stockholder in 1937. The business is now conducted by R. J. Nolan, president. Makers of sterling and plated silver holloware, dresserware, cigarette and vanity cases and novelties.

W. H. SAART CO.
Attleboro, Massachusetts
(See Saart Bros. Co.)

SACKETT & CO., LTD.
Philadelphia, Pennsylvania

Listed in J C-K in 1896 in the sterling silver section. Out of business before 1904.

G. T. SADTLER & SONS
Baltimore, Maryland

Listed in Baltimore City Directories 1900-1901 under silverware, solid and plated. Successor to Philip Sadtler, silversmith, 1824 (?).

ST. LOUIS SILVER CO.
St. Louis, Missouri

SALOSICO WARE

First appeared in the 1893 St. Louis City Directory as The St. Louis Silver Plate Company at 207 Chestnut Street and in 1904 as the St. Louis Silver Company at 118 Chestnut. No listing after 1912.

SALOSICO WARE
(See St. Louis Silver Co.)

SANDLAND, CAPRON & CO.
North Attleboro, Massachusetts

S. C. & Co.
STERLING

Listed in J C-K in 1896-1904 in the sterling silver section. Out of business before 1909.

PHILIP SAUTER
Baltimore, Maryland

Listed in Baltimore City Directories 1855-1871 as silverplater, manufacturer and dealer in door plates, bell pulls, railing knobs, silver and brass letters and numbers, coffin handles, trimmings, German silver, sheet brass and wire.

P. SAUTER & BRO.
Baltimore, Maryland

Listed in 1864 Baltimore City Directory as silverplaters.

WILLIAM SAUTER
Baltimore, Maryland

Listed in Baltimore City Directories 1865-1886 as silverplaters. Beginning in 1871, coffin trimmings are given special mention.

FREDERICK A. SAWKINS
Baltimore, Maryland

Listed in Baltimore City Directories 1864-1896 as a silverplater.

WILLIAM H. SAXTON, JR.
New London, Connecticut

William H. Saxton is listed in the City Directory of New London in 1891 as Collector for port of New London and dealer in watches, clocks and fine jewelry. William H. Saxton, Jr. is listed as watchmaker.

This trademark, No. 20,327 is registered in the name of William H. Saxton, Jr., November 3, 1891, for the manufacture of gold, silver and plated flat and tableware. The type of trademark would indicate souvenir flatware. Listed 1896 in J C-K.

SCHADE & CO.
Brooklyn, New York
(See Harvey M. Schade)

BROOKLYN PLATE CO.

HARVEY M. SCHADE
Brooklyn, New York

Reported as successor to Brooklyn Silver Co. Earliest listing found in the 1887 City Directory. Listed 1898-1904 in J C-K as Schade & Co. and Harvey M. Schade as successor before 1915 and out of business before 1922.

SCHARLING & CO., INC.
Newark, New Jersey

John H. Scharling registered two processes for producing raised metallic designs (silver deposit) on glassware in 1893. The first was on March 7, 1893 and the second was on September 26, 1893.

Listed in J C-K in 1915 in sterling silver section. An advertisement in 1922 indicates they manufactured plated silver holloware. In 1931 pewter ware was also listed. This was the last listing found.

NIC. SCHELNIN CO.
New York, New York

Listed in J C-K in 1904 in the sterling silver and jewelry sections. Out of business before 1909.

WILLIAM SCHIMPER & CO.
Hoboken, New Jersey

Successors (?) to William Schimper, listed as a silversmith in New York in 1841. William Schimper & Co. was listed in J C-K 1896–1922 as manufacturers of dresserware, bonbon baskets, picture frames, match safes, calendars and hair brushes in sterling and plated silver.

J. SCHIMPF & SONS
New York, New York
(See Adelphi Silver Plate Co.)

Made sterling silverware c. 1890. Later made silver and gold plated wares as Adelphi Silver Plate Co.

JEROME N. SCHIRM
Baltimore, Maryland

Listed in 1901 Baltimore City Directory as a silversmith.

SCHMITZ, MOORE & CO.
Newark, New Jersey

Manufacturers of sterling silver dresserware. Listed in J C-K 1915. Succeeded by Moore & Hofman between 1915–1922.

SCHOFIELD CO., INC.
Baltimore, Maryland
(See Baltimore Silversmiths Mfg. Co.)
(See Jenkins & Jenkins)
(See C. Klank & Sons)

Founded in 1903 by Frank M. Schofield as the Baltimore Silversmiths Mfg. Co.

Schofield was from a family of silversmiths and worked as a die-cutter. He is said to have cut the dies for the "Baltimore Rose" for The Stieff Company.

Heer-Schofield Co. was the company name from about 1905–1928 when it was changed to Frank M. Schofield Co.

Around 1930 it was changed to Schofield Co. and incorporated a few years later.

Manufacturers of sterling silver flatware and holloware, Schofield Co., Inc. has been operated since 1948 by Berthe M. Schofield, widow of the founder.

Their trademark has been unchanged except that the letter B in the diamond was changed to an H when the company name was changed to Heer-Schofield.

In 1905 they bought out C. Klank & Sons which continued to be listed under its own name through 1911. Shortly after 1915 they also purchased the tools and dies of Jenkins & Jenkins and also the Farreals Co. Schofield's purchased by Oscar Caplan & Sons in 1965.

A. B. SCHREUDER
Syracuse, New York

H. & S.

Andrew B. Schreuder was born in Norway, 1828. Listed in Utica, New York City Directories in 1852–1853 as a silversmith and later joined the firm of Hotchkiss & Schreuder in Syracuse. The exact date of the founding of the A. B. Schreuder Company not located. Out of business before 1904.

SCHRIER & PROTZE
Baltimore, Maryland

Listed in 1888 Baltimore City Directory as silverplaters. Firm name changed to Novelty Plating Works in 1890.

A. G. SCHULTZ & CO.
Baltimore, Maryland

(Hollow Ware.)

Listed in Baltimore City Directories 1899–1950 as manufacturers of sterling silver holloware.

Successors to Schultz & Tschudy & Co., first listed in 1898. Andrew G. Schultz and Otto Rosenbauer were listed as members of the firm. From 1902–1905, James L. McPhail was also listed as a member of the firm and was listed at C. Klank & Sons during those same years.

SCHULTZ, TSCHUDY & CO.
Baltimore, Maryland

Listed in 1898 Baltimore City Directory as silversmiths. Succeeded by A. G. Schultz & Co. in 1899.

SCHULZ & FISCHER
San Francisco, California

Began the manufacture of silverware in San Francisco in 1868 and occupied a prominent position as workers in precious metals. Their first listing in the San Francisco Directory was in 1869.

Their products included spoons, forks, and table silverware, as well as presentation pieces. One of their epergnes was 27 inches high —the largest piece of its kind made on the Pacific Coast. They were also importers of plated silverware and fine table cutlery. No listing found after 1887. No trademark found.

SCOFIELD & DE WYNGAERT
Newark, New Jersey

Listed 1904 J C-K in the sterling silver section and in 1915 in jewelry. Became F. P. Scofield & Company before 1922 after which no further listing was found.

JACOB SEEGER
Baltimore, Maryland

Listed in Baltimore City Directories 1864-1869 as a silverplater.

SELLEW & COMPANY
Cincinnati, Ohio

SELLEW & CO.
CINCINNATI
(On britannia)

The Cincinnati City Directory lists Sellew & Company as pewterers in 1834. The 1836-1837 Directory lists Enos and Osman Sellew, makers of britannia ware.

About 1860 they discontinued making pewter and devoted their attention to britannia ware.

Out of business in the late 1870's.

WILLIAM H. SEYFER
Baltimore, Maryland

Listed in 1884 Baltimore City Directory as a silversmith.

JOS. SEYMOUR MFG. CO.
Syracuse, New York

J. S. & Co.

(c. 1850-1887)

∗ S ∗

(1887-c. 1900)

(c. 1900-c. 1909)

Began with Joseph Seymour of Utica, New York. He learned the silversmiths' trade in New York City and was listed in the City Directory in 1835 as a silversmith. From 1842-1847 he was listed in the Utica City Directories as a silversmith. About 1850 he became a partner in Norton & Seymour (B. R. Norton) in Syracuse. The company name was changed to Norton, Seymour & Co. after 1850.

Shortly afterwards he went into business for himself under the name of Joseph Seymour & Company.

In 1859 he patented a process for making spoons and in 1863 patented a spoon design.

About 1887 the company name had become Jos. Seymour, Sons & Co., and c. 1900 was changed to Jos. Seymour Mfg. Co. It went out of business before 1909.

3. M. SHANLEY, JR. CO.
(See Pryor Mfg. Co., Inc.)

Consolidated with Pryor Mfg. Co. between 1915 and 1922. Last record found was c. 1935.

GEORGE B. SHARP
Philadelphia, Pennsylvania

Silversmith in Philadelphia c. 1848-1850.

This mark is an example of a type of quality mark used by a few American silversmiths. The American shield was used as an equivalent of an English hallmark.

George and William Sharp worked together, perhaps a bit earlier. Their silver was stamped W. & G. SHARP.

George Sharp apparently worked for Bailey & Co. (later Bailey, Banks & Biddle). A Bailey & Co. advertisement of 1850 includes this mark accompanied by the statement that "All Silver Ware sold by them manufactured on the premises—Assayed by J. C. Booth, Esq., of the U. S. Mint."

CHARLES C. SHAVER
Utica, New York

C.C.S.

Charles C. Shaver was born in Germany. He served his apprenticeship under Willard & Hawley (William W. Willard and John D. Hawley) of Syracuse. He moved to Utica in 1854 and was listed there in the City Directories as silversmith and jeweler until 1858. He died in 1900.

GEORGE E. SHAW
Putnam, Connecticut

GEN. PUTNAM

Listed in J C-K in 1896-1922 in sterling silver section.

The Gen. Putnam trademark was registered in U. S. Patent Office, No. 19,736, June 16, 1891, for flatware, solid and plated. This trademark was for two souvenir spoons to commemorate the Revolutionary hero.

SHEETS ROCKFORD SILVER PLATE CO.
(See Rockford Silver Plate Co.)

Began in 1873 as Rockford Silver Plate Company and was succeeded by Sheets-Rockford Silver Plate Company c. 1921.

They were manufacturers of sterling and plated silver holloware and flatware. Last record found was c. 1935.

SHEFFIELD A1 PLATE

Known only from name stamped on flatware.

SHEFFIELD CUTLERY CONCERN
Boston, Massachusetts

Published an illustrated catalog in 1882. Plated silver novelties, including fancy figure napkin rings were illustrated.

SHEFFIELD PLATED CO.
(See Holmes, Booth & Haydens)
(See International Silver Co.)

SHEFFIELD SILVER CO.
Brooklyn, New York

(1908-1950)

THE SHEFFIELD SILVER CO.
MADE IN U. S. A.
(1950-present)

Registered trademark U. S. Patent Office, No. 107,747, December 28, 1919 for plated silverware and holloware.

Incorporated in the State of New York in 1908. Their basic product is plated silver holloware.

SHELDON & FELTMAN
Albany, New York
(See Smith & Company)

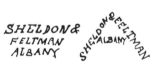

Britannia workers 1846-1848. Thought to have made a small quantity of plated silver with the mark below. The upper ones most certainly were used only on britannia wares. Succeeded by Smith & Feltman in 1849; and by Smith & Co. in 1853.

SHEPARD MFG. CO.
Melrose Highlands, Mass.

S

In business before 1890. Listed J C-K 1896-1915. Out of business before 1922. Manufacturers of sterling silverware.

SHEPARD & RICE
(See Bernard Rice's Sons)

EMMONS F. SHERMAN
Baltimore, Maryland

Listed in 1868-1869 Baltimore City Directory as a silverplater.

GEORGE W. SHIEBLER & CO.
New York, New York

Successors before 1890 to Thomas Evans Co. Out of business before 1915. They were manufacturers of sterling silverware. The "winged S" trademarks are found on souvenir spoons of the 1890's.

SHIELDS, INC.
Attleboro, Massachusetts

Founded c. 1920 as the Fillkwik Company, it was incorporated in 1936 under the present name. In January 1939 the company was bought by Rex Products Corporation of New Rochelle, New York.

During World War II, Shields produced insignia and medals, and now manufactures men's jewelry, fancy display and jewelry boxes.

SHOEMAKER, PICKERING & CO.
Newark, New Jersey

 Sterling

Listed in J C-K 1896 in sterling and jewelry sections. Out of business before 1915.

Trademark identical to Frank Kursh & Son, Co.

SHREVE, BROWN & CO.
(See Shreve, Crump & Low Co. Inc.)

SHREVE & CO.
San Francisco, California

SHREVE & CO.

Two brothers, George C. and S. S. Shreve first opened a jewelry shop in 1852 and were active in its management all their lives. The company was incorporated shortly before 1900.

Ownership and management

has remained in the hands of San Franciscans, though since 1912 no member of the Shreve family has been part of the corporation. Present ownership is in the hands of the Joseph C. Hickingbotham family whose sons, Joseph C. and Howard J. are now Chairman of the Board and President respectively.

Shreve & Co., a San Francisco institution with a history almost as old as the city itself, has made silver services for several battleships and cruisers; the State of California's gift to Queen Elizabeth on her coronation; gifts for the delegates at the founding of the United Nations and has fashioned pieces to the special orders of kings, presidents, shahs, sheiks and people of the entertainment world. They also produce 18 exclusive flatware patterns.

SHREVE, CRUMP & LOW CO.
(See Shreve, Crump & Low Co., Inc.)

SHREVE, CRUMP & LOW CO., INC.
Boston, Massachusetts

CHRONOLOGY

John M. McFarlane	1796
Jones & Ward	1809
Baldwin & Jones	1813
Putnam & Low	1822
John J. Low & Co.	1828
John B. Jones Co.	1838
Jones, Low & Ball	1839
Low, Ball & Co.	1840
Jones, Ball & Poor	1846
Jones, Shreve, Brown & Co.	1854
Shreve, Brown & Co.	1857
Shreve, Stanwood & Co.	1860
Shreve, Crump & Low Co.	1869
Shreve, Crump & Low Co., Inc.	1888

According to tradition, John McFarlane, originally from Salem, proprietor of a modest watchmaker's shop in 1796, was the founder of the company that is now known as Shreve, Crump & Low Co., Inc.

In the early 1800's Jabez Baldwin moved to Boston and formed a copartnership with a neighboring craftsman, and under the title of Baldwin & Jones continued the business begun by McFarlane.

Among the apprentices of Jabez Baldwin in Salem were John J. Low and Edward Putnam, who in 1822 established the firm of Putnam & Low. Three or four years later they separated and in 1839 John J. Low and his brother Francis, joined with George B. Jones, son of Mr. Baldwin's partner. In 1852 Benjamin Shreve was admitted to the firm and 17 years later Charles H. Crump joined. In 1888 the firm was incorporated as Shreve, Crump & Low Company under the law of Massachusetts, with Benjamin Shreve as president.

The Shreve, Crump & Low Company tradition so ably started by the Salem craftsmen and apprentices almost 150 years ago is being carried on today by Richard Shreve, great-grandson of the first Shreve.

The company does no manufacturing, but, has always sold designs made by the finest of American silversmiths; some of the designs being created exclusively for them.

SHREVE, STANWOOD & CO.
(See Shreve, Crump & Low Co., Inc.)

VICTOR SIEDMAN MFG. CO., INC.
Brooklyn, New York

Manufacturing silversmiths c. 1920-1930. Makers of sterling silver holloware, picture frames and candlesticks.

A. L. SILBERSTEIN
New York, New York

Successor to Silberstein, Hecht & Co. before 1904.

Succeeded by Griffon Cutlery Works before 1915. Still in business under that name.

GRIFFON

(All Above on Cutlery.)

SILBERSTEIN, HECHT & CO.
New York, New York

Founding date unknown.

Succeeded by A. L. Silberstein before 1904. Manufacturers of sterling silverware.

SILVERCRAFT
(See Farber Bros.)

F. W. SIM & CO.
Troy, New York

Registered U. S. Patent June 6, 1891 for manufacture of souvenir sterling silverware. No other record.

SIMMONS & PAYE
North Attleboro, Mass.
(See Paye & Baker)

S. & P.

SIMONS BRO. & CO.
Philadelphia, Pennsylvania

Established in 1839 or 1840. Listed in J C-K 1896 to present in sterling and jewelry sections. Now listed as Simons Bros. Co.

SIMPSON-BRAINERD CO.
Providence, Rhode Island

ENGLISH SILVER

Listed J C-K 1915–1922 in plated silver section.

SIMPSON, HALL, MILLER & CO.
Wallingford, Connecticut
(See International Silver Co.)

(Flatware.)

(Cheaper Grade.)   *(Hollowware.)*

AMERICAN SILVER PLATE CO.

Samuel Simpson was well known for his britannia ware in Wallingford. In 1866 he organized Simpson, Hall, Miller & Co. to do silverplating. He was extremely successful and in 1878 made a contract with William Rogers, Jr., to supervise the manufacture and marketing of Simpson, Hall, Miller & Co. Rogers "Eagle" Brand.

In 1895 they started the manufacture of sterling silverware and were one of the original companies to become part of the International Silver Company in 1898. The Wallingford factory became International's sterling center.

SIMPSON NICKEL SILVER CO.
Wallingford, Connecticut
(See International Silver Co.)

Incorporated in 1871 by Samuel Simpson, E. W. Sperry, Albert A. Sperry, Alfred W. Sperry and R. L. McChristie. They made nickel silver flatware blanks which were sold to Simpson, Hall, Miller & Co. for plating and marketing. They did not use a trademark because they sold their products to other silver manufacturers. They began the manufacture of sterling silver flatware shortly before the organization of the International Silver Co. The nickel silver operations were moved to other factories after the company became part of the International Silver Co. in 1898.

WM. AND GEO. SISSONS
Sheffield, England

W. S.

C. S.

(On plated silver)

(On sterling silver)

Successors to Smith, Sissons & Co. who were makers of Sheffield plate and silversmiths in 1848.

Listed in J C-K 1909–1922 in sterling and plated silver sections.

A. F. SMITH CO.
Omaha, Nebraska

Founded in 1894 as Reichenberg-Smith Co., wholesale jewelers. A. F. Smith, President, Louis Reichenberg, Vice President and Max Reichenberg, Sec. Last listed under this name in 1905.

The 1906 City Directory carries the listing of the A. F. Smith Co. with Arthur F. Smith as President. They were incorporated in 1932. In 1936 the listing is A. F. Smith & Co. with G. A. Smith as President-treasurer; L. P. Smith, Vice President and A. F. Smith, Secretary.

The 1938 listing is Smith & Co., with Franklin & Gordon A. Smith (sons) listed as owners. The 1941 listing is A. F. Smith & Co., Inc. and is the last listing under the Smith name.

It was later known as the Allgaier-Smith Co., Inc. in 1942; Allgaier Jewelry Co. in 1945 and John Byrne Inc. 1948–1964.

SMITH & COMPANY
Albany, New York

Listed in the Albany City Directory 1846–1848 as Sheldon & Feltman, Brittania (sic.) and Argentina Manufactory. Listed 1849–1853 as Smith & Feltman, Argentine and Brittannia Works. Listed 1853–1856 as Smith & Company, Argentine and Brittania Works.

The Argentina and Argentine are thought to have been britannia ware plated with silver.

E. H. H. SMITH KNIFE CO.
Bridgeport, Connecticut

PAT. 3.99.

(*Knives.*)

In business in 1899 as manufacturers of plated silver knives. Out of business before 1915.

Probably related to E. H. H. Smith Silver Co. but this could not be established.

E. H. H. SMITH SILVER CO.
Bridgeport, Connecticut
(See Albert Pick & Co., Inc.)

× × × ×

◁ S ▷

(*Flatware.*)

The E. H. H. Smith Silver Company was first listed in the Bridgeport City Directory in 1907. Listed in the J C-K in 1904. U. S. Patent No. 44,191 was issued in their name on February 14, 1905. They were manufacturers of "artistic cutlery and sterling effects in quintuple plated spoons and forks." They were last listed in the 1919 City Directory and were succeeded by the Albert Pick Company in 1920.

SMITH & FELTMAN
(See Smith & Company)

FRANK W. SMITH SILVER CO.,
INC.
Gardner, Massachusetts
(See The Webster Co.)

TRADE MARK.
925/1000 FINE

Founded in 1882 by Frank W. Smith, with sterling flatware and holloware as the principal products.

In October, 1958, all of the flatware tools, and dies, along with the trade name and trademark, were purchased by the Webster Company and the flatware portion of this business moved to North Attleboro, Mass.

FREDERICK L. SMITH
Denver, Colorado

The business was first listed as the C. H. Green Jewelry Company in 1889 with F. L. Smith as secretary-treasurer and L. H. Gurnsey, manager. In 1890 it was known as the C. H. Green Jewelry Company with the Gurnsey name no longer listed. In 1892 the name was changed to the Green-Smith Watch and Diamond Company. Harper's Magazine, July 1892, carried an advertisement listing them as manufacturers of souvenir spoons made of Colorado silver, "Protected by letters Patent, dated Feb. 16, 1892." In 1894 the business listing was dropped and the only entry was under Smith. In 1895 the listing was Frederick L. Smith as manager of John W. Knox—successor to Green-Smith Company.

GEORGE W. SMITH
Albany, New York
(See Rogers Brothers)

Holloware silverplater in Albany, New York before he joined with Wm. Rogers and founded the Rogers, Smith & Co. of Hartford, Connecticut in 1856. Went out of business in 1862.

LAWRENCE B. SMITH CO.
Boston, Massachusetts

Founded in Boston in 1887. Made sterling and plated silverware. Out of business about 1958.

SMITH, PATTERSON & CO.
Boston, Massachusetts

Founded in 1876, became part of Jordan Marsh, New England's largest department store, in 1956. Agents for "several of the best manufacturers." Importers of watches, clocks, silverware and jewelry.

SMITH & SMITH
Attleboro, Massachusetts
(See Wallace Silversmiths)

S & S

Manufacturers of sterling cigar boxes and novelties.

W. D. SMITH SILVER CO.
Chicago, Illinois

(Nickel Silver-Hollowware.)

(Plated Flatware.)

Rudolph J. Bourgeois, vice-president of the company, registered U. S. Patent No. 148,714 on November 22, 1921 for the manufacture of silverware, particularly holloware, flatware, jewelry and precious metal ware. In applying for this patent registration, it was stated that this trademark had been used continuously since 1913.

The company was incorporated under the laws of Delaware and was located in Chicago.

SO. AM.
(See David H. McConnell)

SOCIÉTÉ PICARD FRERES
Paris, France

Registered trademarks U. S. Patent Office No. 30,171, June 8, 1897 for table, kitchen, dresserware and utensils of copper and pure silver. No record after c. 1920.

A. M. SOFFEL CO., INC.
Newark, New Jersey

Manufacturers (?) of sterling silverware c. 1920.

SOUTHINGTON CO.
(See Barbour Silver Co.)
(See International Silver Co.)

SOUTHINGTON CO.

GEORGE A. SPARKS
Brooklyn, New York

S-C-A G

Manufacturers (?) of plated silver
c. 1920.

J. E. SPARKS
Brooklyn, New York

$ SPARK $

Manufacturer (?) of sterling silver
c. 1920.

SPAULDING & CO., INC.
Chicago, Illinois

Successors before 1891 to S. Heard & Co., founded in 1885. Spaulding & Co. was owned by The Gorham Company 1920–1945. It is still in business in Chicago and is listed under the Gorham Company name—probably as a Chicago outlet for Gorham products.

D. S. SPAULDING
Mansfield, Massachusetts

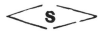

(On plated silver)

Listed J C-K 1896–1922 in sterling and plated silver sections.

(Sterling Silver Top and Plated Back

(On sterling silver)

SPAULDING-GORHAM, INC.
Rochester, New York

Begun by Newell Matson, a businessman, not a silversmith. He was born in Simsbury, Connecticut in 1817 and started in business at the age of 15 selling coin silver.

He established a small store in Louisburg, Connecticut in 1840. In 1845 he opened a larger store in Owego, New York where he not only sold silverware, but employed several silversmiths whose main output was spoons marked with his name. He started and sold several businesses. One was in Milwaukee, Wisconsin, where he established a partnership of Matson, Loomis & Hoes with a branch in Chicago. The Chicago store grew so rapidly that he sold the Milwaukee store only to be driven out by the fire in 1871. Soon afterwards he began business again, first in his home and later under the name N. Matson & Co., with George E. Johnson, L. J. Norton and W. E. Higby. They carried a large stock of the usual jewelers' goods—the silver being from Gorham's. Later, the firm name became Spaulding & Company and in 1944 was Spaulding-Gorham, Inc.

BEN. SPIER
New York, New York

Successor to Spier & Forsheim about 1909. Wholesaler (?) of silverware, jewelry and related articles.

SPIER & FORSHEIM
New York, New York
(See Ben. Spier Co.)

Listed J C-K 1896. Succeeded by
Ben. Spier Co. c. 1909.

S. & S. NOVELTY CO.
Providence, Rhode Island

Manufacturers (?) of plated silver
novelties c. 1915–1922.

STANDARD SILVER CO. OF
TORONTO
Toronto, Canada
(See International Silver Co.)
(See International Silver Co. of
Canada, Ltd.)

(*E. P. on Copper.*)

MONARCH SILVER CO.

MANF'D AND
GUARANTEED BY

TRADE MARK FOR
HOLLOW WARE.

Organized in 1895 as Standard
Silver Co. for the production of
silverplated flatware and hollo-
ware and hotel ware. One of the
original companies to form the
International Silver Co. in 1898.
Merged with International Silver
Co. of Canada, Ltd. about 1912.

STANDARD S. P. CO.

Known only from name stamped
on flatware.

STANDARD SILVERWARE
COMPANY
Boston, Massachusetts

NEVADA SILVER METAL

Retailer and jobber of plated silverware. First appeared in the
Boston City Directories in 1883,

which probably means that it was
founded the previous year. Last
listed in 1921. Edward C. Webb was
head of the firm and was associated with it from about 1903
through 1921.

STANLEY & AYLWARD, LTD.
Toronto, Canada

Wholesalers of plated silver holloware c. 1920.

STAR CUTLERY CO.
(See Elgin-American Mfg. Co.)

I. J. STEANE & CO.
Hartford, Connecticut and New
York
(See Barbour Silver Co.)

Isaac J. Steane, a watchmaker at
Coventry, England, came to America about 1866 to collect a bad
debt. He was forced to take over
his debtor's stock, which he auc-
tioned off at a profit of $6,000. He
continued in the auction business
for some time; returned to England, wound up his business
affairs and came again to the
United States where he formed the
firm of Steane, Son & Hall, consisting of Isaac J. Steane, Isaac J.
Steane, Jr., and J. P. Hall. Mr. Hall

retired in 1886 and the firm name
was changed to I. J. Steane & Co.
Mr. Steane bought the Taunton
Silver Plate Co., and took stock to
New York for auction. He later
bought the Albany Silver Plate Co.,
combining the affairs of these two
companies with that of I. J. Steane
& Co.
In the early 1880's, Mr. Steane
purchased the old silverware stock
of the Cromwell Plate Co., of Cromwell, Connecticut. The sale was
made by A. E. Hobson, who in 1881
had left the Meriden Britannia Co.
to become a salesman for Cromwell.
About this same time, the Barbour Bros. Co. was formed by S. L.

Barbour, from Chicago, joined by
his brother Charles, who was in
business in New Haven. I. J.
Steane & Co. produced the goods
that the Barbour Bros. Co. marketed. Mr. Hobson was associated
with I. J. Steane at this time. At the
suggestion of W. H. Watrous, the
business was moved to Hartford
and two years later the Hartford
Silver Plate Company business was
also acquired. Mr. Steane, Sr. retired and returned to England in
1888.
The I. J. Steane Co., the Barbour
Bros. Co. and the Barbour Hobson
Co., all of Hartford, united to form
the Barbour Silver Company in
1892.

STEANE, SON & HALL
New York, New York
(See Barbour Silver Co.)
(See I. J. Steane & Co.)

THE STEEL-BRUSSEL CO.
New York, New York

Listed in J C-K 1896 in sterling silver section. Out of business before
1904.

H. STEINACKER
Baltimore, Maryland

Listed in 1868–1869 Baltimore City
Directory as a silverplater.

STERLING COMPANY
Derby, Connecticut

Published illustrated catalogs of
fine silverware in 1893 and 1898.
On the catalogs is the statement,
"Established 1866."

STERLING CRAFT
Toronto, Canada

Sterling silver manufacturer (?) c. 1920. Related (?) to Spurrier & Co., London.

STERLING PLATE B
(See American Silver Co.)

STERLING SILVER MFG. CO.
Baltimore, Maryland

Listed in Baltimore City Directories 1894–1896 as silver manufacturers.

THE STERLING SILVER MFG. CO.
Providence, Rhode Island

Listed in the City Directories 1909–1932. Samuel A. Schreiber, president-treasurer; Max L. Jocby vice-president; L. C. McCaffrey, sec. Manufacturing silversmiths. Made sterling flat and holloware and souvenir spoons.

STERLING SILVER PLATE CO.
(See Holmes, Booth & Haydens)
(See International Silver Co.)

STERLING SILVER SOUVENIR CO.
Boston, Massachusetts

In business before 1890. Advertised that they were makers of sterling silver souvenirs. Out of business before 1915.

LOUIS STERN CO., INC.
Providence, Rhode Island

L.S. & Co.

Established in 1871 as chainmakers and silversmiths. Wholesalers of chains, bags, watch bracelets, bracelets, knives, buckles and jewelry. Last record found 1950.

S. STERNAU & CO.
Brooklyn, New York
and
New York, New York

Listed in 1896 Jewelers' Weekly as manufacturer of plated silver chafing dishes and miscellaneous lines. Last record c. 1920.

(Metal Wares.)

STEVENS & LEITHOFF
Irvington, New Jersey

Listed J C-K 1915 in sterling silver section. Out of business before 1922.

STEVENS SILVER CO.
Portland, Maine
(See Colonial Silver Co.)

Incorporated in 1893. Alfred A. Stevens was president. He left Woodman-Cook Company to form the Stevens Silver Company which was later the Colonial Silver Co. Manufacturers of plated silverware.

STEVENS & SMART
Portland, Maine
(See Woodman-Cook Co.)

The firm of Alfred A. Stevens was listed in 1879 and known as Stevens & Smart, manufacturers of britannia wares until 1883 when it was succeeded by Stevens, Smart & Dunham. Alfred A. Stevens and Nehemiah Smart were the partners.

STEVENS & SMART
Portland, Maine
(See Woodman-Cook Co.)

Successor to Stevens, Smart & Dunham in 1887. Succeeded by Stevens, Woodman and Company in 1890.

STEVENS, SMART & DUNHAM
Portland, Maine
(See New England Silver Co.)
(See Woodman-Cook Co.)

Successors to Stevens & Smart when Joseph Dunham joined the firm in 1884. Were makers of britannia ware. Became Stevens & Smart once again when Joseph Dunham left the firm in 1886.

STEVENS, WOODMAN &
COMPANY
Portland, Maine
(See Woodman-Cook Company)

Successors to Stevens & Smart in 1891; succeeded by Woodman-Cook Co. in 1892. Advertisements in 1890 mention silver plating. Alfred A . Stevens and Fred H. Woodman, partners.

THE STIEFF COMPANY
Baltimore, Maryland

STIEFF STERLING

"Hallmark" used on Williamsburg Restorations. Used in Virginia in the 17th and 18th centuries as a shipper's or maker's mark. Used in England as early as the 16th century—apparently to indicate the highest quality.

Founded in 1892 as The Baltimore Sterling Silver Company by Charles C. Stieff, father of the present Chairman of the Board, Gideon N. Stieff, Sr. In 1904 the corporation name was changed to The Stieff Company.

They are manufacturers of sterling silver flatware and holloware. Their "Rose" pattern is so identified with Baltimore that it is often called "Baltimore Rose." They are the exclusive makers of Williamsburg Restoration, Historic Newport and Old Sturbridge Village sterling silver and pewter reproductions.

STIEFF-ORTH CO.
Baltimore, Maryland

Not listed in Baltimore City Directories which were checked from the 1890's through the 1930's. Listed in J C-K 1909 sterling silver section. Out of business before 1915.

G. B. STOCKING
Tacoma, Washington

RHODODENDRON

Jeweler, watchmaker, optician 1893–1896. Registered U. S. Patent No. 22,807, April 18, 1893 for manufacture of jewelry, spoons and other flatware.

ARTHUR J. STONE
Gardner, Massachusetts
(See Stone Associates)

STONE ASSOCIATES
Gardner, Massachusetts

Founded by Arthur J. Stone, who was born in Sheffield, England in 1847. After an apprenticeship of seven years and a working practice as a designer and chaser for ten years, he came to this country in 1884 and was employed by a firm in Concord, New Hampshire. He later became superintendent of a silverware company in Gardner, Massachusetts.

He opened his own shop in 1901 with the assistance of his young American wife. Hand wrought silverware was made in the shop

In 1913 he received the first medal for excellence in craftsmanship and service given by the Society of Arts and Crafts of Boston.

At first he worked alone, gradually adding assistants until 1932 they were 11 in number. Pieces made by the assistants had their initials placed beside the shop mark.

Mr. Stone's associates and successors followed his own high standards until they went out of business between 1950-1955.

STONE STERLING SILVER CO.
New York, New York

Registered their trademark U. S. Patent Office, No. 28,350, June 4, 1896 for silverware and jewelry. Listed in J C-K 1896. Out of business before 1904.

L. S. STOWE
(See H. J. Webb & Co.)

A. STOWELL, JR.
Baltimore, Maryland

Silversmith c. 1855. Listed as member of firm Gould, Stowell & Ward in 1855-1856 Baltimore City Directory.

STRATHMORE CO.
Providence, Rhode Island

SOLID STRATHMORE SILVER
T.S. CO.
STRATHMORE MESH
DIAMOND MESH

Manufacturers of sterling flatware and plated silverware, holloware, picture frames and gift shop novelties. Listed J C-K 1915-1922.

R. STRICKLAND & CO.
Albany, New York

Ralph Strickland listed in Albany City Directories 1857-1884 as manufacturer of plated wares.

STRONG & ELDER CO.
No address

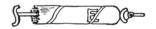

Listed in J C-K 1896 sterling section as out of business.

STRONG MFG. CO.
Winsted, Connecticut

In 1856, Markham and Strong of East Hampton, Connecticut made a small line of coffin tacks, screws and handles from white metal. Mr. Markham continued the business while the two Strongs, David and Clark were in the Union service. In 1866 David Strong bought out the company and moved to Winsted, Connecticut. The articles were considered of great beauty and were silver plated. It is reported that General Grant's casket was adorned with gold handles made by them. Also, handles and plates were furnished for the caskets of ex-president Harrison and Cornelius Vanderbilt. The company is last listed in 1934 city directory. No trademark has been located.

SUCKLING, LTD.
Birmingham, England

Successor to Wm. Suckling & Sons between 1915-1922. Manufacturers of plated silverware.

WYNDHAM A. SULLIVAN
Baltimore, Maryland

Listed in Baltimore City Directories 1900-1915 as a silversmith in the firm of Ritter & Sullivan.

SUNDERLIN COMPANY
Rochester, New York

This silversmithing business began with three Burr brothers; Albert, who was apprenticed to Erastus Cook, and died shortly after starting his jewelry business; Alexander J., who was Albert's apprentice and Cornelius. The business went through a series of partnerships from 1838 and was known as C. A. Burr & Company after the death of the two brothers. In 1864 it was sold to Sunderlin & Weaver; became Sunderlin & McAllister; L. Sunderlin & Company and in 1944 was the Sunderlin Company. Out of business in 1952.

SUPERIOR
(See Middletown Plate Co.)

THE SWEETSER CO.
New York, New York

Listed in J C-K 1904-1915 in sterling silver and jewelry sections. Out of business before 1915.

CHAS. N. SWIFT & CO.
New York, New York

Listed J C-K 1904 sterling silver section. Out of business before 1915.

SYRACUSE SILVER MFG. CO.
Syracuse, New York

Listed 1896-1904 in J C-K as manufacturers of sterling silverware.
Syracuse Silver Mfg. Co. listed in
Syracuse, New York City Directories 1895-1900. Under the first
listing, J. Barton French was president and business manager,
A. Hubbs, Secretary and E. Elmer
Keeler, treas. In 1896-1897, Benjamin F., Simon and Solomon H.
Lesser were listed as owners. In
1898-1900, it was listed as Silverware Manufacturers, A. Lesser's
Son. In 1900, the listing was
A. Lesser Son, watch materials.

T

TABER & TIBBITS, INC.
Wallingford, Connecticut

Listed in the City Directory 1919-
1941. Makers of silverplated hollowares and novelties. Trademark
was a tabor (small drum).

H. H. TAMMEN CURIO CO.
Denver, Colorado

In business from c. 1881 to 1962.
Was purchased by Con Becker in
1957 and is now the Thrift Novelty
Company.

First begun by H. H. Tammen as
a curio shop, the business was expanded to include the manufacture and wholesaling of souvenir
novelties and jewelry. Among their
widely distributed souvenirs were
sterling silver spoons depicting
people and places of the West. By
1887, after several moves for expansion, a museum established in
connection with the business, advertised that "it was lighted by
electric light," and was considered
a place no traveler should miss.
The business managed to survive
the panic of 1893 and went on to
become the largest of its kind in
the West.

TAUNTON BRITANNIA
MANUFACTURING COMPANY
Taunton, Massachusetts
(See Reed & Barton)

T. B. M. CO.

TAUNTON BRIT.
MANFG. CO.

The Taunton Britannia Manufacturing Company was the successor
to Crossman, West & Leonard
when the need for additional capital for expansion brought about
the establishment of this joint-

stock company on August 18, 1830.

There were eight shareholders in the new company. Of these, only William Crossman, Haile N. Wood, Daniel Cobb and William West were experienced in the britannia business. James Crossman had been a merchant tailor, real estate investor and was at that time a director of the Cohannet Bank in Taunton. Haile Wood, Sr., dealt in real estate and Horatio and Z. A. Leonard were prominent in the metal and textile trades.

Immediately a new factory at Hopewell, on the Mill River, was built. Water was planned as the main source of power, but, the old steam engine from the Fayette Street shop was installed for power during summer droughts.

By 1831, the manufacturing of britannia ware had all been shifted to the new factory. Throughout that year, many addi-

tions to their product line were added. Among them were castor frames, tankards, church cups, christening bowls, soup ladles and candlesticks. In 1832, toast racks, soda dispensers and fruit dishes were added. Sales of the tea sets, that had been the backbone of the business, dropped after 1831.

The Taunton Britannia Manufacturing Company was noted for the production of some of the most beautiful lamps made in America. New designs in these lighting devices and an increased supply of whale oil on the market promoted their popularity.

Castor sets were to be found on every dining table in America; many of them were made by this company. Their revolving sets were considered the epitome of luxurious living.

In 1832, William Crossman, William West and Zephaniah Leonard sold their interests in the

company to Horatio Leonard and in 1833, Isaac Babbitt, superintendent of the plant, left the company.

On February 16, 1833, a new corporation, with Horatio Leonard, James Crossman, Haile Wood, Daniel Cobb and Haile N. Wood was formed under the same name —the Taunton Britannia Mfg. Company. General business uncertainty of the period, competition from other britannia ware establishments, as well as a strong preference for foreign articles brought about the total failure of the company in November, 1834.

Three people still had great faith in the enterprise. They were the company agent, Benjamin Pratt; Henry Reed, a spinner; and his friend, Charles E. Barton, the solderer. On April 1, 1835, they reopened the factory and eventually formed what is now Reed & Barton.

TAUNTON SILVER PLATE CO.
(See I. J. Steane & Co.)

F. C. TAYLOR & CO.
Baltimore, Maryland

Listed in 1881 Baltimore City Directory as silverplaters.

THE TENNANT COMPANY
New York, New York
(See Hartford Sterling Co.)
(See Phelps & Cary Co.)

STERLING
TRADE MARK

Silversmiths before 1896. Makers of holloware and dresserware in sterling silver only. Trophies, pres-

entation pieces. Succeeded (?) by Hartford Sterling Co. c. 1901. Trademark is identical to one used by Hartford Sterling Co. and by Phelps & Cary Co., with the exception of the initials in the shield.

THE COLUMBIA
(See G. I. Mix & Co.)

THIERY & CO.
Newark, New Jersey

Listed J C-K as jewelers; out of business before 1909. Trademarks found on souvenir spoons.

THE THOMAE CO.
Attleboro, Massachusetts

TRADE   MARK

The trademark has been used with little change since 1920 and was a personal mark used by Charles Thomae to mark his own work before that.

Chas. Thomae & Son, Inc. was established August 1, 1920 by the late Charles Thomae and his son, Herbert L. Thomae. They make novelty goods of 14k gold and sterling silver, religious medals, photo etching on gold and silver and make bronze memorial plates and signs.

Charles Thomae was superintendent of the Watson Co. for several years and developed enameling and a line of novelties and dresserware till it reached the importance of a separate business. The Thomae Co. was formed as a division of the Watson Co. In 1920, Charles Thomae resigned from both firms and started a new business with the name of Chas. Thomae & Son.

The firm's founder died in 1958. It is now run by his two sons Herbert L., President and Charles G. Thomae.

THOMPSON, HAYWARD & CO.
Mechanicsville, Mass.
(See Walter E. Hayward Co., Inc.)

THORNTON & CO.
New York, New York

H. & S.

*Old Mark of
Holbrook & Simmons.*

Manufacturers of sterling silverware. Successor to Holbrook & Simmons before 1896. Out of business before 1904.

TIFFANY & CO., INC.
New York, New York

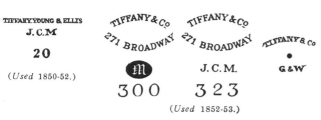

TIFFANY.YOUNG & ELLIS
J.C.M
20
(*Used* 1850-52.)

J.C.M.

(*Used* 1852-53.)

(*Used* 1854-55.)

(*Used* 1854-70.)

TIFFANY & C?
MAKERS
STERLING-SILVER
925-1000
M

(*Used* 1875-91.)

(*Used* 1891-1902.)

TIFFANY & CO.
12345 MAKERS 67890
STERLING SILVER
925-1000
M

TIFFANY & C?
14786 MAKERS 5885
STERLING SILVER
925~1000
C

(*Used since* 1902.)

*The figures at the right and left of the word
"Makers" are the pattern and order numbers,
and vary accordingly.*

*The following marks were used on silverware made
for International Expositions in addition
to the usual one:*

1893	1900	1901
World's Columbian Exposition Chicago.	*Exposition Universelle, Paris.*	*Pan-American Exposition, Buffalo.*

Founded by Charles L. Tiffany in 1837 with John B. Young under the name Tiffany & Young. They first stocked their store with stationery, Chinese bric-a-brac, fans, pottery, umbrellas and desks. They purchased almost all of their silverware from John C. Moore who had begun the manufacture of silverware in 1827 and who was later joined in business by his son, Edward C. Moore.

Called Tiffany, Young & Ellis in 1852. Became Tiffany & Co. in 1853.

In 1868 Tiffany was incorporated and the silverware factory of the Moores became part of the organization with Edward C. Moore becoming one of its directors. From then on, and until Mr. Moore's death the silverware made in the factory bore not only the mark "Tiffany & Co." but also the letter "M." Ever since then, both the name Tiffany & Co., and the initial of the incumbent company president appear on all Tiffany-made silver.

In 1852 Tiffany introduced the English sterling silver standard to America for Tiffany silver. This standard was later adopted by the U. S. Government and made into Federal law determining the minimum amount of fine silver required for articles marked "Sterling Silver."

CHRONOLOGY

Tiffany & Young	1837
Tiffany, Young & Ellis	1852
Tiffany & Company	1853
Tiffany & Co., Inc.	1868

TIFFT & WHITING
North Attleboro, Mass.
(See Gorham Corporation)

Founded in 1840 in North Attleboro, Massachusetts. Succeeded by Whiting Manufacturing Company, Newark, New Jersey in 1866. Purchased by the Gorham Corporation in 1905.

TILDEN-THURBER CO.
Providence, Rhode Island

Roots of Tilden-Thurber Company go deep into the history and business development of Rhode Island. In 1856, when the doors of the new firm opened, the sign above the window read GORHAM CO. AND BROWN. Gorham Thurber, great-grandfather of today's president, was listed as one of the officers. An unusually active man in business, in addition to his interest in Gorham Co. & Brown, he formed a co-partnership with John Gorham, forming the firm of Gorham & Thurber, one of the predecessors of the Gorham Manufacturing Company.

In 1878, Gorham Co. & Brown moved across the street from its first location and changed its name to Henry T. Brown & Co. Members of the board were Mr. Brown, Henry Tilden and Gorham Thurber. The firm remained there until 1895 when it moved into the present Tilden-Thurber building. Gorham Thurber died shortly afterwards.

In March, 1880, the name of the firm was changed to Tilden-Thurber & Co. In the same year, William H. Thurber, grandfather of the present officers and son of Gorham Thurber, joined the firm,

becoming a partner in 1885.

On June 23, 1892, the company became incorporated under the present name Tilden-Thurber Corporation. At this time Henry Tilden was elected President and William H. Thurber, Treasurer. William H. Thurber's contributions to the development of the company were an increased volume of business and addition of a number of new departments added to the original line of jewelry and silverware. Following Mr. Tilden's death in 1907, Mr. Thurber was elected President and Treasurer.

Henry C. Tilden, son of Henry Tilden, joined the firm and became manager of the sterling silver department. In 1915, he moved to Chicago and joined Spaulding & Co., leading jewelers and eventually became president of that firm.

In 1956, when the company celebrated its 100th anniversary, Frederick B. Thurber was Presi-

dent and William Gorham Thurber, Treasurer. Tracy Gorham Thurber, son of W. G. Thurber, joined the company in 1951. Another son, William H. Thurber, is currently President.

Since 1878, Tilden-Thurber has been noted as the source of rare and beautiful importations. Fine paintings and etchings are displayed in the Tilden-Thurber Art Galleries.

Working with the Gorham Manufacturing Company, Tilden-Thurber furnished a complete sterling silver service for the Battleship **Rhode Island,** later placed on display in the State House. They also furnished the silver service for the Cruiser, **Providence,** later exhibited at Brown University.

Service to the community and active interest in its employees have been outstanding characteristics of this company. This has been demonstrated in the establishment of a Brown University scholarship for a local student, assistance in the establishment of a rigorous educational and training program for jewelers; a company-paid pension plan and, most recently, a profit-sharing plan for employees.

TILLINGHAST SILVER CO.
Meriden, Connecticut

TILLINGHAST SILVER CO.

Manufacturers of sterling silver hollow handle serving pieces. In business c. 1920–1935.

EDWARD TODD & CO.
New York, New York

Established in 1869. Manufacturers of sterling silverware and gold pens. Listed J C-K 1896–1922.

EUGENE S. TONER CO.
New York, New York

Manufacturers (?) of sterling silverware. Listed J C-K 1909 as out of business.

Note similarity of trademark to that of Depasse Mfg. Co.

JOHN TOOTHILL
(See Metropolitan Silver Co.)

TOOTHILL & McBEAN SILVER CO.
Ottawa, Illinois

QUADRUPLE PLATE

Listed J C-K 1898 in plated silver section. Out of business before 1904.

TORONTO SILVER PLATE CO.
Toronto, Canada

STERLING

STERLING 🏵 ⊞ T.S.P.

(On sterling silver)

Sterling marks not used after 1915.

(On plated silver holloware)

Manufacturers 1887–c. 1920 of sterling silver and plated holloware, knives and tableware.

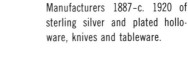

TORONTO SILVER PLATE C(
(Flatware.)

TORSIL METAL
TORSIL STEEL
TORSIL E. P.—N. S.

(Knives.)

A. F. TOWLE & SON CO.
Greenfield, Massachusetts
(See Lunt Silversmiths)
(See Rogers, Lunt & Bowlen)
(See Towle Silversmiths)

A. F. Towle & Son, successors to Towle & Jones, were the links between the Moultons, of Newburyport, and the Towle Silversmiths. Anthony F. Towle was an apprentice to William Moulton IV and bought his business and that of Joseph Moulton IV in 1873. In 1882, with others, the business was incorporated as Towle Silversmiths. Anthony F. Towle & Son moved to Greenfield, Massachusetts in 1890 and operated until 1902. At that time their business was taken over by Rogers, Lunt & Bowlen, now known as Lunt Silversmiths.

They were manufacturers of both sterling and plated silverware. Registered trademark, U. S. Patent Office, No. 27,286, November 19, 1895 for electroplated ware.

E. J. TOWLE MFG. CO.
Seattle, Washington

E. J. T. Co.

Began as Joseph Mayer & Bros. c. 1895; Jos. Mayer, Inc. before 1922; Northern Stamping & Manufacturing Co. (still used for some items) and was succeeded by E. J. Towle Manufacturing Company c. 1945.

Were wholesalers of diamonds, watches, jewelry, sterling silverware, plated silver goods, cut glass and optical goods.

Medals and other presentation pieces have been and are still made. Some of the finest die work in the country is still done by this company.

Their work is now mainly the designing and manufacturing of silver jewelry, charms, religious goods and souvenir silverware.

TOWLE SILVERSMITHS
Newburyport, Massachusetts

(On plated silver)

La Fayette Silverware

Paul Revere Silverware

(On sterling silver)

William Moulton II, born in 1664, settled in old Newbury, later Newburyport, to become the first silversmith in a long lineage of craftsmen now the Towle Silversmiths. He was succeeded by Joseph I, William III (who moved to Marietta, Ohio and became not only the first silversmith in The Northwest Territory, but, also one of the founders of Marietta), Joseph II, Joseph III, Ebenezer William IV, Enoch, Abel and Joseph IV—all silversmiths.

Anthony F. Towle and William P Jones, apprentices of William IV began business under the name Towle & Jones in 1857, later buy-

THE MOULTON MAKER'S MARKS

WILLIAM MOULTON, II 1720–1793	W.MOULTON / WMoulton	WM / W·M
JOSEPH MOULTON, II 1724–1795	I·MOULTON	J·M / J·M
JOSEPH MOULTON, II 1744–1816	JM MOULTON MOULTON / I·M I·MOULTON MOULTON	
WILLIAM MOULTON, IV 1772–1861	W.MOULTON / W MOULTON / W.MOULTON	WM / W·M / W.MOULTON
EBENEZER MOULTON 1768–1824	MOULTON	
ENOCH MOULTON 1780–1815	E.MOULTON. EMOULTON / E MOULTON	
ABEL MOULTON 1784–1840	AM *·M· A.MOULTON	
JOSEPH MOULTON, IV 1814–1903	J.MOULTON J·MOULTON	
TOWLE & JONES 1857–1873	TOWLE & JONES	
A. F. TOWLE & SON 1873 Inc. 1880 1882	A F TOWLE & SON	

ing the business of William IV and Joseph IV. Anthony F. Towle and Edward F., his son, engaged in business as A. F. Towle & Son in 1873, and this partnership was the germ of the A. F. Towle & Son Co., Inc. in 1880, which in 1882 became the Towle Manufacturing Company, Anthony F. Towle and Edward F. Towle retiring. The company is now known as the Towle Silversmiths.

About 1890 the familiar "T enclosing a Lion" was first used as a trademark.

Towle Silversmiths manufacture an extensive line of both sterling and plated silverware.

They have been leaders in establishing an exhibit gallery where artist-silversmiths skills are presented to the public. Other exhibits of silver craftsmanship have been prepared in cooperation with museums.

NOW

THE TOWLE SILVERSMITHS

IRA STRONG TOWN & J. TOWN Montpelier, Vermont		Advertised 1830–1838 as clockmakers and silversmiths—"silver work of every description manufactured to order on short notice."
IRA S. TOWN & ELIJAH B. WITHERELL Montpelier, Vermont		Successors to Ira Strong Town and J. Town. Formed a partnership that took over the business until it was dissolved in 1845. Advertised that "they made all the silverware bought at their shop and it was warrented to be the best quality."
THE TOWNSEND, DESMOND & VOORHIS CO. New York, New York	**T. D. & V. CO. STERLING.**	Listed J C-K 1896–1904 in sterling silver section. Out of business before 1909.

TUCKER & PARKHURST CO.
Ogdensburg, New York

Listed in J C-K in sterling silver section as out of business before 1904.

JAMES W. TUFTS
Boston, Massachusetts

Trademark registered February 2, 1875 for plated silverware by James W. Tufts, Medford, Massachusetts. Incorporated 1881. Out of business before 1915.

TUTTLE SILVER CO.
Boston, Massachusetts
(See Tuttle Silversmiths)

TUTTLE SILVERSMITHS
Boston, Massachusetts

FINE STERLING

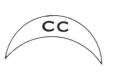

In 1890, Boston silversmith Timothy Tuttle was first commissioned by wealthy families to copy old English silver. His original pieces were dated in the English custom with the crest of the reigning monarch. During the term of office of President Calvin Coolidge, Tuttle adopted this custom, marking each piece with a crescent and the initials of the incumbent President of the United States. Today this date mark is unique with Tuttle.

Timothy Tuttle used the Pine Tree Shilling symbol as his trademark. The Pine Tree Shilling was one of the earliest silver coins minted in the American colonies by Hull and Sanderson in 1652. Used as the Tuttle trademark it is the stamp of quality and prestige appearing on all Tuttle sterling pieces, including authentic reproductions of Early American, European and modern design.

In 1915, the company was listed as Tuttle Silver Co. By 1922, it was incorporated.

In 1955 Tuttle Silversmiths was purchased by R. Wallace & Sons Mfg. Co. (now Wallace Silversmiths) and became an acquisition of the Hamilton Watch Company of Lancaster, Pennsylvania when Hamilton purchased Wallace Silversmiths in December 1959. Every piece of Tuttle silver is sterling. They make no plated silver.

TIMOTHY TUTTLE
Boston, Massachusetts
(See Tuttle Silversmiths)

Silversmith in Boston, Massachusetts in 1890. Founder of Tuttle Silversmiths.

TYSON, TRUMP & CO.
Baltimore, Maryland

Listed in 1867–1868 Baltimore City Directory as silverplaters.

U

UNGER BROS.
New York, New York

Listed J C-K 1896–1915 in sterling silver and cut glass sections. Out of business before 1922.

UNION SILVER PLATE CO.
(See Holmes, Booth & Haydens)
(See International Silver Co.)

UTOPIAN SILVER DEPOSIT &
NOVELTY CO.
New York, New York

Listed J C-K 1915 in sterling silver section. Out of business before 1922.

V

THOMAS J. VAIL
Connecticut
(See American Sterling Co.)
(See Curtisville Mfg. Co.)
(See Williams Bros. Mfg. Co.)

During the Civil War Thomas Vail produced war materials. Between 1865 and 1869 Vail probably was in the silver plating business as in the Hartford Directory for 1869 he is listed as manufacturer of German Silver and plated ware, etc. In 1871, The American Sterling Company took over the property from the trustee, Leavitt Hunt.

VALENTINE LINSLEY SILVER CO.
Wallingford, Connecticut
(See Wallace Bros. Silver Co.)
(See The Wallingford Co.)

V. L.
(Silver Plated Hollowware.)

MADE AND PLATED BY
WALLACE BROS. SILVER CO.

Listed in the City Directory 1895-1899. Makers of plated silverware. Succeeded by The Wallingford Co. in 1899.

VAN BERGH SILVER PLATE CO.
Rochester, New York

BRITANNIA METAL CO.

Founded in 1892 by Frederick W. Van Bergh and Maurice H. Van Bergh, who were President and Secretary, respectively. A third brother is said to have joined the firm in 1898 (not confirmed). The company was incorporated July 1, 1904. In 1925 all assets were transferred to a new corporation, The Van Bergh Silver Plate Company, Inc., set up by Oneida Community Limited. This new corporation was merged into Oneida Community Limited in 1926 and moved from Rochester to Oneida, New York.

CLARENCE A. VANDERBILT
New York, New York

STERLING—V

Manufacturers of sterling silverware, baskets, salt and peppers, cups, candlesticks, cigarette cases, vanity cases, picture frames, napkin rings and flasks from c. 1909-1935.

W. K. VANDERSLICE & CO.
San Francisco, Calif.

Founded in 1859, it was the pioneer silver plate company west of the Rockies. Went out of business between 1904–1915.

P. M. VERMASS
Minneapolis, Minnesota

Successors to F. L. Bosworth before 1921. They were jobbers who bought wares "in the metal" and plated them in their own shop. No record after 1922.

VICTOR SILVER CO.
(See International Silver Co.)

VICTOR S. CO.

Trademark of Derby Silver Co. on less expensive line. Variation used after 1922 by International on silverplated flatware for hotels, restaurants, etc.

GEO. L. VOSE MFG. CO., INC.
Providence, Rhode Island

Successor to Geo. L. Vose & Co. between 1904–1915. Manufacturing jeweler. Last listed c. 1920.

W

J. WAGNER & SON, INC.
New York, New York

Used since 1909

First listed in J C-K in 1909 as the Central Sterling Company. Suc-

ceeded by Weber Wagner Co. between 1909 and 1915. Listed as Weber-Wagner & Benson Co., Inc. 1915–1931 and as J. Wagner & Son, Inc. in 1950. Not listed in 1965.

Manufacturers of sterling silver holloware.

THE WALDO FOUNDRY
Bridgeport, Connecticut

(*Aluminium-Gold Flat and Table Ware.*)

Listed in J C-K 1896–1904. Out of business before 1915. Manufac-

turers of aluminum-gold flat and tableware.

Note similarity to trademarks of the W. H. Glenny & Co. and H. H. Curtis & Co.

WALDORF SILVER CO.
(See Woodman-Cook Co.)

WALDORF SILVER CO.

Thought to be trademark of Woodman-Cook Co. No confirmation.

WALLACE BROS. SILVER COMPANY
Wallingford, Connecticut
(See Wallace Silversmiths)

QUADRUPLE
PLATE

ESSEX SILVER CO.
ESSEX SILVER CO.
QUAD PLATE

(Silver plated britannia)

MADE AND PLATED BY WALLACE BROS. SILVER CO.

In July 1875, Robert Wallace and his sons, Robert B., William J., Harry L., George H., Frank A., and sons-in-law, W. J. Leavenworth and D. E. Morris formed a co-partnership with the name Wallace Brothers to manufacture plated silver flatware of cast steel. On June 23, 1879 the corporation of R. Wallace & Sons Mfg. Co. bought the business of Wallace Brothers.

R. WALLACE & SONS MFG. CO.
Wallingford, Connecticut
(See Wallace Silversmiths)

(*Flatware.*)

(*Nickel Goods.*)

(*Hollowware.*)

900
(*Steel Flatware.*)

(On sterling silver knives about 1898)

Successor to Wallace, Simpson & Co. in 1871. Name changed to Wallace Silversmiths in 1956.

R. WALLACE
(*Silver Soldered.*)

SILVER SOLDERED

WALLACE SILVERSMITHS
Wallingford, Connecticut

WALLACE STERLING

WALLACE STERLING

ROBERT WALLACE was born in Prospect, Connecticut in 1815. He was the grandson of James Wallace, who had come from Scotland and settled in Blandford, Mass., late in the 18th century. At 16, Robert was apprenticed to Captain William Mix of Prospect to learn he art of making britannia poons. Two years later, in 1833, e set up shop in an old grist mill o make spoons on his own. About year later he saw a German silver poon, made by Dixon & Sons of heffield, England. He recognized ts superior strength and color and vith Deacon Almer Hall (later head f Hall, Elton & Co.) began the manufacture of German silver poons—the first in this country.

From 1834 to 1849 he made hese spoons for Deacon Hall, for all, Elton & Co., and in 1849 enered into a co-partnership with . B. Pomeroy to manufacture hem on contract for Fred R. Curis Co. of Hartford and made briannia spoons for Hall, Elton & Co. and Edgar Atwater of Wallingford.

In 1854, Robert decided to take p farming, but soon returned to Vallingford to continue the manufacture of German silver orks, spoons and similar articles vith Samuel Simpson of Wallingord. This ten-year partnership was ormed May 1, 1855, under the ame of R. WALLACE & CO. On May 15, 1855, Simpson's artners in the Meriden Britania Co., H. C. Wilcox, W. W. Lyman nd Isaac C. Lewis, were admitted, vith the firm name remaining the ame. This contract was termiated in 1865 when a new contract

was made and the corporation WALLACE, SIMPSON & CO. was organized.

In 1870, Wallace purchased two-thirds of Simpson's interest and in 1871 bought the remainder. On July 17, 1871 the corporate name was changed to R. WALLACE & SONS MFG. CO. with his two sons, Robert B. and William J. and a son-in-law, W. J. Leavenworth members of the firm.

In 1875 the company started production of forks and spoons of sterling. In July 1875, Robert Wallace with his sons, Robert B., William J., Henry L., George H., Frank A. and sons-in-law W. J. Leavenworth and D. E. Morris formed a co-partnership under the name of WALLACE BROTHERS for the manufacture of silverplated flatware on a base of cast steel. Manufacture of silverplated holloware also began at this time. On June 23, 1879, the corporation of R. WALLACE & SONS MFG. CO. acquired and took over the business and good will of WALLACE BROTHERS.

New machinery and mass production methods made possible great expansion. All types of flatware, holloware, dresser silver and practically all lines of articles in which silver is a component, as well as stainless

steel, were added.

In 1924 a Canadian plant was opened in Cookshire, Quebec, for production of tinned spoons and forks. In 1944 sterling flatware was added to the line. In 1945 the Canadian branch was incorporated as R. WALLACE & SONS OF CANADA, LTD. It was sold in 1964.

In 1934, William S. Warren, designer for the company, conceived the idea of three-dimensional flatware patterns—for which the Wallace Company is noted. The Watson Company of Attleboro, Mass. was bought by Wallace in 1955, moving to Wallingford in 1956. The name R. WALLACE & SONS MFG. CO. was changed to WALLACE SILVERSMITHS in 1956. The Tuttle Silver Company and Smith & Smith were acquired by Wallace and moved to Wallingford. WALLACE SILVERSMITHS, in 1959 was purchased by the Hamilton Watch Company of Lancaster, Pennsylvania and is now a Division of that firm. Manufacturing continues in Wallingford, but office facilities are in Lancaster.

CHRONOLOGY

Robert Wallace	1834
Robert Wallace & Co.	1855
Wallace, Simpson & Co.	1865
R. Wallace & Sons Mfg. Co.	1871
Wallace Silversmiths	1956

HE WALLINGFORD CO., INC.
Vallingford, Connecticut
See Wallace Bros. Silver Co.)

ESSEX SILVER CO.
(Quadruple Plate.)

QUADRUPLE
PLATE

The Wallingford Co. was listed in the City Directory 1903-1941.

V. L.
(Silver Plated Hollowware.)

MADE AND PLATED BY
WALLACE BROS. SILVER CO.

JOHN WANAMAKER
Philadelphia, Pennsylvania

Founded 1861 as Wanamaker & Brown. Became John Wanamaker in 1870. It was the first American system store—actually a collection of exclusive stores under one roof.

Like Marshall Field's, Macy's and others, they sold silverware stamped with their own trade mark.

ANDREW E. WARNER, JR.
Baltimore, Maryland

Listed in Baltimore City Directories as a gold and silversmith from 1864 till 1893. Listed as Andrew E. Warner & Son, 1867- 1870. Andrew E. is listed alone from 1874-1889. The listing from 1890-1893 is A. E. Warner.

ANDREW E. WARNER, SR.
Baltimore, Maryland

Andrew Ellicott Warner was born in 1786 and died in 1870. He was listed as a gold and silversmith from c. 1805 till his death. Andrew and Thomas H. Warner (1780-1828) worked together c 1805-1812.

GEORGE C. WARNER
Baltimore, Maryland

Listed in 1855-1856 Baltimore City Directory as a silver chaser.

WARNER SILVER COMPANY
(See Weidlich Bros. Mfg. Co.)

WARNER SILVER MFG. CO.
Chicago, Illinois

Listed in J C-K 1896-1904 Manufacturers of plated silverware. Out of business before 1915

THOMAS H. WARNER
Baltimore, Maryland

Thomas H. Warner c. 1780-1828 He and Andrew Ellicott Warner worked together c. 1805-1812. From 1814 to 1824, and perhaps longer, Thomas H. Warner was assayer for the city of Baltimore. His duty was to "test silverwares to see that they were of no less fineness than eleven ounces pure silver to every pound troy."

ARREN MANSFIELD CO.
ortland, Maine

An advertisement in Leslie's Magazine, November 1904 carried the statement that they were gold and silversmiths, established in 1867. They are not listed in the Portland City Directories.

They published an illustrated catalog with price list of jewelry, spoons, tableware, watches, etc. in 1900. Another catalog, dated 1907, illustrated an extensive line of silverware. No trademark is shown.

ARREN SILVER PLATE CO.
ew York, New York
ee Oneida Silversmiths)
ee Wm. A. Rogers, Ltd.)

NEW YORK
(*Medium Grade Hollowware.*)

Warren Silver Plate Company was a trademark first used in 1901 by Wm. A. Rogers Company on their medium grade holloware. The name apparently was based on the fact that the New York Office was located at 12 Warren Street.

ARWICK STERLING CO.
ovidence, Rhode Island

John F. Brady, treasurer of the company, registered the lower trademark, U. S. Patent Office No.

97,038 on May 19, 1914 to be used on sterling silver, flatware, holloware, tableware, dresserware, desk articles, sewing articles, silver trimming for leather, glass, wood, metal, fabrics and jewelry. He stated that this trademark had been used continuously since January 1, 1913. No record after 1922.

ATROUS MFG. CO.
allingford, Connecticut
ee International Silver Co.)

 STERLING.

 W. M.CO.

(*Silver Plated on Nickel Silver Hollowware.*)

Successor to Maltby, Stevens & Curtiss in 1896. Manufactured sterling silver novelties, vanity cases, cigarette cases, dorine boxes, match boxes, belt buckles and small holloware. One of the original companies to become part of the International Silver Co. in 1898.

WATSON COMPANY
Attleboro, Massachusetts
(See Wallace Silversmiths)

(1879-1905)

(1905-1929)

(1910-1938)

An undated Watson Company catalog shows the trademarks on the left and the dates they were used. Examination of hundreds of pieces made by this company has not turned up a single one with the "pennant enclosing a W." All the pieces stamped with the pennant have had an H enclosed.

Note that the trademark used between 1905-1929 is one Wilcox & Wagoner trademark turned upside down.

Successors to Cobb, Gould & Co., founded in Attleboro, Massachusetts in 1874.

Became Watson & Newell Company in 1894 and the Watson Company in 1919.

Before 1905 they bought Wilcox & Wagoner of New York.

Watson & Newell were among the largest producers of souvenir spoons in the country. J. T. Inman, also of Attleboro, bought the souvenir spoon dies from the Watson Company. The balance of the business was purchased by R. Wallace & Sons (now Wallace Silversmiths). In 1964 these same souvenir spoon dies were sold to Whiting & Davis who are producing them stamped with their own trademark.

CHRONOLOGY

Cobb, Gould & Co.	1874-1894
Watson & Newell	1894-1919
Watson Company	1919-1955

JULIUS R. WATTS & CO.
Atlanta, Georgia

(On Souvenir Spoons.)

Established in 1888 and listed in the Atlanta City Directories through 1958-1959. They are listed as watchmakers and more recently as jewelers and watch inspectors. The Uncle Remus trademark was stamped on souvenir spoons.

JOHN WAUBEL
Baltimore, Maryland

Listed in the 1864 Baltimore City Directory as a silverplater.

WAYNE SILVER CO.
Honesdale, Pennsylvania

Listed J C-K 1896 in sterling silver section. Out of business before 1904.

WEB SILVER COMPANY, INC.
Philadelphia, Pennsylvania

WEB

Successors to the Web Jewelry Manufacturing Co. between 1950-1965. In 1952 they acquired the sterling flatware dies and patterns formerly used by the Weidlich Sterling Spoon Company, Bridgeport, Connecticut.

GEORGE W. WEBB
Baltimore, Maryland

George W. Webb was born in 1812 and died in 1890. The earliest record found for his gold and silversmithing was an advertisement stating that his business was established in 1850. He is listed in the Baltimore City Directories as George W. Webb until 1865-1866

when the name was changed to Webb & Company. G. W. Webb, A. Remick and W. H. Sexton, partners. This listing continued until 1877 when it changed to Geo. W. Webb & Co. The latter listing continued through 1886.

H. J. WEBB & CO.
Springfield, Massachusetts

Successors to L. S. Stowe & Co. between 1896 and 1904. Jobbers and retailers of silver and jewelry. Out of business before 1915.

JOHN WEBB
Baltimore, Maryland

John Webb is listed by Pleasants and Sill (see bibliography) as a silversmith in Baltimore c. 1827-1842. In the Baltimore City Directories John Webb is listed 1855-

1856 as a goldsmith. The 1864 listing is in the name John Webb, Sr. The 1865-1866 listing is John Webb, jeweler.

WEBER-WAGNER & BENSON CO., INC.
(See J. Wagner & Son, Inc.)

WEBER-WAGNER CO.
(See J. Wagner & Son, Inc.)

WEBSTER COMPANY
North Attleboro, Massachusetts
(See Reed & Barton)
(See Frank W. Smith Silver Co., Inc.)
(See G. K. Webster Co.)

Founded by George K. Webster in 1869 in North Attleboro under the name of G. K. Webster & Company. As the business grew, Mr. Webster purchased the interest of his partners. It operated under his direct supervision throughout his lifetime.

On January 1, 1950 it became a subsidiary of Reed & Barton of Taunton, Massachusetts. It continues its independent operation as The Webster Company.

The principal product has always been articles made of sterling silver. They are mostly baby goods, dresserware and picture frames.

In October 1958 they purchased the Frank W. Smith Silver Co. Inc and all the tools and dies, along with the tradename and trademark. The flatware portion of this business was moved to North Attleboro from the original location in Gardner, Massachusetts

---

A. A. WEBSTER & CO.
Brooklyn, New York

Began as Frederick S. Hoffman, silversmith c. 1820; succeeded by C. B. Webster (Clarence B. Webster) between 1896–1904 and by A. A. Webster & Company before 1909. Distributors (?) of sterling silver goods, 14 and 18k gold novelties and leather goods with silver mountings.

E. G. WEBSTER & SON
Brooklyn, New York
(See International Silver Co.)

(On sterling silver)

Webster Mfg. Co., Brooklyn, New York, 1859; E. G. Webster & Bro. 1873 became E. G. Webster & Son 1886. Bought by International Silver Co. in 1928 and moved from Brooklyn to Meriden. Manufacturers of sterling silver and plated silverware.

G. K. WEBSTER
North Attleboro, Massachusetts
(See Reed & Barton)
(See Webster Co.)

Founded in North Attleboro, Massachusetts in 1869. Succeeded by the Webster Co. before 1904

W. E. WEBSTER CO.
Providence, Rhode Island

Registered trademark U. S. Patent Office, No. 27,241, November 19, 1895 for sterling silver, rings, pins and ornamental jewelry. Out of business before 1904.

THE WEIDLICH BROS. MFG. CO.
Bridgeport, Connecticut

POMPEIAN GOLD
THE WARNER SILVER CO.

Founded in 1901 in Bridgeport, Connecticut. Specialized in sterling and plated trophies. Went into voluntary dissolution in 1950. No connection with Weidlich, Inc. 140 Hurd Avenue, Bridgeport, Connecticut.

WEIDLICH STERLING SPOON CO.
Bridgeport, Connecticut

Related to Weidlich Bros. Mfg. Co. of Bridgeport. Made sterling silver souvenir spoons and sterling silver flatware (U. S. Patent 103,304, March 30, 1915). In

1952 the Web Jewelry Mfg. Co., now the Web Silver Co., Inc., silversmiths in Philadelphia, acquired the sterling flatware dies and patterns. No connection with present Weidlich, Inc., 140 Hurd Avenue, Bridgeport, Connecticut.

. M. WEINBERG & CO.
New York, New York

Listed J C-K 1915 in plated silver section. Out of business before 1922.

Note similarity of trademark to that of F. G. Whitney & Co., Attleboro, Massachusetts.

WEINMAN CO.
Philadelphia, Pennsylvania

BRAZIL SILVER

Manufacturers of plated silverware in Philadelphia c. 1900.

WEIZENNEGGER BROS.
Newark, New Jersey

Listed J C-K 1909-1922 in sterling silver section, manufacturers of mesh bags, dealers in diamonds.

WELCH SILVER
(See American Silver Co.)

WELSH & BRO.
Baltimore, Maryland

Listed in Baltimore City Directories 1887-1909 under plated silverware.

WENDELL MANUFACTURING
COMPANY
Chicago, Illinois

TRADE MARK

Listed J C-K 1896-1915. Manufacturers of sterling silver badges and emblems. Retail (or wholesale) outlet in New York listed as Wendell & Company, 1904-1909. Not listed in Chicago City Directories.

WEST SILVER CO.
Taunton, Massachusetts

Founded in Taunton, Massachusetts in 1883. F. B. Rogers successors before 1896.

WESTBROOK BRITANNIA
COMPANY
Portland, Maine

Listed in 1869-1885 City Directories. William Wallace Stevens owner.

C. A. WETHERELL & CO.

Listed in Jeweler's Weekly, 1890 as manufacturers of sterling silverware. Listed in Attleboro City Directories 1892-1897 as manufacturing jewelers.

WHITING & DAVIS CO., INC.
Plainville, Massachusetts

W. & D.

Began as a small chain manufacturing company c. 1876. Operated by William Wade and Edward P. Davis. C. A. Whiting, while still a young boy, entered the business as an unskilled worker. He worked as an artisan, salesman and partner, finally becoming owner in 1907.

Years of experimenting led to the development of the first chain mail mesh machine shortly after 1907. Whiting & Davis is now the world's largest manufacturer of

199

nesh products including such items as safety gloves and aprons, mesh handbags and purse accessories, and jewelry. They also produce an outstanding line of antique reproduction jewelry—many pieces copies of museum masterpieces.

In 1964 they purchased the J. T.

Inman Company and integrated the complete manufacturing facilities into their main plant. The souvenir spoon equipment, dies and tools were bought from the Watson Company by J. T. Inman. The balance of the business was sold to the Wallace Company. These dies are now used to make

souvenir spoons. There are approximately 3,000 designs, according to the Executive Vice President, George J. LeMire. They will be stamped, whenever possible, with the Whiting & Davis registered trademark.

WHITING MFG. CO.
Providence, Rhode Island
(See Gorham Corporation)

Successor to Tifft & Whiting in 1866. Makers of sterling silver flat and holloware and jewelry (U. S. Patent No. 24, 712, May 15, 1894). Purchased by Gorham Corporation in 1905 and moved to Providence, Rhode Island in 1925. The Whiting mark is still used.

FRANK M. WHITING CO.
North Attleboro, Massachusetts
(See Ellmore Silver Co.)

Founded in 1881 as F. M. Whiting Company; became Frank M. Whiting & Company c. 1900. Manufacturers of sterling silver flatware.

Was a division of Ellmore Silver Co. c. 1940. Has been independently owned since 1960.

G. WHITNEY & CO.
Attleborough, Massachusetts

Trademark registered July 12, 1881 for use on jewelry. Note similarity to trademark of E. M. Weinberg & Co. of New York.

WHITNEY JEWELRY COMPANY
Boston, Massachusetts

Barbara Frietchie
No. 19,788

Columbus Before the Queen
No. 19,778

First listed in the Boston City Directories in 1883; probably founded the previous year. It was first listed as Whitney Brothers, jewelers. The brothers were: Edwin A. Whitney of Watertown, Massachusetts, and later of Newton, Massachusetts, and Albert E. Whitney of Fitchburg, Massachusetts. Albert E. was not connected with the firm by 1894, when it was listed as E. A. Whitney Company, watches and jewelry. Was in business through 1911.

U. S. Patents Nos. 19,778 through 19,992 were registered in the name of Edwin A. Whitney, June 30, 1891, for use on gold, silver and plated flatware.

Columbus and the Egg
No. 19,779

Fort Smith
No. 19,790

Monitor & Merrimac
March 9, 1862
No. 19,791

Antietam, September 17, 1862,
No. 19,992

Gettysburg, July 1863,
No. 19,789

The **Santa Maria,** No. 19,780

The March to the Sea
No. 19,781

Appomattox, April 9, 1865
No. 19,782

July 4, 1776, No. 19,784

Sheriden's Ride, No. 19,783

General Stonewall Jackson,
No. 19,785

"The Seven Days" battle used in spoon bowl, General Robert E. Lee is the trademark, No. 19,786

Signing the Emancipation Proclamation, January 1, 1863, No. 19,787

There is a discrepancy between the historical scenes listed in the trademark description and those actually shown. Numbers 19,784 and 19,790 are listed as "July 4, 1776" and "Fort Smith." The two scenes shown are actually of Harpers Ferry, Oct. 17, 1859 and Fort Sumpter, April 12, 1861.

H. F. WICHMAN
Honolulu, Hawaii

H. F. WICHMAN

Manufacturing silversmiths and jewelers. Began in 1890 as Gomes & Wichman. Became H. F. Wichman in 1891 and continues in business under that name.

HENRY WIENER & SON New York, New York	PICADILLY	Distributors (?) of sterling silver-ware c. 1920.

WIEDERER & MOORE Baltimore, Maryland		Listed in 1885 Baltimore City Directory as silverplaters.

CHAS. C. WIENTGE CO. Newark, New Jersey		Manufacturers or distributors of sterling silverware c. 1915–1920.

WILCOX BRITANNIA CO.
(See International Silver Co.)
(See Wilcox Silver Plate Co.)

WILCOX & EVERTSEN New York, New York (See International Silver Co.)		Makers of sterling silver hollo-ware in New York in 1892. Moved to Meriden in 1896. One of the original companies which formed the International Silver Co.

WILCOX-ROTH CO. Newark, New Jersey		Listed in J C-K 1909 in sterling silver section as out of business.

WILCOX SILVER PLATE CO.
Meriden, Connecticut
(See International Silver Co.)

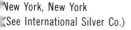

Organized in 1865 by Jedediah and Horace Wilcox, Charles Parker, Aaron Collins and Hezekiah Miller and others to make holloware as Wilcox Britannia Co. In 1867 the name was changed to Wilcox Silver Plate Co. In 1869 they purchased the Parker & Casper Co. They were one of the original companies to become part of the International Silver Co. in 1898.

H. C. WILCOX & CO.
Meriden, Connecticut
(See International Silver Co.)
(See Meriden Britannia Co.)

Organized by Horace C. and Dennis C. Wilcox to market the products of Meriden's britannia ware. A forerunner of Meriden Britannia Co.

WILCOX & WAGONER
New York, New York

Listed in J C-K 1904 in sterling silverware and cut glass sections. Bought by the Watson Co. before 1905.

WILEY-CRAWFORD CO., INC.
Newark, New Jersey

Manufacturers of gold and sterling silver novelties, card trays and jewelry c. 1915-1922.

WILKINSON SWORD CO.
London and Sheffield, England

Manufacturers of plated silver swords. Listed J C-K 1909-1922

WILLIAMS BROS. MFG. CO.
Naubuc, Connecticut
(See American Sterling Co.)
(See F. Curtis & Co.)
(See Curtisville Mfg. Co.)
(See Thomas J. Vail)

Williams TRIPLE PLATE

James B. and William Williams bought the American Sterling Company and founded the Williams Bros. Mfg. Co., in 1880. Manufacturers of plated silver spoons, forks and a general line of flatware. They went out of business in June 1950.

ROGER WILLIAMS SILVER CO.
Providence, Rhode Island
(See Gorham Corporation)
(See Mt. Vernon Co. Silversmiths, Inc.)

R & W

U. S. Patent No. 36,769, July 16, 1901 for certain named metalwares—whole or in part of silver.

Trademark used continuously since June 1, 1901.
Merged in 1903 with the Mauser Mfg. Co. of New York and Hayes & McFarland of Mount Vernon, New York to form the Mt. Vernon Company Silversmiths, Inc. which was bought by the Gorham Corporation in 1913.

JOHN W. WILLSON
Baltimore, Maryland

Listed 1867-1869 Baltimore City
Directories as silverplaters.

WILMORT MFG. CO.
Chicago, Illinois

Manufacturers of sterling and
plated silverware and novelties c.
1920-1930.

WM. WILSON & SON
Philadelphia, Pennsylvania

J. S. Patent No. 9,949, January 9,
1883 for sterling silverware.

U. S. Patent No. 9,950, January 9,
1883 for electroplated wares.

Patent Office records show the
registration of two trademarks by
William Wilson & Son in 1883.
They were also listed in J C-K in
1896 and 1904 and were out of
business before 1909.

WINNIPEG SILVER PLATE
CO., LTD.
Winnipeg, Manitoba

Listed J C-K 1915-1922 in plated
silver section.

WOLF & KNELL
New York, New York

Manufacturers and importers c.
1900 of antique silver in Dutch,
French and English designs.
Decanters, tea and coffee sets,
vases, spoons, tea strainers, etc.
O. Buchholz, U. S. and Canadian
representative. Factory at Hanau,
Germany.

WOLFENDEN SILVER COMPANY
North Attleboro, Massachusetts
(See Crown Silver, Inc.)

Successor to J. W. Wolfenden
Corp. Founded in 1919 by John
W. Wolfenden and now a Division
of Crown Silver Inc., New York.
Dies and equipment were moved
to the Crown factory in New York
in 1955.

WOOD & HUGHES
New York, New York
(See Gorham Corporation)
(See Graff, Washbourne & Dunn)

(*Used* 1833 *to* 1871.)

(*Used since* 1871.)

Silversmiths. Successor to Gale, Wood & Hughes c. 1845 (?). The 1904 J C-K illustrates their earlier mark with the notation that it was used 1833 to 1871. Wood & Hughes is listed in the New York City Directories 1840-1850. Listed in J C-K 1877. Succeeded by Graff, Washbourne & Dunn in 1899.

N. G. WOOD & SONS
Boston, Massachusetts

Registered trademark U. S. Patent Office, No. 20,515, December 29, 1891 for spoons, gold, silver and plated.

Listed J C-K 1896-1922 in sterling silver section. The trademark illustrated was for souvenir spoons made to commemorate the Boston Tea Party and was discontinued before 1922.

MRS. SARAH B. DICKINSON
WOOD
Niagara Falls, New York

The House of Dickinson, well-known jewelry firm of Buffalo was founded by Thomas V. Dickinson in 1849. Associated with him were his wife, Elizabeth, and later his son, Alfred; his grandson, Alfred. Now the great grandson Alfred Dickinson is in charge of the business.

The founder was granted a patent on July 21, 1891 for the manufacture of silver, flat and tableware, using the buffalo head trademark that his daughter (later Mrs. Sarah B. Dickinson Wood) used on souvenir silverware. According to Alfred III, they have no records that the Dickinsons actually manufactured these items themselves. They were probably made for them by one of the many companies who did this sort of work and stamped it with the trademark of the wholesaler or retailer.

WOODMAN-COOK CO.
Portland, Maine

WALDORF SILVER CO.

Began as Stevens & Smart 1879-1883. Manufacturers of britannia ware. Became Stevens, Smart & Dunham 1884-1886; Stevens & Smart, 1887-1890; Stevens, Wood-man and Company, 1891-1892 and Woodman-Cook Company 1893-1914. Manufacturers of plated silverwares. Edward B. Coon, president; C. H. Fessenden, vice-president; Fred H. Woodman, treasurer.

WOODS & CHATELLIER
New York, New York

Successor to Stephen Woods before 1904. Manufacturers of sterling cases, novelties, boxes and jewelry. Listed J C-K 1904–1922.

STEPHEN WOODS
Newark, New Jersey
(See Woods & Chatellier)

RICHARD M. WOODS & CO.
New York, New York

Successor to Woodside Sterling Company c. 1920. Makers of sterling silver holloware, dresserware and novelties. Around 1940 also listed as wholesalers.

WOODSIDE STERLING CO.
(See Richard N. Woods & Co.)

Listed 1896 Jewelers' Weekly. Listed 1904 J C-K. Succeeded by Richard M. Woods & Co. c. 1920.

JAMES T. WOOLEY
Boston, Massachusetts

James T. Wooley was one of the few native-born Americans to work in The Handicraft Shop in Boston. He was born in Providence, Rhode Island in 1864 and learned the silversmithing craft in The Gorham Company. For eighteen years he was foreman at Goodnow & Jenks in Boston. For two years he shared bench room with George J. Hunt in The Handicraft Shop though they worked independently. Around 1908 he opened his own shop. Many of his pieces are excellent adaptations of Colonial silver.

WORDEN-MUNNIS CO., INC.
Boston, Massachusetts

Silversmiths and goldsmiths, founded in 1940. Makers of early American, English and Irish reproductions. The company was purchased in 1964 by Old Newbury Crafters who are producing the sterling holloware line.

WORTZ & VOORHIS
New York, New York

Listed in J C-K 1896 in sterling silver section. Out of business before 1915.

WUERTTEMBERG PLATE CO.
Germany

Listed J C-K 1909-1915. No. record after 1920.

Y

HIRAM YOUNG & COMPANY
New York, New York

In the 1860's they purchased Reed & Barton wares "in the metal" and operated their own plating establishment.

OTTO YOUNG & COMPANY
Chicago, Illinois

Established in 1865. Importers, manufacturers and wholesalers of all types of silverware and jewelers' merchandise.

An illustrated catalog of 1893 (courtesy of the Whittelsey Fund, Metropolitan Museum of Art) depicts silverware, jewelry, optical goods, clocks and watches.

The last record found was 1924.

YOUREX
(See George E. Herring)

YUKON BRONZE W. CO.

Known only from name stamped on plated silver souvenir spoon from California c. 1910.

YUKON SILVER
(See Cattaraugus Cutlery Co.)

GLOSSARY

Acanthus: A form of ornamentation taken from the acanthus leaf, originally used extensively on the Corinthian capital throughout the Renaissance period, 16th–17th centuries.

Ajouré: A French term applied to metalwork which is pierced through, perforated or open-work.

Albata: Alloy of nickel, copper, and zinc, forming a silvery white metal.

Alchemy: A superior pewter used in the 16th and 17th centuries for making spoons and plates; an alloy of tin and copper.

Alcomy: An alloy of various base metals.

Alloy: A substance composed of two or more metals intimately united, usually intermixed when molten.

Alpacca: German silver and nickel silver; are synonomous trade names of an alloy of copper, nickel and zinc.

Annealing: Reheating of silver to keep it malleable while it is being worked.

Anvil: An iron block on which metal is hammered and shaped.

Apocryphal: Classical term for a fake.

Applied: Certain parts, such as spouts, handles, covers, et cetera, are sometimes made separately and applied with solder.

Apprentice: One who is bound by indentures to serve another person with a view to learning a trade.

Argentine: An alloy of tin and antimony used as a base for plating.

Assay: The test made to prove that the metal is of the required quality.

Baltimore Assay Marks: Starting in 1814, silver made in Baltimore was marked at a hall and identified by a date letter; this compulsory marking was abolished in 1830.

Base Metal: An alloy or metal of comparatively low value to which a coating or plating is normally applied.

Bat's-wing Fluting: Gadrooning, graduated and curved to resemble the outline of a bat's wing and encircling holloware.

Beading: A border ornament composed of small, contiguous, bead-like, half-spheres. Popular in late 18th century.

Beakhorn: A sharply pointed anvil.

Bell Metal: A variety of Sheffield Plate consisting of an unusually heavy coating of silver, introduced in 1789 by Samuel Roberts.

Black Pewter: An alloy of 60 per cent tin and 40 per cent lead. Used for making organ pipes and candle molds.

Bleeding: The technical term applied to pieces of plate whereon the copper base is exposed.

Bobêche: Flat or saucerlike rings placed around candle bases to stop wax drippings.

Bright-cut Engraving: A particular form of engraving popular about 1790, in which the metal is removed by bevelled cutting tools. This gives a jewel-like, faceted sparkle to the surface.

Britannia Metal: A silver-white alloy of tin, antimony and copper, sometimes containing zinc and bismuth.

Bronze: An alloy chiefly of copper and tin.

Buffing: Removal of the outer layer of metal with a flexible abrasive wheel or a soft mop, exposing a shiny undersurface but imparting no additional hardness.

Burnisher: Tool with hard, polished working surface such as agate, for burnishing gold and silver.

Burnishing: Electro deposits consist of a multitude of small crystals, with intervals between them, and with facets reflecting the light in every direction. The deposited metal is hardened by burnishing and forced into the pores of the underlying metal. The durability is thus increased to such an extent that, with the same amount of silver, a burnished article will last twice as long as one which has not been so treated.

Butler's Finish: Satin finish produced by a revolving wheel of wire which makes many tiny scratches, giving the article a dull appearance. Patented by James H. Reilly, Brooklyn Silver Co.

C: (See Coin.)

Cable: Molding like twisted rope, derived from Norman architecture.

Cast: Formed in a mold, i.e., handles, ornaments, et cetera are often cast separately.

Chafing-dish: Various forms of dishes for hot foods.

Chamber-candlestick: A tray candlestick in the form of a circular dish stand with a handle.

Champleve: Enameling by cutting troughs in the metal into which the frit is melted; the surface is ground flush and polished.

Chasing: A cold modeling process of ornamenting metal by hammers. Also called embossing.

Cloisonné: Enameling by melting the frit into areas defined by wire soldered to surface to be decorated.

Coin: By 1830, COIN, PURE COIN, DOLLAR, STANDARD, PREMIUM or C or D were used to indicate 900/1000 parts of silver.

Coin Silver: 900/1000 fine, with 100/1000 of copper. Used by early silversmiths to whom sterling was not available.

C-scroll: Usually applied to the shape of a handle in the form of the letter C; also called 'single scroll'.

Cut-cardwork: Silver work in which conventional designs of leaves and flowers are cut from thin sheet-silver and applied to a silver surface.

Cutler: One who makes, deals in, or repairs utensils or knives.

D: (See Coin.)

Date Letter; Date Mark: Proper assay marks on English silver, the date being indicated by a letter of the alphabet. Some American silver is date marked. (See Gorham, Kirk, Tiffany, and Tuttle.)

Dish Cross: An x-shaped support for a dish, some with spirit lamps for warming food.

Dish Ring: A silver stand particularly identified with Irish silver, and sometimes called a potato-ring.

Dollar: (See Coin.)

Dolphin: The sea dolphin used as a sculptured or carved motif.

Domed: Spheroid form of cover, first used in 1715 on tankards, teapots and coffeepots.

Domestic Plate: Silverware for home use.

Double-schroll: A sinuous line of S-shape, or composed of reverse curves, used especially in design of handles.

Drawing Irons: Metal parts of a drawing bench, through which silver is drawn.

Electrolysis: Conduction of an electric current by an electrolyte of charged particles.

Electroplate: Articles consisting of a base metal coated with silver by the process of electrolysis.

Electrum: A natural pale-yellow alloy of gold and silver. Also, an imitative alloy of silver, 8 parts copper, 4 nickel, and 3½ zinc.

Embossing: Making raised designs on the surface of metal from the reverse side, strictly applicable only to hammered work (Repoussé).

Engraving: Cutting lines into metal with a scorper or graver.

EPC: Electroplate on copper.

EPBM: Electroplate on britannia metal.

Epergne: An elaborate centerpiece, especially for a dining table; an ensemble of cups and vases for holding fruits, flowers, et cetera.

EPNS: Electroplate on nickel silver.

EPWM: Electroplate on white metal.

Etching: Surface decoration bitten-in with acid.

Ewer: A jug or pitcher having a wide spout and a handle.

Feather Edge: Decoration of edge of spoon-handle with chased, slanting lines. An engraved, decorative design.

Fine Pewter: Eighty per cent tin and 20 per cent brass or copper. Used for making plates because of the smooth surface, attractive color and strength.

Fine Silver: Better than 999/1000 pure. It is too soft for practical fabrication, and is mainly used in the form of anodes or sheets for plating.

Flagon: Large vessel for serving wine or other liquors.

Flash Plate: Unbuffed, cheap plated ware.

Flat Chasing: Surface decoration in low relief. Popular in England in early 18th century, and widely used in America, 1750–1785.

Fluted: A type of grooving.

Foreign Silver: Other than English sterling, is sometimes of uncertain silver content, in some instances running considerably below the coin standard. The fineness is often stamped on the article. In the Scandinavian countries and Germany solid silver tableware 830/1000 fine has been standardized, and the stamp "830" signifies this silver content.

Forging: The shaping of metal by heating and hammering.

Fusion: An act or operation of melting, as the fusion of metals. Usually accomplished by the application of intense heat.

Gadroon: A border ornament radiating lobes of curved or straight form. Used on rims and feet of cups, plates and other vessels from late 17th century.

German Silver: A silver-white alloy consisting principally of copper, zinc and nickel. During World War I this name was dropped by many and the term nickel silver used.

Gold Plating: The covering of an article with gold.

Goldsmiths' Company: The organization under whose jurisdiction and regulation the English silver industry has been conducted.

Graver: Tool used to engrave silver.

Hallmark: The official mark of the English Goldsmiths' Company used on articles of gold and silver to indicate their genuineness.

Holloware: A general term for articles in the form of hollow vessels, such as mugs, ewers, tankards, bowls and pitchers.

Holloware Pewter: Eighty per cent tin and 20 per cent lead, used for making teapots, tankards, coffee pots and liquid measures.

Ingot: A bar of silver or other metal.

Katé: A Malayan weight equal to 11.73 ounces. Tea was sold by the kate (pronounced katde). It became "caddy"—hence tea caddy. Also spelled kati.

Latten: An alloy of copper and zinc; brass.

Limoges: Enamel painted on metal, covering the surface.

Maker's Mark: The distinguishing mark of the individual goldsmith.

Malleable: Capable of being extended or shaped by beating with a hammer; ductile.

Matted-ground: A dull surface made by light punchwork, to secure contrast with a burnished surface.

Metalsmith: One versed in the intricacies of working with metals.

Nickel Silver: An alloy of nickel, copper and zinc.

Niello: Deep-line engraving on gold or silver with the lines filled with copper, lead and sulphur in borax, forming a type of black enamel which is fired and polished.

N.S.: Nickel silver.

Onslow Pattern: Design for flatware shaped as a volute scroll.

Ormolu: "Ground gold," literally. Ground gold leaf used as a gilt pigment. Also, brass made to look like gold.

Oxidizing: Accented beauty of ornamentation by the application of an oxide which darkens metal wherever applied. Shadows and highlights are created which give depth and character.

Patina: Soft luster caused by tiny scratches that come with daily use.

Pewter: An alloy of tin and copper or any alloy of the low-melting-point metals, including tin, lead, bismuth and antimony. Sad pewter is the heaviest, but not the best. The higher the tin content, the better the pewter.

Pinchbeck: An alloy of copper or zinc used to imitate gold. Invented by Christopher Pinchbeck (1670–1732), London. Also called "Chapman's" gold or Mannheim gold.

Pit Marks: Minute holes usually found on lead or soft metal borders.

Planishing: To make smooth or plain. Oval-faced planishing hammers are used to conceal hammer marks used in forming a piece.

Plate: Used in England and on the Continent when referring to articles made of precious metals.

Plique-á-jour: Translucent enamel without a metal backing, enclosed within metal frames, giving a stained glass or jewel-like effect.

Premium: (See Coin.)

Pricking: Delicate needle-point engraving. Pricked initials were often used on early pieces.

Pseudo Hall-marks: Devices used to suggest English hall-marks.

Pure Coin: (See Coin.)

Raising: Formation of a piece of holloware beginning with a flat circle of silver. It is hammered in concentric circles over a succession of anvils with frequent annealings.

Rolled Plate: (See Sheffield Plate.)

Rope-molding: A type of gadroon bordering made up of reeds and flutes slightly spiralled.

R.P.: Rolled plate.

Repoussé: Relief ornament hammered from the under or inner side of the metal. Usually given added sharpness of form by surface chasing of detail and outline. Has been practiced from early times. Introduced to this country by Samuel Kirk in 1828.

Satin Finish: (See Butler's Finish.)

Scorper: Small chisel for engraving. The blades are of various shapes.

Sheffield Plate: True Sheffield plate was produced by fusing, with intense heat, a thin sheet of silver to one or both sides of a thick sheet of copper. The composite metal was then rolled down to the proper thickness for fabrication. Invented by Thomas Boulsover about 1743.

Silver Edge: An ornamental border of solid silver.

Silverplate: A base metal, usually either nickel silver or copper, coated with a layer of pure silver by electroplating.

Solid Silver: 925/1000 silver and 25/1000 alloy.

Spinning: Process used for forming holloware. A metal plate is cut to proper size, placed against a chuck in a lathe, where pressure against it with a smooth revolving instrument produces the desired form.

Stake: An iron anvil or tongue, on which a silver object is formed.

Standard: (See Coin.)

Sterling Silver: 925/1000 fine, with 75/1000 of added metal, usually copper, to give it strength and stiffness. This is the standard set by the United States Government in the Stamping Act of 1906, and any article stamped "sterling" is of assured quality. It appears on Baltimore silver, 1800–1814, and after 1860, elsewhere.

Stoning: Polishing of silver with an emery-stone.

Swaged: Shaped by the process of rolling or hammering.

Tempering: Strengthening of metal by heat.

Touch: Maker's mark, impressed with a punch.

Touchstone: A hard siliceous stone or modern square of Wedgwood on which a piece of silver or gold of known quality can be rubbed to compare its mark with that of a piece being assayed.

Town Mark: The mark assigned to a city and applied as a hallmark to denote the location of manufacture.

Trifle Pewter: Sixty per cent tin and 40 per cent lead. Of a darker color and softer than better grades of pewter, it was short lived. The alloy was altered to 83 parts tin and 17 parts antimony and was made into spoons, saltshakers, buttons and similar articles which could not be finished on a lathe. Workers in this alloy were called "triflers."

Vermeil: Gold plating process developed in France in the mid 1700's. France banned production of vermeil early in the 19th century because the process involved the use of mercury. Present-day vermeil is produced by a safe electrolytic process.

Victorian Plate: Plated silver ware made during the period c. 1840–1900 by the process of electrolysis.

Waiter: A tray on which something is carried; a salver.

White Metal: Pure tin, nickel, silver, and all-white metal alloys, white brass, albata, electrum, argentine, and other alloys.

Whitesmith: A planishing smith; superior workman in iron, comparable to the armorer. Also a worker in pure tin of the "block" variety, not cast, but hammered and battered, planished and "skum." Originally "whitster."

BIBLIOGRAPHY

Abbey, Staton. *The Goldsmiths and Silversmiths Handbook.* New York: Van Nostrand, 1952.

Albany Silver. Albany, New York: Albany Institute of History and Art, 1964.

Alexander, A. E. "Tiffany's Sterling: History and Status," *National Jeweler*, June, 1963.

American Church Silver of 17th and 18th Centuries Exhibited at the Museum of Fine Arts, July to December, 1911. Boston: Boston Museum of Fine Arts, 1911.

"American Silver," *American Magazine of Art*, August 1919, v. 10, p. 400.

Antiquarian Magazine. 1924–1933.

Antiques Digest. Frederick, Maryland: Antiques Publications, Inc., 1951–1952.

Antiques Magazine. New York: 1922–1966. ⌐

Attleboro Daily Sun, Anniversary Edition. Attleboro, Mass.: 1964.

Avery, Clara Louise. "New York Metropolitan Museum of Art, American Silver of the 17th and 18th centuries." *Metropolitan Museum of Art Bulletin.* 1920.

Avery, Clara Louise. "New York Metropolitan Museum of Art, Exhibition of Early American Silver." *Metropolitan Museum of Art Bulletin.* December, 1931.

Avery, Clara Louise. *Early American Silver.* New York: The Century Company, 1930.

Bartlett, W. A. *Digest of Trade-Marks. (Registered in the U. S.) for Machines, Metals, Jewelry and the Hardware and Allied Trades.* Washington, D. C.: Gibson Bros., Printers, 1893.

Bent, Dorothy. "A Fascinating Biography of Knives and Forks." *Arts and Decoration.* Vol. 25, June, 1926.

Bigelow, Francis Hill. *Historic Silver of the Colonies and its Makers.* New York: The MacMillan Company, 1917.

Biographical History of the Manufacturers and Business Men of Rhode Island at the Opening of the Twentieth Century. Providence, Rhode Island: J. D. Hall & Co., 1901.

Bishop, J. Oleander. *A History of American Manufacturers from 1808–1860,* 2 vols. Philadelphia: Young & Co., 1861.

Boger, H. Batterson and Boger, Louise Ade. *The Dictionary of Antiques and the Decorative Arts.* New York: Charles Schribner's Sons, 1957.

Bolles, Albert S. *Industrial History of the United States from the Earliest Settlements to the Present Time.* Norwich, Conn.: 1879.

Brix, Maurice. *List of Philadelphia Silversmiths and Allied Artificers, 1682–1850.* Philadelphia: Privately Printed, 1920.

The Bromwell Story. Washington, D. C.: D. L. Bromwell, Inc., pamphlet, no date.

Buck, J. H. *Old Plate, Its Makers and Marks*. New York: Gorham Manufacturing Company, 1903.

Buhler, Kathryn C. "Silver 1640–1820," *The Concise Encyclopedia of American Antiques*. New York: Hawthorn Books, Inc., Vol 1., no date.

Burton, E. Milby. *South Carolina Silversmiths 1690–1860*. Charleston: The Charleston Museum, 1942.

Carlisle, Lillian Baker. *News and Notes*. Vermont Historical Society, no date.

Carpenter, Ralph E. Jr. *The Arts and Crafts of Newport*. Rhode Island: Preservation Society of Newport County, Pittshead Tavern, 1954.

Catalog of an Exhibition of Paintings by Gilbert Stuart, Furniture by the Goddards and Townsends, Silver by Rhode Island Silversmiths. Rhode Island School of Design, Providence, Rhode Island: 1936.

Clarke, Hermann Frederick. *John Coney, Silversmith 1655–1722*. Boston: Houghton Mifflin Company, 1932.

Clarke, Hermann Frederick and Foote, Henry Wilder. *Jeremiah Dummer, Colonial Craftsman and Merchant 1645–1718*. Boston: Houghton Mifflin Company, 1935.

Clarke, Hermann Frederick. *John Hull, Builder of the Bay Colony*. Portland, Me.: The Southworth-Anthoensen Press, 1940.

Clark, Victor S. *History of Manufacturers in the United States*. New York: Carnegie Institute of Washington, 1929.

Clearwater, Alphonso T. *American Silver, List of Unidentified Makers and Marks*. New York: 1913.

A Collection of Early American Silver. New York: Tiffany and Company, 1920.

Colonial Silversmiths, Masters & Apprentices. Boston: Boston Museum of Fine Arts, 1956.

Comstock, Helen. "American Silver," *The Concise Encyclopedia of Antiques*. New York: Hawthorn Books, Inc.

"The Craft of the Spoonmaker." *Antiques*, 1929.

Crosby, Everett Uberto. *Books and Baskets, Signs and Silver of Old Time Nantucket*. Nantucket, Mass.: Inquirer and Mirror Press, 1940.

Crosby, Everett Uberto. *95% Perfect*. Nantucket Island, Mass.: Tetaukimmo Press, 1953.

Crosby, Everett Uberto. *The Spoon Primer*. Nantucket, Mass.: Inquirer and Mirror Press, 1941.

Currier, Ernest M. *Early American Silversmiths, The Newbury Spoonmakers*. New York: 1929.

Currier, Ernest M. *Marks of Early American Silversmiths, List of New York City Silversmiths 1815–1841*. Portland, Me.: The Southworth-Athoensen Press. 1938.

Curtis, George Munson. *Early Silver of Connecticut and Makers*. Meriden, Conn.: International Silver Company, 1913.

Cutten, George Barton. *Silversmiths of Georgia*. Savannah, Ga.: Pigeonhole Press, 1958.

Cutten, George Barton, *Silversmiths of Northampton, Massachusetts and Vicinity down to 1850.* Pamphlet.

Cutten, George Barton. *Silversmiths of North Carolina.* Raleigh, N. C.: State Department of Archives & History, 1948.

Cutten, George Barton and Cutten, Minnie Warren. *Silversmiths of Utica.* Hamilton, New York: 1936.

Cutten, George Barton. *Silversmiths, Watchmakers and Jewelers of the State of New York Outside New York City.* Hamilton, N. Y.: Privately printed, 1939.

Cutten, George Barton. *Silversmiths of Virginia.* Richmond, Va.: The Dietz Press, 1952.

Cutten, George Barton. *Ten Silversmith Families of New York State.* Albany, New York: State Historical Assoc., 1946.

Danbury (Conn.) News-Times, December 2, 1938.

Davis, Charles H. S. *History of Wallingford, Connecticut.* Published by author, 1870.

Day, Olive. *Rise of Manufacturing in Connecticut, 1820-1850.* Yale University Press for Tercentenary of Conn.

Depew, Chauncey M. *One Hundred Years of American Commerce.* D. O. Haynes & Co., 1895, Vol. 2.

Descriptive Catalogue of Various Pieces of Silver Plate forming Collection of the New York Farmers 1882-1932.

Detroit Historical Society Bulletin. Detroit, Mich.: November, 1952.

Dreppard, Carl W. *A Dictionary of American Antiques.* Boston: Charles T. Branford Co., 1952.

Dreppard, Carl W. *The Primer of American Antiques.* Garden City, N. Y.: Doubleday & Company, Inc., 1954.

Duhousset, Charles. *L'Art Pour Tous.* Paris: 1879.

Durrett, Colonel Reuben T. *Traditions of the Earliest Visits of Foreigners.* (Filson Club Publications, No. 23) Louisville, Kentucky: John P. Morton & Co., 1908.

Dyer, W. A. "Early American Silver," *Arts and Decoration.* VII (May 1917)

Early American Spoons and Their Makers. Editor and Publisher, Golden Anniversary Issue, July 21, 1934.

Early Connecticut Silver 1700-1830. Gallery of Fine Arts. New Haven, Conn.: Yale University Press, Connecticut Tercentenary Commission, 1935.

Early, Eleanor. *An Island Patchwork.* Boston: Houghton Mifflin Company, 1941.

Early New England Silver lent from the Mark Bortman Collection. Northampton, Mass.: Smith College Museum of Art, 1958.

Eaton, Allen H. *Handicrafts of New England.* New York: Harper & Brothers Publishers, 1949.

Eberlein, H. D. "Early American Silver," *Arts and Decoration.* XI (August 1919).

Eberlein, Harold D. and McClure, Abbot. *The Practical Book of American Antiques.* Garden City, New York: Halcyon House, 1948.

Edmonds, Walter D. *The First Hundred Years, 1848-1948, Oneida Community.* Oneida, N.Y.: Oneida Ltd., 1958.

Ellis, Leonard Bolles. *History of New Bedford and its Vicinity, 1602–1892.* Syracuse, New York: D. Mason & Company, Publishers, 1892.

Ensko, Robert. *Makers of Early American Silver.* New York: Trow Press, 1915.

Ensko, Stephen. *American Silversmiths and Their Marks.* New York: Privately printed, 1927.

Ensko, Stephen. *American Silversmiths and Their Marks II.* New York: Robert Ensko, Inc., Privately printed, 1937.

Ensko, Stephen. *American Silversmiths and Their Marks III.* New York: Robert Ensko, Inc., Privately printed, 1948.

Exhibition of Old American and English Silver. Pennsylvania Museum and School of Industrial Art, 1917.

Fisher, Leonard Everett. *The Silversmiths.* New York: Franklin Watts, Inc.

Forbes, Esther. *Paul Revere and the World He Lived In.* Boston: Houghton Mifflin Co., 1942.

Freedley, E. T. *Philadelphia and its Manufacturers,* 1857.

Freeman, Larry and Beaumont, Jane. *Early American Plated Silver.* Watkins Glen, N. Y.: Century House, 1947.

French, Hollis. *A List of Early American Silversmiths and Their Marks.* New York: Walpole Society, 1917.

French, Hollis. *Jacob Hurd and His Sons Nathaniel and Benjamin, Silversmiths.* Printed by the Riverside Press for the Walpole Society, 1939.

From Colony to Nation, Exhibit. Chicago, Illinois: Chicago Art Institute, 1949.

Galt & Bro., Washington, D. C.: Pamphlet, no date.

Gibb, George S. *The Whitesmiths of Taunton, A History of Reed and Barton.* Cambridge, Mass.: Harvard University Press, 1946.

Gillespie, Charles Bancroft. *An Historic Record & Pictorial Description of the Town of Meriden.* Meriden, Conn.: Journal Pub. Co., 1906.

Gillingham, H. E. "Silver," *Pennsylvania Magazine of History and Biography,* 1930–1935.

Gorham Silver Co. *The Gorham Manufacturing Company Silversmiths.* New York: Cheltenham Press, 1900.

Graham, James Jr. *Early American Silver Marks.* New York: James Graham Jr., 1936.

Grimwade, A. G. "Silver," *The Concise Encyclopedia of Antiques.* New York: Hawthorn Books, Inc.

Halsey, R. T. Haines. *New York Metropolitan Museum Catalogue of Exhibition of Silver Used in New York, New Jersey, and the South.* Metropolitan Museum of Art, 1911.

Hardt, Anton. *Souvenir Spoons of the 90's.* New York: Privately printed, 1962.

Harrington, Jessie. *Silversmiths of Delaware 1700–1850.* Delaware: National Society of Colonial Dames of America, 1939.

Heller, David. *History of Cape Silver, 1700–1750.* 1949.

Hiatt, Noble W. and Lucy F. *The Silversmiths of Kentucky.* Louisville, Ky.: The Standard Printing Co., 1954.

"Highlights of the House of Kirk," *Hobbies*. August, 1939.

Hill, H. W. *Maryland's Silver Service*. Baltimore, Maryland: Waverly Press, Inc., 1962.

Hipkiss, E. J. *Boston Museum of Fine Arts Philip Leffingwell Spaulding Collection of Early American Silver*. Cambridge, Mass.: Harvard University Press, 1943.

Historical and Biographical Sketch of the Gorham Manufacturing Company. Reprint of booklet issued, 1878.

History of New Haven County, Connecticut. Edited by J. L. Rockey, Vol. One.

History of the Spoon, Knife and Fork. Taunton, Mass.: Reed & Barton, 1926.

Hittell, John S. *Commerce and Industries of the Pacific Coast of North America*. San Francisco: A. L. Bancroft & Co., 1882.

Hoitsma, Muriel Cutten. *Early Cleveland Silversmiths*. Cleveland, Ohio: Gates Publishing Co., 1953.

The House of Kirk, Our 150th Year, 1815–1965. Baltimore: Samuel Kirk & Son, Inc., 1965.

Hoving, Walter. "The History of Tiffany," *Christian Science Monitor*. April 9, 10, 11, 1959.

"How America's $400 Million-a-Year Silver Manufacturing Industry Grew," *The Jewelers' Circular-Keystone*, Directory Issue. Philadelphia, Pa.: 1965.

Hower, Ralph Merle. *History of Macy's of New York, 1858–1919*. Cambridge, Mass.: Harvard University Press, c. 1943.

Hughes, G. Bernard. "Sheffield Plate," *The Concise Encyclopedia of Antiques*. New York: Hawthorn Books Inc., Vol. Two.

Hungerford, Edward. *The Romance of a Great Store (Macy's)*. New York: Robert M. McBride & Co., 1922.

Index of Trademarks Issued from the United States Patent Office, 1881.

Jacobs, Carl. *Guide to American Pewter*. New York: McBride, 1957.

James, George B., Jr. *Souvenir Spoons*. Boston, Mass.: A. W. Fuller & Co., 1891.

Jayne, H. F. and Woodhouse, S. W., Jr. "Early Philadelphia Silversmiths," *Art in America*. IX (October 1921).

Jeweler Buyers' Guide, A McKenna Publication. New York: Sherry Publishing Co., Inc., 1960.

The Jewelers' Circular & Horological Review. New York: D. H. Hopkinson, no date.

The Jewelers' Circular-Keystone. Philadelphia Pa.: Chilton Publication, 1869–1966.

The Jewelers' Circular-Weekly, 50th Anniversary Number. New York: Jewelers' Circular Pub. Co., 1919.

The Jewelers' Dictionary. New York: The Jewelers' Circular-Keystone, no date (c. 1950).

Jobbers' Handbook. 1936–1937.

Jones, E. Alfred. *Old Silver of Europe and America*. Philadelphia: Lippincott Co., 1928.

Keddell, E. Avery. "Romance of the Spoon," *Art Journal*. January 1907.

Keir, Robert M. *Manufacturing in Industries of America*. Roland Press, 1928.

Kelley, Etna M. *The Business Founding Date Directory*, (1687–1915). Scarsdale, N.Y.: Morgan & Morgan, 1954.

"Kentucky Silversmiths before 1850," *Filson Club History Quarterly*. XVI, No. 2, April 1942, 111–126.

Kerfoot, J. B. *American Pewter*. Boston and New York: Houghton Mifflin Co., 1924.

The Keystone Jewelers' Index. Phila.: The Keystone Publishing Co., 1922, 1924, 1931.

Kirk in U. S. Museums. Baltimore, Maryland: Samuel Kirk & Son, Inc., 1961.

Kirk Sterling—A Complete Catalog of America's Finest Sterling by America's Oldest Silversmiths. Baltimore: 1956 (?).

Knittle, Rhea Mansfield. *Early Ohio Silversmiths and Pewterers 1787–1847*. (Ohio Frontier Series.) Cleveland, Ohio: Calvert-Hatch Company, 1943.

"Knives for a Nation," *Industry*. September, 1961.

Kovel, Ralph M. and Kovel, Terry H. *A Directory of American Silver, Pewter and Silverplate*. New York: Crown Publishers, 1961.

Lambert, Isaac E. *The Public Accepts; Stories Behind Famous Trademarks, Names and Slogans*. Albuquerque, N. M.: Univ. of N. M. Press, 1941.

Langdon, John Emerson. *Canadian Silversmiths & Their Marks, 1667–1867*. Lunenberg, Vermont: The Stinehour Press, 1960.

Lathrop, W. G. *The Brass Industry in the United States*. Mt. Carmel, Conn.: Wilson H. Lee Co., 1926.

Laughlin, Ledlie I. *Pewter in America*. Boston: Houghton Mifflin Co., 1940.

Macomber, Henry P. "The Silversmiths of New England," *The American Magazine of Art*. Oct. 1932.

Masterpieces of New England Silver 1650–1800. Gallery of Fine Arts, Yale University, 1939.

May, Earl Chapin. *A Century of Silver 1847–1947*. New York: Robert McBride Co., 1947.

Mazulla, Fred M. and J. *The First Hundred Years, Cripple Creek and the Pikes Peak Region*. Denver, Colorado: A. B. Hirschfeld Press, 1956.

Meeks, E. V. *Masterpieces of New England Silver*. Cambridge: Harvard Univ. Press, 1939.

Meriden, the Silver City. Connecticut Tercentenary Committee, 1935.

The Meriden Daily Journal, 50th Anniversary Number. April 17, 1936.

Miller, V. Isabelle. *Silver by New York Makers, Late Seventeenth Century to 1900*. New York: Women's Committee of the Museum of The City of New York, 1938.

Miller, William Davis. *The Silversmiths of Little Rest*, Rhode Island. D. B. Updike, The Merrymount Press, 1920.

Nationally Established Trade-Marks. New York: Periodical Publishers Assoc. of America, 1934.

"New England Silversmiths, news items gleaned from Boston newspapers, 1704–1705." *Art in America*, X (February 1922), 75.

The New England States. William T. Davis, Ed. Vol. II: 832,833.

New York State Silversmiths. Eggertsville, N. Y.: Darling Foundation, 1965.

New York Sun. Antiques section.

Okie, Howard Pitcher. *Old Silver and Old Sheffield Plate.* New York: Doubleday, Doran and Company, 1928.

"Old American Silver," *Country Life in America.* February 1913–January 1915.

Ormsbee, Thomas H. *Know Your Heirlooms.* New York: The McBride Co., 1956.

Parke-Bernet Galleries catalogue. January 1938–1965.

Elias Pelletreau, Long Island Silversmith and his Sources of Design. Brooklyn, N. Y.: Brooklyn Institute of Arts and Sciences, Brooklyn Museum, 1959.

"Pennsylvania Museum and School of Industrial Art Loan exhibition of Colonial Silver, special catalogue." *Pennsylvania Museum Bulletin.* No. 68, June 1921.

Percy, Randolph T. "The American at Work, IV: Among the Silver-Platers," *Appleton's Journal,* New Series, No. 30. (Dec. 1878).

"Philadelphia Silver 1682–1800," *Philadelphia Museum Bulletin,* LI, No. 249 (Spring 1956).

Phillips, John Marshall. *American Silver.* New York: Chanticleer Press, 1949.

"Pioneers of the American Silver Plate Industry," *Hobbies.* April, 1947.

Pleasants, J. Hall and Sill, Howard. *Maryland Silversmiths, 1715–1830.* Baltimore: The Lord Baltimore Press, 1930.

Porter, Edmund W. "Metallic Sketches," *Taunton Daily Gazette.* March 19, 1906–Sept. 28, 1907.

Prime, Alfred Coxe. *The Arts & Crafts in Philadelphia, Maryland and South Carolina, 1721–1785.*

Prime, Alfred Coxe. *The Arts & Crafts in Philadelphia, Maryland and South Carolina, 1786–1800.*

Prime, Mrs. Alfred Coxe. *Three Centuries of Historic Silver,* Philadelphia: Pennsylvania Society of Colonial Dames of America, 1938.

The Providence Plantations for 250 Years. Providence, R. I.: J. A. & R. A. Reid, Pub., 1886.

Randolph, Howard S. F., "Jacob Boelen, Goldsmith of New York and his family circle," *New York Genealogical and Biographical Record.* October, 1941.

Retrospect, A publication of the Historical Society of Glastonbury, Conn. No. 10, Feb. 1948.

Revi, Albert Christian. Nineteenth Century Glass. New York: Thomas Nelson & Sons, 1959.

Robertson, Constance, *The Oneida Community.* Pamphlet, no date.

Roe, Joseph Wickham. *Connecticut Inventors.* Tercentenary Commission of Connecticut, N. Y. Press, 1935.

Rogers, Edward S. *The Lanham Act and the Social Function of Trade-Marks, in Law and Contemporary Problems.* Durham, S. C. Quarterly, pub. by Duke Univ. School of Law, V. 14, No. 2, 1949.

William Rogers and his Brothers in the Silverware Industry. Philadelphia: Keystone, Keystone Publishing Company, August and September, 1934.

Romaine, Lawrence B. *A Guide to American Trade Catalogs, 1744–1900.* New York: R. R. Bowker Company, 1960.

Rosenbaum, Jeanette. *Myer Myers, Goldsmith.* Philadelphia: Jewish Publication Society of America, 1954.

Rumpp, Leaders for a Century in Fine Leather Goods. Philadelphia: C. F. Rumpp & Sons, Inc., 1950.

Schild, Joan Lynn. *Silversmiths of Rochester.* Rochester, N. Y.: Rochester Museum of Arts and Sciences, 1944.

Seeger and Guernsey. *Cyclopaedia of the Manufactures and Products of the United States.* New York: 1890.

Selwyn, A. *The Retail Jeweller's Handbook.* New York: Chemical Publishing Co., Inc., 1950.

Semon, Kurt M. *A Treasury of Old Silver.* New York: McBride Company, 1947.

"Silver by New York Makers," *Museum of the City of New York.* New York: 1937.

"The Silversmiths of New England," *American Magazine of Art.* October, 1932.

"The Silverware Industry in America," *The Jewelers' Circular-Keystone.* New York: November and December 1946.

Sniffen, Philip L. *A Century of Silversmithing.* Reed & Barton Silversmiths. Taunton, Massachusetts: 1924.

Snow, William G. *Silverplating in Connecticut.* 1935.

Souvenir Spoons of America. New York: The Jewelers Circular Publishing Co., 1891.

The Spinning Wheel. Hanover, Pa.: 1945–1966.

The Spoon from Earliest Times. Meriden, Conn.: International Silver Company, 1915.

Sterling Flatware Pattern Index. N. Y. and Phila.: Jewelers' Circular-Keystone, 1949.

Stieff Sterling Silver, The Stieff Company. Baltimore: Barton-Gillet, c. 1930.

The Story of Daniel Low. Salem, Mass.: Daniel Low & Co., Catalog for 1917.

The Story of Sterling. Newburyport, Mass.: The Towle Silversmiths, 1954.

The Story of Sterling. New York: Sterling Silversmiths Guild of America, 1937.

The Story of the House of Kirk. Baltimore: Samuel Kirk & Son, Inc., 1914 and 1939.

Stow, M. *American Silver.* New York: Barrow & Co. 1950.

Stutzenberger, Albert. *The American Story in Spoons.* Louisville, Ky.: Privately printed, 1953.

"Tammen Curio Company of Denver," *Denver Post.* January 29, 1957.

"Tammen's Curio Shop," *Rocky Mountain Life.* Denver, Colorado: March 1949.

Taylor, Emerson. *Paul Revere.* New York: Dodd, Mead & Co., 1930.

Taylor, Gerald. *Silver.* London: Unwin Brothers, Ltd. 1956.

Thorn, C. Jordan. *Handbook of American Silver and Pewter Marks.* New York: Tudor Publishing Company, 1949.

Those Green River Knives. Russell Harrington Cutlery Company (Reprinted in part from Indian Notes, Vol. IV., No. 4 Museum of the American Indian, Heye Foundation, New York: October, 1927.)

"Three Centuries of European and American Silver," *M. H. de Young Memorial Museum Bulletin.* San Francisco: October 1938.

Tilton, George P. *Colonial History* (catalogues of Benjamin Franklin, La Fayette, Paul Revere, Newbury and Georgian flatware patterns in addition to the histories of the persons and places.) Newburyport, Mass.: Towle Manufacturing Company, 1905.

Trade Marks of the Jewelry and Kindred Trades, New York and Philadelphia: Jewelers' Circular-Keystone Publishing Co., 1869, 1896, 1898, 1904, 1910, 1915, 1922, 1943, 1950, 1965.

Tryon, R. M. *Household Manufactures in U. S.* Chicago: University Press, 1917.

Twyman, Robert W. *History of Marshall Field & Co., 1852–1906.* Philadelphia: University of Pennsylvania Press, 1954.

U. S. Bureau of the Census, Digest of Accounts of Manufacturing Establishments in the United States and of Their Manufactures. Washington, D. C.: 1823.

U. S. Tariff Commission. A Survey of the various types of silverware, the organization of the industry and the trade in silverware, with special reference to tariff consideration. Washington, D. C.: U. S. Gov't. Printing Office, 1940. Report No. 139, Second Series.

Wallace, Floyd, Sr. *Wallace News.* June 1947. Credit to Miss Emma Dray.

Wardle, Patricia. *Victorian Silver & Silver Plate.* Victorian Collector Series. Thomas Nelson & Sons, 1963.

Wendt, Lloyd & Kogen, Herman, *Give the Lady what She Wants.* History of Marshall Fields, Chicago: Rand McNally, c. 1952.

Wenham, Edward. *Practical Book of American Silver.* New York and Philadelphia: J. B. Lippincott Co., 1949.

Westman, Habakkuk O. "The Spoon: Primitive, Egyptian, Roman, Medieval & Modern," *The Transactions of the Society of Literary and Scientific Chiffoniers.* New York: 1844.

White, Benjamin. *Silver, its History and Romance.* New York and London: Hodder & Stoughton, 1917.

Williams, Carl Mark. *Silversmiths of New Jersey 1700–1825.* Philadelphia: G. S. McManus Co., 1949.

Woolsey, Theodore S. "Old Silver," *Harper's Magazine,* 1896.

Wroth, Lawrence C. *Abel Buell of Connecticut, Silversmith, Typefounder, and Engraver.* 1926.

Wyler, Seymour B. *The Book of Old Silver.* New York: Crown Publishers, 1937.

Wyler, Seymour B. *The Book of Sheffield Plate, Including Victorian Plate.* New York: Crown Publishers, 1949.

Family Tree of the American Silverware Industry: 1815-1965

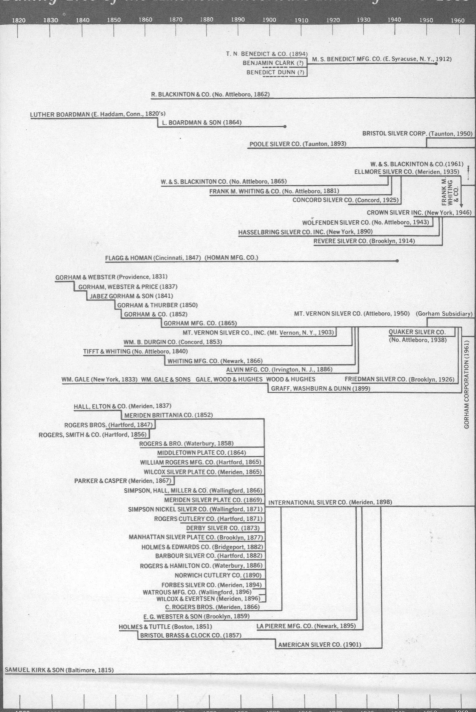